Last

Native American Prophecies
Tales of the End Times
by Robert Ghost Wolf

LIBRARY OF CONGRESS
CATALOGING-IN-PUBLICATION DATA

Last Cry:
Native American Prophecies: Tales of the End
ISBN: 0-9660668-5-5

Copy Right © 1994-95-96-97 Robert Ghost Wolf /
Wolf Lodge Cultural Foundation
Tales of the End Times © 1993 Robert Ghost Wolf /
Wolf Lodge Cultural Foundation

Mistyc House Publishing
P.O. 10196, Spokane, WA 99209

Cover Art and Illustrations by Robert Ghost Wolf
Dream Catcher Illustration by Robin Ryan
Cover and Interior Design Robert Ghost Wolf / Cindee Delgado
Editing by Lori Stebbins M.B.A. and Cindee Delgado

Printed in the United States of America

This book is designed to provide information in regard to the subject
matter covered. The purpose of is to educate and entertain. The Author,
Editors, and Publisher shall have neither liability nor responsibility to any
person or entity with respect to any loss or damage caused, directly or
indirectly by information contained in this book.

Table of Contents

To the Wigmunkee Oyate –
The People of the Rainbow

*T*here are not words that I have found in this English language that could express the Gratitude I have for those who enabled me to complete this work: On the Earthly plane, Grandfather Fools Crow, John Lame Deer, Pete Catches, Wallace Black Elk, Grand Father Bear Heart, Mad Bear and Rolling Thunder, Grandmother Kitty, No Eyes, and Evelyn Eaton. My friend Sun Bear who taught me to hold my vision of spiritual unity before the criticisms of the world. Those brave hearts, who taught me the healing ways of ceremony and the meaning of Sacred, as well as who my Grandpa and Grandma really were and why we had to unite the Sacred hoop. And Buddy Redbow for what you left us in songs. Your songs will always remind me that we are spirit riders who will ride forever, for we have no endings in this dream.

I send my Gratitude to my Sister Wolf Moon Dance who rekindled my remembrance of self purpose, to Brook Medicine Eagle who taught me to walk with grace and courage. To Storm, who opened the doors to the wisdom or the Metis, and to Judi Pope who taught me harmony through conflict. Though we walk in different worlds, I remember you in the wind.

To Len and Lori Toye who helped keep the violet flame of the Masters lit in my heart when I walked through my dark night of the soul. They would come and lift the pain from my being. To Sharon White Arrow, who taught me to look Deep into the eyes of someone's heart. To Grandmother Conni Mirabell who kept carrying her bundle with unconditional love for everyone. To Larry Konosha, my pipe brother, who gave me the gift of friendship, and safe harbor in the storm. To my Little Sister Robin and my brother John who taught me to sail and play with the Dolphins. To Clay Larson and to all those who saw the vision and helped make this printing possible.

To my daughter Gabrielle, through whom I have learned unconditional love by loving her from a distance. At her birth, I experienced the appearance of Sai Baba, and the awakening to my spiritual inheritance and true path. And to my sister Marri, the Hummingbird, who has always challenged my truth, and creativity. For we are Eagle Clan, we are each a little piece of forever.

To all those who have come to ceremony and danced with the Wolf, and who have dared to open their hearts to their unlimited potential. To those who have cooked the food, taken care of the sick, the weak, and the insane, put up the teepees, built the lodges, carried stones, cried at the wonder, and stood tall against adversity, even when its form could not be identified, holding to the pathway of heart. To those who still dare to dream, and love. To those who own themselves.

Cindee, Louie for helping carry the vision the last mile. Patrice and Michael, when we were shot down you helped with love and tools -- no questions asked. Lori for fighting with my words, so others could understand the written message. There Are no Words. Rodney, Kay, Danny and Grandmother Turtle who proved that angels still happen. To you, the reader of these works.

I send my Gratitude to Grandfather Stalking Wolf who taught me how to truly be the Wolf. To Storm who prepared me for the outside world. And to my Hopi Grandfathers Martin and Dan, who stand by me in these times of change. To Grandfathers David and Titus. I will see you on the other side of this veil.

I send my Gratitude to those wondrous *Above Beings*, who reached through dimensions to touch my heart and soul with the spark of divine fire, Waicomah Tete, Deganaweda, Stalking Wolf, Crazy Horse, Joseph, Mahto Hana, Sananda, Kuthumi, El Morya, Kuan Yin, the Calf Women, St Germain, Zarathustra the gentle wise one, who reminded me of my higher commitments, and yes my beloved RAM, Grandfather, the grandest teacher of them all.

To my beloved Mother *Unchi Maka* upon who's body I walk this incredible journey. My Mother who never stopped giving and nurturing, who took me into her deepest confidence and shared with me her secrets of creation, healing, and the power of dreaming, who's beauty and humor continue to inspire me, when humanity leaves me with only my tears -- sometimes coming as the Butterfly, sometimes as the Cougar, sometimes as the Dolphin.

I send my Gratitude to the God I AM, who created this world and continues to create my reality, and gives us the courage from within to stand up against the whole of the world for the sake of divine truth. I AM awakening! I carry this message for the people! For all the elders who kept the medicine alive that so that it is still here with us this day. For the pipe carriers who held the spirit of the people. For the Sundancers and the Ghost Dancers. For the Grandmothers who kept their hearts, and dreams alive. For the children that continue to be our hope for tomorrow. Through our children we witness the continuing dream for humanity, and the possibility of change and rebirth to be all that we can be, that we might again dance within the grace of the Sacred Hoop.

I thank the little people, the devas, and the Star People, and to those I might not have named here but hold in my heart, I send my Gratitude, for you have made my life one of abundance..................

Aho Mitakyue Oyasin, All my relations, *Piyamala emello, I send a voice, I give thanks!*

Last but not least, I give thanks to my Twin Flame, Laura Lee, who helped heal this bleeding Heart and led me back again to the beauty path, with whom I now walk into the light of forever.

May we always continue to walk this beauty path! May each of you keep walking through the grass and hold the vision, using your Heart as your Shield.

AUTHORS NOTE:

I have found that with many of us who are teachers and light workers, often our words and teachings seem to reflect what one other is saying. We must now blend all knowledge into one tapestry for the good of hu-manity.

There are many of those teachers and authors who I have come to respect. Some I have been blessed in my life to know as personal friends. Others, though I have not met them, I am familiar with the body of their work and feel good about their sources & intent.

You are seeking answers. In your quest for truth and knowledge be certain to listen to your heart. Follow your instincts and learn from the tapestry of life - we are all connected in the web of life.

Foreword —
A Message to the Reader

When asked to write this message, my thoughts went back to some of the extraordinary events that shaped the outcome and delivery of this writing. I have been able to observe the construction of this inspiring book from a bird's eye view. What I have read and seen transpire has been no less than miraculous.

I have witnessed and participated in such a dichotomy of events that now polarity swings seem almost ordinary!! These events ranged from feeling the presence of masters and light beings assisting Robert as he put into print the history and truths of our existence, and all the love and support, physical help, and encouragement from the most unlikely places, to the horrendous and steady stream of energies trying to discourage and threaten us into giving up on this project entirely! At times I jokingly told my friends, "I feel like I'm living in a Sci-Fi-Spy movie!!".

Presently, my adventure here seems to be to create a multitude of experiences and opportunities to practice the concepts I've learned from this experience. First and foremost, we must not buy into fear, but rather go to center, breath, feel the love vibration, and transmute everything else with that energy -- then laugh a lot! I think what helped me the most was to constantly remind myself and those around me that it's just a hologram -- it's not reality. No one is actually going to be hurt, so let's have a good time, see the bigger picture, remember that love is the only thing that is real, and then ask, "What's funny about all of this? What's the cosmic joke here?"

It was in this state that I realized the contents of this book of wisdom and prophesy must be pretty darned important to the awakening and personal sovereignty process of certain people. These printed words must have the capacity to impact and alter lives and future events. No wonder we've been getting such a wide variety of relentless opposition and blatant attacks from all levels! It all became so clear as I expanded my view to see the bigger picture!!

I now offer to you my feminine viewpoint. I think it is important to realize that there isn't anything to be afraid of, not even fear, for there are lessons to learn in every experience we encounter. When we do feel the grips of fear running through our systems, remember that there is always something to learn and the sooner we go neutral, the sooner we will *"get it"*, move through it, and boldly come out on the other side stronger and wiser. Keep this in mind as you step into the pages of this book, for there are some things inside this cover that may be perceived as uncomfortable, or even fearful if not taken in the context of *"where do love and humor fit into all of this?"*

Last but not least, I would recommend that you check everything you read or discover in these pages with your own internal <u>truth detector</u>. What rings true, embrace -- what doesn't, put on the back burner for a little while, let it simmer, and see what it turns into before you throw it away. Maybe all you need is a few of your own ingredients to add to it to make it palatable to you. If you feel like something needs to be thrown away or recycled, you're the boss! You call the shots in this movie you're starring in!

Keep in mind that in this movie/drama/holographic illusion/adventure game we're in, you get to write the rules to your own game! You are the dream master. What you embrace or repel can determine and have a profound effect on the outcome of this **exciting and soul expanding drama!**

Know this. Within the pages you are holding are some very ancient keys and codes that have been kept silent -- until now. Some of these keys may have a blueprint that resonates to you, and will aid and unlock some of the previously dormant knowledge stored within you. Be advised that some of the things you read could trigger memory so ancient, yet somehow familiar and recent, that it may greatly alter and redirect your life's journey forever. If you should feel rattled or unstable from time to time in this adventure, go to the core of your being and ask for directions or instructions. You are sure to find the help you need there. (You are probably simply getting ready for a quantum leap, so pat yourself on the back and get excited about your progress!!)

I now leave you to ponder the immortal words of the Moody Blues at the end of *KNIGHTS IN WHITE SATIN*.

Red is grey and yellow white,

but we decide which is right

... and which is an illusion.

May the love and laughter of the
goddess penetrate to your being
...and know that you are dearly loved!!!

I wish you love and passion for your
adventure
on this planet,

Laura Lee Mistycah -
"Morning Star"

Eagle Dances

Orcas Island, Spring Equinox 1996

March had entered upon the Islands like the proverbial Lion. After a six week stretch of Northeastern torrential rains and dealing with wind chill factors often 50 below zero, the equinox, the coming of spring would be a welcomed experience.

After 62 days of rain, even Ducks will begin to have dreams about the desert. Walking along the rocky, moss-covered cliffs of the Washington coast, taking in the gentle weather, I needed a break from writing the prophecy book. Ever since I had undertaken the task of compiling the information I was receiving from the Grandfathers into the book, many new elements had come into play in my life. The Islands of the Pacific Northwest Coast are reminiscent of ancient Scotland. They can be misty and moody, and one often looses their sense of time while walking out their thoughts along trails of tangled introspection. I found myself dreaming about the ranch in Arizona.

I was living in two worlds. I had come to find myself. I seemed to be walking through a dream these days, waiting for the mythical *Bird of Freedom* to lift me from these Islands of eternal gray fog. Part of me seemed to still be back in Arizona, walking amongst the red rock cliffs of the ceremonial grounds on the ranch. As I walked the ocean cliffs, the Albatross sang messages in my ears.

Its message was carried to me upon the wind, "It is going to be a hard summer there this year in your southern home. The desert will be burning up." I am shown visions of a very dry desert landscape, brush fires burning everywhere. Later that afternoon I would talk to a friend in Cave Rock, who would inform me that they have passed through their usual monsoon season without a single drop of rain.

As always, when I think of Arizona I think of my friends the Hopi. I have spent over twenty years now, walking this "Good Red Road." There are many stories that can only be remembered. Stories that will never be spoken. I remembered Grandfather Dan saying, "People live in two worlds now. The Hopi way will soon disappear from this Earth."

Walking along the cliffs, my mind goes back to just a few short months ago when I was in Hotevilla. I was in ceremony with the traditional elders in prayer circle. These elders are properly and respectfully referred to as "the Sinom," which translates more or less to mean those old wise ones who carry the memory of the original teachings of Creator for the People.

We sit together in an ancient kiva for four days talking to the old ones, and asking the Kachinas for assistance, exactly as their ancestors had done over twelve thousand years ago. We call for understanding and truth to help us understand these times of changes, asking the Kachinas to give us clarity for the future. In the Hopi way we are "Crying for a Vision." My experience in the kiva leads me to new clarity.

I emerge from the kiva feeling as if I have awakened from a dream. I walk into the Hopi cornfield, staring out at the stars that create a surreal blue luminescence upon an ancient landscape.

I stand looking at a world that is exactly as other eyes have seen it millenniums ago. I wondered what they must have thought as they received their visions of potential future events. They stood here as I now do trying to understand the visions of a very bazaar future reality. Did they think themselves mad?

I stood there naked in the moonlight, having made it through to the other side of a labyrinth. I found myself struggling to make my new eyes see, to allow my consciousness to touch and comprehend a new expanded reality. I was struggling to see through veils of illusion, painfully tearing through the bondage of cultural and genetic programming that leaves one blind to what is illusion and what is truly real--what to most is unreachable and lies hidden behind a cloak of invisible reality, accessible only through *the Eye of the Shaman*.

Life in many ways has become an abstract science fiction movie, starring myself and those friends that I have in my immediate world that manage to hold on to some degree of clarity of mind. How does one determine a degree of sanity in a world in which the rules that dictate our realities seem to shift in the moment? At times it is very difficult to differentiate between dream states. Quite frankly, sometimes there is no difference as they merge. There are no longer any rules in man's created consciousness that apply to the game of life. The Hopi Prophecy keeps coming to mind, "in that time man will find that he lives in two worlds..." My life has certainly become a testament to that.

The sounds of Eagles playing in a nearby tree overhead brings me back to the reality of the ocean and the cliffs of Orcas Island. In that moment of hearing the Eagles cooing as they played, I became aware that there had been a lot of unusual incidents with Eagles recently. In fact, ever since I had made the commitment to doing the prophecy book and started working on it, Eagles were making their presence known very strong in my life. They brought to me the message that I was to call my work, *Last Cry.* Both for myself and those who came to see me on my Island retreat, the Eagles would touch our souls forever!

The other day there was one sitting on the fence post, a huge female, by the side of the road. I slowed the car and rolled down my window. Softly but quietly, not being more then six feet away from her, I asked, "Sister, what are you doing on that fence post. You're not a Raven or a Crow you know!"

Well, she just turned around and shot me a look that said, "Are you speaking to me?" Then with slow motion, rendering my reality to the world of special effects, she spread her eight foot wingspan, lifted off, and began to spiral upwards towards the Sun.

Two days ago, in the early morning while walking Mountain Lake, I literally almost walked right into a big Grandmother as I came around a large rock outcropping. I startled her. She flew off with a huge Salmon in her talons. The sound of her huge wings stopped my heart. She took off through the branches and flew over my head in a very close clockwise circle. She must have been only thirty feet or so above my head. I could see the Salmon she held in her talons, still dripping with blood!

Two Eagles were circling over my house every afternoon, one spotted and one mature bald male. They were doing flight training, mastering the thermals, calling their excitement to father sky. They appeared to be father and son.

Just yesterday while I was hiking in the woods, taking an afternoon break from carpentry work in the house and several weeks on the road doing retreat workshops, two Eagles were trying their skill at acrobatics, flying through the branches of the trees. I've seen Hawks do that on occasion, but never Eagles. Believe me, it is an awesome site to be witnessing two huge raptors not twenty feet away performing such acrobatics.

This evening I have been sitting with my Sacred Pipe by the fire, half drifting off and out of my body, listening to Owls--maybe three, but at least two--in the grove of fir trees behind the house. These Night Eagles were singing messages to me very loudly. Does the Owl Spirit bring me a divine message, or is it warning me of something mysterious, something passing from this dream forever?

As I sat there, half drifting off into a dream state, wondering what this all meant, I kept pondering what the message to me was in all this... Then, it came! I shook myself upright with a start at hearing my own voice! "That's it!" I cried out loud as if there were anyone who could hear me. I was, after all, totally alone in my fire-lit log cabin. Every time I closed my eyes there was before me a great White Eagle. I distinctly heard the voice of the Eagle saying to me:

"Look at me. Observe me. How do I live?

"Look at me. What do you see about my true nature?

"Am I not always alone? And why is it, do you suppose, I never seem to gather in groups larger then two or three at a time?

"I Master my capabilities without comparison to any other living thing. I do not suffer the stress of competition with others.

"I simply am; living constantly within my power; fishing, living, playing, hunting, flying, watching, being a part of all that is around me.

"We gather in numbers only occasionally; at great Migratory gatherings, or during the mating season when we gather as did your tribes of old.

"When we do gather in numbers, be sure that all the other creatures in the forest take notice.

"All creatures acknowledge our power and grace of nobility, with an ageless familiarity, as the spirit of our eternal intent emanates from us.

"Even Man, the most arrogant creature of them all, acknowledges us!"

There was a silence for a moment. The Eagles turned from me as if acknowledging the presence of unseen others. Then they flapped their wings, letting loose the sound of rolling thunder that echoed through the forest hillsides. Turning once again towards me, one stared at me through two huge yellow eyes with renewed intensity.

"Fulfill yourself! It is only when you yourself are beyond need that you can affect change. For it is only when you are in your full power and not coming from the emotion of lack that you are fully capable of manifesting your chosen reality. When you make your moves from the seat of your power, you will be truly be capable of affecting the world and changing condition.

"You, who are beginning once again to see the web of life and the truth of things, you should be careful lest the Dark Hunters find you. Do not gather in numbers, for you are then easy prey for these Dark Hunters. Young dreams need time to mature. Like young grass, you must establish a strong root system. The roots that support the great tree of your knowledge need time to grow and seek the wisdom the Earth has to offer.

"Love all beings, but trust no one with untested certainty. For this is the time of the Coyote Moon. There is a madness in the air! Many seem caught in a spell of harsh madness and self destruction. Be still; you can sense it moving towards you from the void! What seems like a block might well be the answer. Counter-intention can be there to strengthen you as well as slow you.

"The Dark Hunters are everywhere; they are hiding in the shadows of your dreams and in the places where your doubts lie. The Dark hides in shadows because it is afraid to be seen. The moment that it is in the fullness of the light it transforms. You will know the Dark Hunters because they have no face of their own! They have no form of their own! They are shape shifters and soul snatchers! They ride upon your spirit! They will drain your energy, for they are not creators and have no dreams of their own.

"The Dark Hunters take on the nature of all that is going on around them. They are the great Chameleons, taking on the character and coloring of their hosts. They are the necromancers, possessing no life of their own. They always come from our unresolved past; they cannot exist in *the Now*. One can live in fantasy of the past or the future. These are phantom worlds. But to exist in *the Now* takes power, for it is by right use of will and will alone that one can claim enough power to exist in *the Now*! Know that it is only through *the Now* that one can manifest any expression of reality.

"Look at me! Look closely into my eyes; what do you see? We have a contract, your kind and mine, that is from ancient times. The true nature of it is older than your memory can access. Only your heart can access the dimension of my reality--only your heart.

"Great change is coming. Nothing shall remain as it has been. This change will come as a great wind. It will come suddenly, giving but the slightest forewarning of impending change. Then in a moment it will be upon you, and envelop all that you are.

"If you wish to survive this experience of change, then *BE AS I AM*. Be in the moment, be in the silence. For here in the silence you will find your power. Here in the silence of your own being you will remember your own Heart. It is in your heart that your origins lie.

"Fulfill yourself! It is only when you yourself are beyond need that you can affect change. For it is only when you are in your full power and not coming from the emotion of lack that you are fully capable of manifesting your chosen reality."

"Listen closely. We give you now the wisdom of the Eagle nation. Go and gather all around you those who are a part of your heart. Gather around you all that brings you joy. All that you dream of being is yours to experience when you gather these things. Hold those dreams very close to your heart!

"Realize and embrace the sweetness in the gift of living the human drama, for the nature of Earth's reality is about to change dramatically. Quickly, as is her nature, you will not be able to avert the force of the tumblers of change as they begin to roll across the landscape of the dream. The very essence of the dream shall shake and fracture. Only the human heart remains the same though all your evolutionary changes.

"The Dark Hunters, which are a part of your perception of reality, are phantom overseers, watching, observing, waiting for you to succumb to a moment of fear. For fear closes the Heart and opens the back doors to your dreams, leaving you vulnerable to the phantoms of human fear. They are the vampires in the holographic dream you would call reality. For they need to steal your dreams for their life essence. They need to feed off what you have created. They are the true vampires.

"Do you not remember who you are, little God? Let your spirit loose, and fly with us through the clouds. All below you and its true intent will come into clarity. And that which blocks your progress along the crooked labyrinths of life's petty dramas shall become as small boulders from these magnificent heights.

"So lift yourself and spiral upwards towards Great Spirit. Care not for the explanations; **follow your intuitive knowing**. That is the

Pathway of the Heart. It is GOD'S compass showing you the direction of the Road back home!

"I AM the spirit guardian that danced with your ancestors. I AM THE WHITE EAGLE.........LISTEN WITH YOUR HEART..............

THIS MAY WELL BE ... *THE LAST CRY!*"

Otipemsiwak
Those who own Themselves

With each moment that one experiences joy, by whatever action, they allow the inner union with the totality of themselves. That totality is God I AM. The creator has never judged—only man has judged man, bound by his smallness of spirit and addiction to ignorance. For the creator, the great Mystery, God I AM, the creator of all that is.....is lawless.

Strive always for happiness and joy, for these are the attributes that allow LOVE to find you. These are the emotions that, like invisible radio waves, lead us to the creator, the great Mystery. The Path, the Good Red Road, is anything but narrow, for in essence it encompasses all that is, for all that is, is God. Thus, in truth we can never stray from it. Aye, even within the nucleus of the atom can creator be found; in a tiny speck of blue light, the flame that burns eternal. Knowing this, why then would you deny creator's existence within your own heart..........?

Native American Prophecies--
Tales of the End Times

To accurately relate the prophecies of even one of the Native American Peoples, whether they be Lakota, Cherokee, Hopi, Inca, or the Mayan, would take volumes. I am called Ghost Wolf. I am Metis (me·tā), having in my genetic line the blood of both the Lakota and Haudenosaunee (Iroquois) People. I am equally proud of my European heritage of mixed blood. Creator has made me, beyond question, a mongrel in this life. I have come to understand through my inter-dimensional teachers that I also have the genetics of over 22 races from beyond the Sun, so I am truly a Child of the Rainbow. The Lakota have a name for my people; we are the *Wigmunkee Oyate* -- the Rainbow Nation. In my travels I have been adopted by many of my Native American relatives, *Hunka*, the making of relatives. In short, I have returned to the ways of the first nations' people. The Metis are the largest community of People in America. We are the tribe without borders.

I carry the Sacred Pipe, the Chanupa. It was given to me by my elders. It was they who taught me to carry it, to respect it, and how to use it. I worked alone for many years before I was told that I had the right to carry it 'for the people,' if I chose to take the responsibility. I accepted and as is tradition, I made the pipe I would use for ceremony for the people with my own hands.

My Earthly teachers have been elders from a variety of people, Apache, Sioux, Hopi, Osage, Ojibiwa, Cherokee, Comanche, Haudenosaunee. When Grandfather first put the Chanupa in my hands he told me, "You must go and learn the spiritual ways of all peoples. I see you working with people from many cultures in the times that are ahead of you. They will all be coming back here to the turtle, for this is where all their journeys began. Go and learn how they see spirit and Creator. Then you can help them heal their minds, that they might heal their own hearts. In your time a new world will be born. You will see many strange things. Judge no one for their ways of expressing spirit, for the Creator allows all beings to express in their own way.

"You must learn to connect with your own individual consciousness. It has always been the consciousness of the few that transcended the opinion of the many and brought change. The few move the many. Knowledge can come from hearing prophecy, but wisdom comes from learning how to use the knowledge about the prophecies. Otherwise we can become frozen in the dream, as if caught in ice."

"Another part of your journey will be that somehow you are to help reconnect the people of the Condor with the people of the Eagle. If you and the others succeed, then this land and its people might become one again. Many secrets will open that have been closed. You will know when you have accomplished your task, for there will be no time, but you will still be here. Go, be the peacemaker."

It is a prophecy of the Baha'i faith that the original peoples of the Americas will become awakened, and in their awakening they shall illuminate the world. That indeed it is the destiny of the Native People of the Americas to lead the world back to their spiritual heritage -- and that this shall result in the day of Creator. For on this day, the day of Man, the day of the Prophets will be past. It will be the beginning again, the day of God. All people will gather and have the opportunity to build the new nation. It is my prayer that this prophesy of the end times comes to pass, for it will mean the beginning of a golden age where humankind has once again returned to their awareness of their divine beginnings.

I tell you now that if this prophecy is ever to pass, all people, even the Native People, must give up arguing about their differences and join together as one people. And the rest of the world must recognize the Native People as a sovereign people, and hear what we have to say. Our stories must go out to the world unfiltered, not distorted by the intellect. It must be a story of the heart.

You have come to me in a good way, as my people say. You bring sage and herbs, and come without agendas. I see you have an open heart. So I will speak to you and share what the Grandfathers and Grandmothers have shared with me. But to accomplish such a thing we must smoke the Pipe, so we will know what passes between us will be truth, uncolored by our own purpose or fears.

She asked for visions of the days that were coming. What were the messages of the Native People? I lifted the Pipe and I asked Grandfather for truth. The following is the reading after the pipe ceremony which I allowed to be recorded.

We have smoked the pipe together, so these words will be truth. You came here on a journey to ask about prophesy. Prophecies always follow a twisting road, yet they can end up at the same place, if they are truth. There are so many truths with all the different people. Creator has many eyes.

Western consciousness is imploding. The consciousness that came here, that conquered everything without caring, without listening to the Buffalo or the Eagle, is dying, and the signs are everywhere. It is good that you should ask us about prophesy. We have been trying to tell you for centuries. But you have not had on your ears, so you did not hear us. Our prophets have never been heard by your people. But I hear that prophets are often not heard in their own land.

We also have our stories of the Messiah. We, too, have our saints, our prophets, our ascended masters. But in many ways the traditional native people of this turtle are ahead of modern society in the awakening process. You see, we honor our sacred women, as well as the men. It has always been the stories of Grandfather *and*

Grandmother we have been telling. Without the balance of the male and female, life would cease to be, for creation itself could not occur.

There are many misconceptions about the Indian ways. We do not worship beasts and we do not worship stones. We honor them, and we honor the consciousness that is within them. Because we are all *Mitakyue oyasin* -- we are all relations, we are one with all things even unto the universe. We are connected to all of life by a web of light. This light is invisible to most. But the medicine people can see it, if their medicine is real. We see it in everything -- all of life is connected. We are all brothers and sisters with the Eagle, the Rabbit, the Tree People, even with the stones. Everything is alive, and that aliveness is the Creator that is in all things.

In my life I have come to walk with the elders of many nations. I too asked the same questions that you ask of me now. What about the prophecies? I learned much from the Hopi. But there are many prophecies. Each people that are on this turtle have a part of the story. The prophecies are all woven together like a blanket. That is part of the reason we are all one people. And even though each of us expresses our spirituality in our own way, the stories all come together in the end. That is how we know if it is truth or not.

There are many clans, and many nations. We are a sovereign people. But always, as the Hopi say, "Under it all, every blanket is made from the wool of the sheep." So we are all made from the same stuff, we just look different on the outside. That is our individual cultural expression. But we are woven together just like that blanket. We are one family, born to one Mother and to one Father. We are one tribe -- we are called Human beings. Our seeds are so mixed that there are no pure ones left on this surface world...but that is a story for another time.

My uncle, Pete Catches, said once, "We have come to a time when we should be together. There should not be divisions amongst people, there should be peace amongst men. In saying this, I would pray Great Spirit blesses anyone who hears these words and opens their hearts to the truth."

A great prophet came to the people somewhere around the time of your stories of Jesus. He was our messiah, and it is possible that he was the same man. I know he was, because that is what my heart tells me, and my heart has never lied to me. Much of our history and our ways in both North and South America are connected to this Pale Prophet who came from across the waters, riding upon the wind.

The Lakota people called him *Wacuma tete wakan* (way-cu-ma tet-taye wakon), the Lord of the Wind. He had many names. He was *Ee-me-see* to the Choctaw, the Wind God. The Yakima people call him *Tiacoma*, the Wind God. The Hawaiian people called him *Wakea*. The Algonquin people call him *Es-see co-ti*, the feathered serpent. To the Papago in Arizona, he is known as *E-see-cotl*. The Toltec people called him *Kate-zahl*. To the Mayan he was *Quetzalcoatl*, the plumed white serpent from the sea.

"There are many clans, and many nations.
We are a sovereign people. But always, as the
Hopi say, 'Under it all, every blanket is made from
the wool of the sheep.' So we are all made from the
same stuff, we just look different on the outside. That
is our individual cultural expression. But we are woven
together just like that blanket. We are one family,
born to one Mother and to one Father. We are one
tribe – we are called Human beings.
Our seeds are so mixed, there are no pure ones left on
this surface world..."

To the Haudenosaunee people he is known as *Deganaweda*, the Peacemaker. He created the Great Peace. It is the way of the Great Peace that united the Iroquois Confederacy for hundreds of years before the coming of the white man. Deganaweda spoke about how to be human beings, and how a warrior race could live in unity and peace. He and his helper, Hiawatha, taught the people how to create a form of self-government that was based upon the spiritual understanding of the human family. It is upon this form of government which your entire constitution is based -- the great claim to freedom of America.

There were others who brought great prophecy to our people. Black Elk, the *Oglala* holy man, spoke much prophecy. His vision was the story of the Rainbow Nation, the *Wigmunkee Oyate*. He foresaw, as did Grandfather Fools Crow, a coalition of all human kind, a great Hoop made up of all Creator's children. It is to this vision that I am also committed to which I speak, and the to end to which I work. We are all Children of the Sun. A Rainbow Nation without Borders.

Heal the Women — Heal Humanity

I will tell you a story that was given to me by a Grandmother of the Ojibiwa people. She told me that we must work with the women, we must help them at all costs to heal their pain. In these times that are coming, she told me to help the women reclaim their power. If the women do not reclaim their power, all will be lost. Because in these times the men will no longer act like men. They will not be noble and proud of who they are, who they come from, and their connection to the land. They will not hold the words of Creator close to their hearts. They will only hold the words of other men to their hearts, and men can be wrong. Two-leggeds make mistakes.

Men have become sick with altered ego and greed. They have lost their connection to their inner spirits. They have a material God now. There are no longer leaders among the People, so our children do not learn, and they now wander aimlessly through life like lost souls, without connection to their spirit. A human being without spirit is like a ship without a sail. All they can do is float around, hoping that luck will bring them to a safe harbor. They are without personal power and not really alive. They are a leaf at the mercy of the wind.

Grandmother told me that in the times that were coming, it would be the women who will remember who they are first, because women have known who they are for many generations. Once, as the bearers of life, it was the women who were the teachers of life's mysteries. Long ago the people made a choice, and many of them left the good red road and began to walk the black road. The stories of the women who followed their men down this black ribbon were suppressed, because they kept telling the men that they were walking in the wrong direction. They kept telling them that they were walking away from the sacred ways, and that one day they could loose even their memories of these ways entirely. But the men did not want to hear that they might be wrong. Today we know that the women were right in their fears about this black ribbon road. Most of us do not even know how to speak our own language.

The men brought the sacred bundles to us for safe keeping, but it was already too late. Our way of life was disappearing from this Earth faster than the snow melts in spring. With the coming of the white man's ways, women were not allowed to speak. It was taught that the devil spoke through their mouths. Only the men could speak, so we watched in silence as the world fell apart. Today we are beginning to wake up. We are remembering our beginnings; it is as our elders have always taught us. The time is near for us now when we will see the new world.

The women have help from Grandfather Grizzly, Mahto, who had given secret medicine ways to the women and taught them the ways of the herbs and the healing power of the plants. He taught them also about the Dream time power, and how to heal the mind. I ask you, was it not always the women who taught the men the ways of the people? And in the end, when they saw their world crumbling, the men brought the sacred bundles to the women, who then took them to the safety of the mountains. The women cried for vision, and begged the Creator to show them where to bury these sacred bundles, so that there would be something left for their children to know the ways.

So it is the Grandmothers that to this day hold many of these sacred bundles, and the sacred pipes, for the people. And this is how it should be, for the women are the bearers of life. They have the ancient wisdom that has always been with them. They create the bodies that we use when we come into this world. They have a very special relationship with the Mother, for she is the one who gives the women the formula for doing this.

Heal the women. Then they can heal themselves. Once the women have been healed, then they can heal the men. With strong hearts they can help heal the fear that has consumed men, which is what happens when you lose contact with you spirit. When the men are healed, then we can dream the new dream for this Earth and use the Ghost Dance Medicine that Mahto has given us. Then we will dance with Sitting Bull and the Porcupine once again. Then we will return to the ways of the Great Peace, *Kia neri Kowa*. This is the story that Grandmother told me.

Tales of the End Times

I will speak to you now of another prophecy. In the next decade, the Star People that you call meteorites and comets, will come to this Earth in answer to the Mother's call for help. You see, we are all relations. So the Star People are the beings we call stars and planets. Sometimes they are not these beings, but in fact are great ships that travel through dimensions, yet they are all living organisms. There are many living beings inside these ships who sometimes come here to visit us. We have always known of their existence.

The ones who have visited me most often have had blue skin. Some are white and appear to float. I believe these are the older ones, their holy ones. They have told us of the Mother's cry for help being heard throughout the universe. The sacred Mother is screaming for life and the meteorites and comets will hear her cry and answer her cal for help. They will hit the Earth as they come from the heavens. They will hit the Earth with such force that many internal things will happen, as well as external things. The Earth's tectonic plates will move as a result of the velocity of the impacts. We have been told that this will occur just before the turn of the century.

This will cause the sacred fire, the source of all life to the Mother, to move through her body. She is like a great bird within the egg, trying to crack out of the shell. When the Meteorites hit, the rings of fire will move from South where all life comes from. They will move North, in a contrary manner, because all of this action is contrary to the dance of life. It will be as though the Mother is having her period and making new eggs for the new life forms she will birth.

The clouds that bring the rains will change their direction and the winds will alter their course. What has occurred for 3,000 years will be changed forever, and what has existed for over thousands upon thousands of years will no longer exist. Everything will be inside out. Where there is summer, there will be fall. And where there is fall there will be winter. And where there is winter there will be spring.

The animals and plants will become confused. The animals will think it is spring in the winter, and the cherries will come to blossom and die in the frost. And in the summer, the winds will come from the North, and the blanket of purification will fall and the fruit and wheat will die. The animals that you raise will no longer be able to graze, because they will try to graze in the summer upon winter fields. The time is getting very near for the dimensions to open up. Very soon we will experience a merging of worlds as we enter the fifth world. When this happens things will get very confusing. These are some of the ways in which the Mother will warn us, so we will know that this time is near. Then we must stay in the mountains, away from the cities.

There will be great plagues that your doctors will not understand. Many of these plagues are born of the experimentation your scientists are doing. Their intentions have gone awry, and they think they can control nature. Your scientist have let monsters loose upon the land. Some are from this dimension, some are from others that have long been asleep. Some are like mechanical bugs that they have created for purposes of war and population control. They appear to be living things, but they are more like little machines.

These plagues will spread through your waters, which will become poisoned. You will only be able to drink deep rock water in these times. These plagues will poison your blood from the food you eat. The whole food chain will be disrupted, as well as the natural chain of events by which the Mother cleanses herself with the waters.

Only those who have learned to live off the land where the water runs pure from deep within the Earth, and the rain that falls from the sky is washed by the trees to clean the acid from it, will have a chance to find sanctuary from the turmoil that will result. You must go to where the Eagles fly, to where the Wolf roams, to where the Bear lives. Here you will find life, because they will always know to go to where the water is pure and the air can be breathed.

Live where the trees are old. They are the lungs of this Earth and they purify the air. Go to where these standing people take the poisons from the breath of the Dragon. They can change it by breathing, and they give the clean air back to you, so that you may live. Where the snow falls you will find protection from the plagues and viruses. The snow is a great purifier. Go to where the Mother's blanket heals your body as well as your emotions, where she will give you new dreams of the emerging world. If you learn to live in these places, you will live through these times.

"This is a time to relearn how to live with the Earth. It is a time to honor Spirit. It is a time to listen to the Mother. It is time to reawaken our feminine emotional awareness so we can communicate with the higher octaves of reality as we did once long ago when we were all living free upon this sacred egg we call Earth... It is time once again to feel the wind upon your face, to smell the Earth after the newly fallen rain, to learn the power of living in the cold without freezing, because what you think with your body is what you create."

You will see the great ships returning. The Dragons will come back to their home from long ago. They will come from the heavens. For long ago, this was their world. We were left as the caretakers, the guardians. This has been foretold -- the return of the red Kachina. Most will call it a comet, but it is a Dragon ship. Then the Blue Kachina will come in answer to the Red "comet". These are our friends. They are messengers from the Gods of old, letting us know that we are not forgotten.

The degree and intensity of the changes depends upon the consciousness that you hold. The consciousness held at this time is the consciousness of many beings. You are made up from many beings, "star seeds" if you will. You must learn to connect with your own individual consciousness. It has always been the consciousness of the few that transcended the opinion of the many and brought change. The few move the many. Knowledge can come from hearing prophecy, but wisdom comes from learning how to use the knowledge about the prophecies. Otherwise, we can become frozen in the dream, as if caught in ice.

In the times to come you must cut off the voices that constantly rattle in your head. These are the voices that tell you what you shouldn't have done or said. The voices that insist it is crazy to think you are getting messages from the spirits, and that the others will laugh at you. When you are busy worrying about what people say or think about you, you cannot see the truth. One can only see the truth when one is experiencing the truth. It happens in the moment, not in the past or the future.

It is hard to tell you everything that will happen, because your society and the way it thinks and sees life is as inconsistent as your consciousness. Your social consciousness swings back and forth like a pendulum. Your society has called upon itself a consciousness of self-destruction. This consciousness, created from so many maligned thoughts, will pass from this plane as did the Mammoth and the Dinosaur. Once the people were across the land like the Buffalo, and this wisdom and understanding of the ways of the Earth were everywhere. Now we, like the Buffalo, are also very few in number.

Prophecies can be heard in the cry of the Eagles, in the voice of the ocean as it ebbs and flows, from the whale and the dolphin that come upon your shores crying, pleading with you not to end this reality. Once they were you, once you were they. We are brothers and sisters that come from another world. Prophecies can also be heard within the stones in the Inipi lodge, if you learn to listen to the sound of the silence.

You must look deeply into the simplicity of what you are, not into the complexity of what you create. For too long you have lived in the complexity of your thoughts of what you are. As a result, you have lost touch with your inner reality. You have named everything upon the Earth, and still you know nothing about this Earth. Now you would even attempt to name the heavens of which you know even less.

You have formulated everything and tried to make the Earth bend to the will of your technology and science, but you still cannot control her. Now the very nature of your reality is collapsing, because you refused to listen to the living song of creation -- her Song. You must see that she is a living being who has given life to you! Until you realize that, there is nothing you can do to deal with what she will bring forth during her birthing of the fifth world.

The times that are coming will teach us our technology will no longer work. It is against natural laws and physics. What will work is a little common sense -- very simple common sense. New technology that works with the human consciousness is already available to us. The native people have methods of healing that will rock modern allopathic means of remedy for illnesses. There have always been ways we could apply our consciousness to create new technology that would surpass anything we presently have available to the scientific community.

The spiritual awakening will happen of its own accord. We do not have to concern ourselves with what is the proper way. There is no cultural or ethnic secret formula for evolution. Most of it is a matter of opening the heart, which will open the mind to new avenues of applied reality. Mostly we have to create an environment free from fear. We do not need to get lost in whether we hold a pipe in the Lakota way or the Ojibiwa way, or if the Tibetan way or the Buddhist way is correct. Creator does not care if you are Christian or Aborigine. Great Spirit hears the human heart. From there we all speak the same language, and from there we are all the same. We are all relations.

When the Dali Lama visited our holy people, they understood each other. They spoke a common language. When our *Witchasha Wakan* visits leaders of other countries, they understand each other. It is only our scientists and social religious leaders that do not seem to understand the commonality between us. It all comes down to fear. Let go of fear and we find the answers.

The common language is simply this. Live with the Earth instead of against it. Love the Earth, and love yourself. If you are in harmony with the Earth, you cannot help but be in harmony with yourself. The person living in joy and harmony in a little hut on the side of a mountain with a clear stream running through his or her front yard is going to survive it all.

I know it is hard when you go to the reservation and look for Crazy Horse and Sitting Bull and Chief Seattle, and all the other "hero" Indians you have made movies about, and instead find poverty. You satisfy yourselves by assuming we want to live like that! You ease your conscience by pointing at all the drunk Indians on the streets of Gallop. It is easier to look at the poverty and see the alcohol and the other symptoms of an out of balance world, than to look at the cause and the responsibility your government has had in implementing policies of genocide in many nations, both here and around the world!

"All the races must be honored and recognized. Separation must end. Supremacy of a chosen few must end. It is long enough that the Catholics have lived the only way, and long enough that the Buddhists have lived the only way. No longer is the only way the Red way, or the blue way. There is only the way of the people. We the people are the dream of the Earth; we are her gift to the universe."

You have to understand that until 1978, when president Carter signed the Native American Religious Freedom Act, it was against the law for us to practice our ways. Our children were not even allowed to speak our native language in public places. To my people the Chanupa, the Sacred Pipe, is a tool for prayer. It is as sacred to us as the bible is to the Christians.

The Pipe is our church, our Sacred altar, and until just a very short time ago we could be imprisoned and have our children taken away for praying with it. Today we can go to a Potlatch ceremony any time you want, but until President Carter signed that bill we were not allowed by law to hold such events. This is what we have had to live with. Perhaps we are all learning to leave the ignorance of our past experiences behind us. I would hope so.

So when you go to the reservations, you shouldn't be surprised that only maybe two percent of the people still practice the native ways, or the people are reluctant to talk to you about them. But it is alright. It doesn't matter how many. How many of the people who conquered this land and its people, and proclaimed their religion so loudly, really practice the ways of their own religion? How many Christians are really Christ-like -- maybe two percent? That is all behind us now. What is here and coming from within us and from the heavens will soon make all of that seem like a bad dream.

My people are very shy by nature. They are very shy about sharing their ways. Perhaps now you can understand why! In reality, Western intellectual consciousness has controlled this country for almost 200 years. And where are we? The land no longer can sustain life in many places, and the people are filled with disease. We can't eat the fish from the rivers and oceans. The water we all need for life is poisoned.

We have created so much garbage that there is no place left on Earth to dump it all. I hear that there are many ships that just float around the ocean with the garbage, because there is no place to put it all. I have seen trainloads of garbage coming out of LA and being secretly dumped on reservation land in New Mexico -- train loads!

We have so much violence in our society these days, along with drugs, suicide, and prison buildings in some cities in America bigger than their hotels. When the Earth was in the care of the Native People, there were millions of people here, and cities existed that were larger than the cities in Europe. Then there was no need for prisons. You do not find ancient prisons at the ruins sites, now do you?

The People are angry! The youth is angry! We are experiencing *Kyanosquatsi,* the world out of balance! They are angry at the government which is out of control. They are angry at a legal system that invades our privacy and abuses our human rights, destroys families and persecutes the poor, and steals land from its citizens and then gives it over to the UN. The anger is growing. Soon it will not be so easy to cover up the truth with all of us asking questions. They will not be able to handle the cover-up with a whole nation of angry people, locked up in their cities.

The Earth is moving. Everyday there are Earthquakes. You read about them in the news papers, or find out about them on the Internet before they even get to the 11 o'clock news. What you do not see on the news or read in the papers is what is happening beneath the Earth's surface. Under the ocean, where she is moving and steaming in silence, the lava is moving, and new land formations are forming all throughout the Pacific Rim. Whole mountain ranges are rising hundreds of feet in the Atlantic ocean. There is a lot of hydro-thermal activity beneath the ocean's surface. The steam is rising up and warming the atmosphere. The Mother's skin is scratching and itching and stretching.

All this stretching and shaking is causing many rivers to change their course. Some are drying up. Lakes are dropping their levels. The water level at Lake Tahoe is 50 feet lower than it was ten years ago. A lot of this is an indirect result of what humankind has done unconsciously.

You think where you sit upon the Earth is solid, but it is always moving. The mountains are moving. On the West coast of America, the land mass that makes up California is moving Northward on the average of 6 to 18 inches every year. The continents are definitely moving. The land also needs to breath. All the concrete and asphalt is stopping the Earth from breathing. This is not a solid rock; it is a living organism. We have forgotten that in contemporary society, where even our souls have become commodities.

Once, long ago, when we all walked upon the Earth and lived our lives in freedom, we knew how to follow the signs. We knew to follow the changing course of the river. The storm clouds spoke to us. We could call the rain. We could call the good weather as well. We did this with our minds because our hearts were open.

The Government is building huge underground structures all over the world. It is no longer the US government -- it is a world Government; they just haven't told you. That is why your politicians do not listen to what you tell them, why it seems they do not know how you feel. Not everyone in high places is from this Earth, either. The government is covering up a lot of things. But you know, those walls are cracking, and the truth is leaking out. We the people, the people of the land, are not going away!

We must be concerned about these underground complexes that the government has built. They are building them so when the Earth Changes start they can move the elite underground to "safety." Well, it won't work. But they have created other problems. There will be many underground explosions from gasses and chemicals that are in these tunnels below the surface world, some of which run for miles and are essentially cities below the surface. They cannot hide from the changes. Unless they change their consciousness and take responsibility for participating in this game, this change will affect every molecular structure upon the Earth, to the very core of the planet.

*"Learn to listen to your own heart.
If you learn that, you will know the wisdom of the
ages. Learn to speak your own words, and sing your
own song, while you learn to allow others to enjoy the
same state of being. Allow, allow, allow!"*

This is a time to relearn how to live with the Earth. It is a time to honor Spirit. It is a time to listen to the Mother. It is time to reawaken our feminine emotional awareness so we can communicate with the higher octaves of reality, as we did once long ago when we were all living free upon this sacred egg we call Earth, that the Star brothers call Terra. It is time once again to feel the wind upon your face, to smell the Earth after the newly fallen rain, to learn the power of living in the cold without freezing, because what you think with your body is what you create.

The spiritual awakening will happen; we do not have to look for it. We just have to get ready for it to arrive. We have to allow it to occur. It is like Grandma is coming for the weekend, but we are just not sure of when she will arrive since she likes to window shop. Do not concern yourself so much with which is the right way. But I will tell you this, whatever the world governments tell you they are trying to do to help the Earth and her people will not work, until all of her people are heard and honored.

All the races must be honored and recognized. Separation must end. Supremacy of a chosen few must end. It is long enough that the Catholics have lived the only way, and long enough, Grasshopper, that the Buddhists have lived the only way. No longer is the only way the Red way, or the blue way. There is only the way of the people. We the people are the dream of the Earth; we are her gift to the universe.

Learn to listen to your own heart. If you learn that, you will know the wisdom of the ages. Learn to speak your own words, and sing your own song, while you learn to allow others to enjoy the same state of being. Allow, allow, allow!

We must learn to respect all life -- respect the planet, respect the Insect, respect the Rattlesnake -- as well as the Eagle, the rock, and the tree. It is all consciousness. It is all life. We are all related, just different expressions of divine intelligence. It is all in the song of creation, and the song is made up of many notes.

If you can no longer get up in the night to listen to the falling rain, or to listen to the sound of the owl outside your window with joy in your heart, if you can no longer enjoy the wind rustling through the grass or the warmth of the sun upon your face, if there is no longer a song in your heart and a dream in your head, then you have lost it all anyway. Best to go find what you have left behind -- you are going to need it.

You must make the conscious decision to change your life. I'm not talking about changing roles or just using different words. This is not the time to redecorate the box we are all stuck in. I am talking about being different -- NOW! Everything is going to change. It will be like going from the dream time to wake up time. There is a big difference in those realities, is there not?

If you do not love yourself enough to change, then you will not be able to come into alignment with the new frequencies. And about change, remember what my people always kept in mind: "Change so that when you yield this robe, your children will still have a mother to enjoy. Always remember seven generations. For in seven generations, you will return to harvest your actions and your dreams." Is it worth all the judgement that you harbor and the angry energy that you throw around without regard for where it falls?

If my people have a prayer for you, it is that you would wake up tomorrow and walk this Earth consciously. I pray that every movement you live will have a purpose, that every word you speak has a meaning, and that every thought you have be a prayer of gratitude for being alive, knowing that you are the "bringers of the dawn."

Aho   Mitakyue Oyasin, hechetu wealo.

It is so!

Arizona Pipe Circle

*I*n July 1994, the people of America watched the media coverage of the Jupiter comet collisions with anxious anticipation (heavily dosed with intermittent interruptions by the O.J. Simpson trial.) Simultaneously, a small group of people met in the mountains of Arizona to do ceremony, and though this meeting went unnoticed in the eyes of the world, it was the most important event of the century to that point in its impact on the fate of the world as we know it.

We were spoon fed the Jupiter collision like kindergarten children on our first field trip to the museum, as the scientists tried to give us hypothetical possibilities for something they knew nothing about. Science had little, if any, understanding of the monumental effects to our planet or our solar system that would result from this occurrence.

Without a balance of spiritual understanding and a full grasp of the true nature of Quantum Physics and the higher octaves of reality, there was little they could offer to help people comprehend the chain of events that was just beginning with the comets impact on Jupiter. During one network's coverage, they explained the belief that millions of years ago, a comet crashed onto the Earth's surface, causing the Earth to heat up so much that the dinosaurs disappeared and life on Earth altered forever. If one comet striking Earth could do all that, imagine what radical shifts occurred from twenty-one of them hitting Jupiter!

From the Native American perspective one might ask, "If the Earth is a living being, and Jupiter also a living being, what will these occurrences mean to us in the patterns of our future? What will this mean to the balance of our solar system and the beings who make up the family known as the Milky Way?" There are many instances of findings of the ancient Meso-American civilizations which hold the keys to the answers to these and other questions. While much evidence has been destroyed during the conquest of the Americas by the invading

Europeans, still countless examples remain locked away in the underground archives of the Catholic Church in Rome. Records of ancient beings are imprinted upon the living rocks, or buried in obscure locations beneath the Earth's surface. The pyramids and mounds of North America, the pyramids and tombs of the Mayan, Inca, and Aztec people in South America contain examples of these records.

"God is simple, simple, simple. If it is complicated, it is not from the Divine. Life lived in balance brings joy. Joy is our natural state, so simply put, seek Joy in your life – joy in a smile, the smell of a flower floating upon the wind, the falling of rain upon the parched Earth, the laughter of children playing without any sense of time to clutter their feelings. Allow the God within you to come forth, to live in accordance with the Great Plan. Do you have the courage to place Joy at the top of the list, no matter what criticism you may attract? Remember, statues were never built to honor critics; they were built to honor those who had the courage to be criticized."

It is this information that the small council of human beings had come to discuss in July of 1995. Through ceremony, each of us shared in our own manner, the knowledge we were given from our ancestors and our own personal experiences in the spirit world. The Hopi have long been my friends. We call each other family. I was greatly honored to have the opportunity to sit in council with them as, for three days and nights, we shared the sacred pipe and sang sacred songs handed down through our different heritages.

I am Metis, a mixed blood, born of the Indigenous blood of the Iroquois and Lakota as well as the European, representative of the new blood. The Hopi Elders, who were members of our circle were of ancient lineage, going back to the beginnings of humankind's appearance in this mysterious land we now call America. They were well aware that they may, in fact, be the last pure bloods of their civilization. The world is changing rapidly. Genetic intermingling is now a global phenomenon. Perhaps the next generation will see the new breed of Homo Sapiens as we are fast becoming a mongrel race. It is felt that soon there will be no pure bloods among the Indian people, an eventual reality of all the races.

However, this is not necessarily a bad thing. This is evolution -- part of Creator's plan. We are destined to become the Earth Race, one people of one planet, one Mother, one Father. The races are coming together in accordance with the balance of life that must occur if humankind is to survive. The separatism we have known, as it has been taught through our many religions, cultures, and nation, has outlived its usefulness. There is being born through this experience a Rainbow People, possessing the knowingness of all the races, all the religions and all the cultures.

The time of the old civilizations with their separate tribalized cultures is passing quickly, as is the world circumstance that influenced their development in the course of our evolutionary process. Perhaps this is why it is so important at this time to uncover and bring to the surface the deeper understandings of the different peoples of this Earth, to unveil the mysteries of the past and release what knowledge they might hold -- knowledge, which, in many instances, has been deliberately kept from us by the organized religions of the world. Organized religions now find themselves in much the same situation as the dinosaurs who also once dominated life on this planet.

In the books *The Celestine Prophesy* and *The Tenth Insight,* which have recently taken American readers by storm, we are told of the causes and effects of the human drama we call Life. To most of us the word *coincidence* takes on a whole new understanding as a result of these publications. With this in mind, I say to you that it is no coincidence that there is a growing global awareness of our entering into a New Age, that we are at the precipice of a radical change in our present consciousness, that life as we have known it, is perhaps abruptly coming to an end.

What seems the hardest thing for most of us to grasp in trying to understand the true nature of these changes, is that the final outcome will depend upon our personal choices in how we play out the human drama. There will be no one road, there will be no one event to point to, and the future is not yet written in stone. What is occurring is a change in the entire universe while we are still stuck, if you will, in "I, Me, My." A galactic change is occurring, and we beings of Earth have a small but important role to play in this grand drama.

Change is a natural state of existence here on the Earth plane. No thing remains the same; all of life is flow. All things have their seasons. Our present global civilization is entering into its season of winter. The hope of the coming spring and the new life it will bring, should be our focus at this time. The dreams we have now will directly affect the events that are to come in the spring. We are being allowed the time to reflect, if you will, on our past experiences, that which we call our history as the Human Race, as well as the events in our personal lives.

This may at first seem overwhelming to the seeker, until he or she finds a direction to follow. There are so many different roads we have followed. Why else would there be over 11,000 forms of organized religions in our little world, most claiming to have the one truth. We also have had so many different lifetimes of human experience to sort through, we can easily succumb to despair and confusion. It is a lot like working our way out of a maze.

The first step out of the maze is to come to terms within your own being, your own human drama. What you were in the past is of little importance in *the Now*. What you are now is the first key. Everything you have been, every lifetime, has been for the accumulated experience of personal desire. That desire was experienced through your dreams. The dreams were the thoughts of the feelings you wanted to experience. What would it be like to be the king? What would it be like to fly, to be the warrior, to be the fool? These desires lead you onward into the foreverness of the human drama, for all that you think consciously shall come to pass. And they will manifest soon -- almost instantly.

Your desire is what gave you hope and new direction each time your dream called Life, seemed to collapse. Desire is the emotional drive that gave you the instinct to survive and continue. All of your past experiences culminate in each experience you develop in the moment. What you feel, how you perceive the world, how you perceive others, how you view your life, your choice of relationships, all are the result of your *choosing* in each experience. You have had choice in each lifetime, as you now have choice during the passing of each day. Our life here is about Human interaction, the root of the human drama; it is why we are here.

"...the final outcome will depend upon our personal choices in how we play out the human drama. There will be no one road, there will be no one event to point to, and the future is not yet written in stone".

The Iroquois people have a great understanding of the patterns of human life and social structure. Everything is an extension of the self. The self is realized through interaction with other beings. This is the basic human experience. The first part of this experience is the male/female relationship since we live in a world of duality, positive, negative; male, female. From this relationship comes the family. From the family comes the community. From the community comes the society. From the society comes the nation, and so forth. But it all begins with self.

Another aspect of our human-ness which binds us together, which contributes to our interaction, is our biology. Within us exist natural dualities. Both genders possess male as well as female hormones. We are made up of spirit as well as flesh. All of these factors require expression. That is how we attain self-realization, through our manner of expression. This expression allows us to feel. Through feeling we understand our nature. We live on the Earth, a being who possesses the same elements we do. She, our Mother, has shared with us the elements that comprise our physical bodies. The body is the vehicle through which we are able to participate in the human drama upon the Earth plane. Therefore, we have to establish our relationship with Her.

Earth, Terra, Ghia, is feminine energy, the Goddess. She also possesses within Her being the God Force. The God Force is neither male nor female; it is the state of "is-ness". It is the Source. It is within all elements that comprise Life everywhere throughout the entire universe. We are, in essence, Her children. We also possess this God Force. The same elements that comprise our bodies are also within every physical life form upon the Earth. The elements are simply arranged in different balances, so to speak, causing different life forms to manifest upon this plane. It is much like wearing a space suit.

Therefore, what is in the tree is within us. That which is in the great eagle is within us. That which is within the rock is within us. That which is within the great star is within us. We are truly One with all things. We are expressions of this great God Force contained within a physical embodiment, for the purpose of unique expression of the God Force. Expression is a manifestation of how the God Force realizes Itself. We are the eyes, ears, mouth, hands and emotional heart of Creator upon the Earth Plane. An old Indian wisdom, we are all One. *Aho Mitakyue Oyasin,* we are all relations.

By understanding this fundamental truth, we are able to come into harmony with what we call our Earthly existence, the human drama. We and all upon the Earth, are very much connected. This understanding can be extended into our relationships with our mates and other human beings. They are what we are; we are what they are. Each of us different particums of the greater expression of one consciousness, Human consciousness. Each one of us is entitled to self-expression. This self-expression can be defined in simple terms, as personality. No two leaves on the tree are exactly the same, yet all together they make up the character of the tree.

For the process of creation to occur upon this Earth Plane, both the Female element and the Male element are necessary. It is Universal Law. This is because the existence of physical mass (our bodies) occurs through the lowering of light until it becomes electrical energy. This is accomplished by slowing down the light, causing it to form into coagulated particums. The light particums coagulate because they are moving at a slower rate of speed (a slower vibration) than when they were pure light and without form. This results in a field of electrical energy. It is only within a field of electrical energy that physical mass can exist.

This electrical energy must have a positive and negative charge to exist; that is its nature. As Earth beings made up of physical mass, existing in an electrical field of energy, we possess both the positive and negative aspects of that energy. Our very existence is the result of the polarity of energy in that field. The very existence of the human body places us in a situation of duality.

The God Force, the Creator, is the source of all life forms, all energies, therefore, 'It' is neither the positive nor the negative energy. 'It' is both, and the cause of both existing. 'It' is, in essence, both together in equal balance. 'It' exists in the middle. 'It' is the zero point. Albert Einstein began to see this through his theories on the science of relativity ($E=mc^2$) which is, for the most part, common knowledge today. This understanding is what has given birth to our current limited realization of Quantum Physics. Thought Creates. Literally, everything that exists is all the result of *thought*. We are, in essence, the result of Creator's dream of us. We are but a thought in the River of Life, a potential experience realizing itself moment by moment.

"We and all upon the Earth, are very much connected
... Each of us different particums of the greater
expression of one consciousness, Human consciousness
... No two leaves on the tree are exactly the same, yet
all together they make up the character of the tree."

Where are you in all this potentiality? You are where your thought comes from. You are not the thought, but the one having the thought. Reality is what happens in between, the result of the thought realized. What does this all mean? How does it relate to our relationship to the Earth, to the Creator, to our interaction with other human beings? My Native American side would explain it in the following manner.

In the beginning there was Creator. Creator was all things, yet also no thing. In the contemplation of all that Creator was and could be, Creator dreamed. In the dream Creator felt emotion, awareness, and all the Universe was born of this realization in an explosion of light particums that filled the void. In the dream the Mother (Earth,) the female side of Creator, was also conceived. Together they dreamed the Dream of Life and the Five Worlds were created, each unfolding in accordance with the Great Plan. The Great Plan was Life unfolding and experiencing itself.

The *First World* was of a spiritual nature, much like the dream state -- real, but possessing no form, for form had not yet been conceived. It was simply consciousness and energy. All things potentially, yet no thing materially. The *Second World* was in the nature of physical things, the world of minerals, the basic elements of physical life. These became the crystals, the rocks, the water, the embodiment of the Earth Herself. This is what we call physical mass.

The dream continued to evolve into the *Third World*, and the plant world came into existence -- trees, lichen, flowers, the grasses and so on. Then there came the *Fourth World*, the animal world. There were many expressions in this world also. This is the world that we came into so as to participate in the Dream of Creation. Creator wondered, "How do I make a foot work? How will the eye work, the hand, the mind?" Mother dreamed us and Creator fulfilled Her dreams, for whatever is desired is given. And behold! We were born onto this plane of reality.

The *Fifth World* is the one we are about to enter. In this new world we will learn to balance our spiritual and physical natures. This is described in the prophecies as the age when Man's kind learns to walk upright, as one with Creator. In Tibetan, the term *Hu* means God. So we are about to truly become *Hu-Man*, God-Man realized, Man's kind realized. This is part of what will occur as the *Fifth World* unfolds in its evolutionary process. This is why we call it the awakening, for we, *Hu-Man* kind, is awakening from our dream of the previous four worlds. As the child realizes its potential, it becomes the adult. In our case, we are becoming the Christed Ones.

As children, we saw life around us as one-sided. We only perceived life as it affected our immediate desire. That desire was most often one of self-gratification. First, we must learn to assert our power. We require affirmation of our own existence or identity. As children, we find it hard to see the inter-dependence on each member of the family. As children, it is hard to see the levels of relationship, but as we grow in our awareness, we not only see our own position, we also become aware of the necessity of each member of the tribe and their individual role in the larger community. This awareness occurs as we move into the role of those who preceded us. Simply said, we become aware of what it means to be a member of the human family as we learn to become human through experience.

That expansion of our personal awareness and our input into the society, expressed through creativity and action, results in the evolution of the human species. We connect with the consciousness around us, if we are allowed to expand freely with our genius for personal expression. The evolution of each civilization, experienced in each race, has followed this basic pattern since our first appearance upon this plane. Along the way there have been great civilizations, and some not so great. As some civilizations reached the limitations of the collective thought and they regressed and declined, new civilizations were born to carry on the dream. The moment we achieve perfection we cause change. Perfection is a completion. Completion is an ending. So life, which must continue, mutates and the resulting change allows the River of Life to keep flowing. Eternal experience is unlimited and never-ending.

There have been individuals and even whole groups of people who have transcended this plane together, many more then we presently are aware of. Such was the case with the people who inhabited Easter Island in the Pacific, Machu Picchu in Peru, and the cliff cities at Mesa Verde in Colorado. Many of the physical records of these great civilizations will be discovered within the next decade. As the Earth opens up and flexes Her body during the Earth Changes, she will reveal some of these records. Other records will be revealed as we open our awareness and allow the higher vibratory realities, already existing upon this plane, to be realized within us.

Already great shifting occurs beneath our oceans, as the tectonic plates react to the gradual shifting of our magnetic poles and Her re-birthing process continues. We will also become very aware, collectively, of the existence of the inner worlds and inhabitants who live within our planet. It is estimated, at the time of this writing, that mass open contact will be made with our brothers of the Inner Earth within two to three years. Their existence is known to many, but has been veiled for the most part, since we, as a people, have been closed to the possibility of their existence. We are mostly a fearful lot, and religions have made us closed-minded. We hardly have enough tolerance for our own kind, much less those who might be different than ourselves in their physical form. These Inner Earth inhabitants have been waiting and watching for eons. These are the ones we call the Watchers. They are waiting for us, as a race, to evolve to the point of being capable of interaction on a large scale.

The Fifth World is already here, in a manner of speaking. We have already called it forth. The lack of balance within the human societies that presently exist upon this plane have reached such a level that we are on a pathway of complete annihilation of all life forms on the planet if we are allowed to continue in our present pattern. As a whole, we are fast losing our abilities to dream, to exercise choice. If we fail to dream and choose, life will come to an abrupt halt.

What we have forgotten is our connectedness to all life, to Creator, and to the Earth Herself. What has been overlooked in the madness of our society is the will of the Mother as a sovereign being possessing her own free will. It is a situation where we must totally reconstruct the values by which we live our lives. What we have forgotten she will, once again, remind us of, as she has in the past. The Earth will survive; be assured. She will renew Herself. The continuation of humankind, however, is a matter of choice.

What we have created with our thoughts and actions can be recreated; we possess that kind of power. It is a matter of taking responsibility for our thoughts and actions which empowers our walk on the Pathway. In order to attain Christhood, we must assume responsibility for all that we are. Within all of us there lies the seed of knowingness, the God Force. Therein lies the dream of how this life can be. That is the spark of the Divine Dream. We can choose to live as we have been, lifetime after lifetime, or we can change. We begin our change within. The exterior world and our experience of it is simply the result of our inner desires.

We have fallen victim to the social belief that everything is outside of us. God is out there living on a piece of real estate called Heaven. Spirit is something strange existing in another reality. It is amazing that we even have the ability left to live as the animals. Divide and conquer was the cry of the ancient warriors, the Caesars, the Napoleons, the tyrants of old. As we have been divided from our own spiritual heritage, life grows more hopeless with each passing day. That is the result of allowing ourselves to be divided, allowing our own houses to be divided. We are the temples of the living God, yet we exist outside of our own house. We are looking for the answers, looking for God everywhere, except where God truly dwells -- within. "The Kingdom of Heaven is within."

There will be no Divine Intervention. There has been to much of that in the past, and we did not get the message. All of the great teachers, all of the Holy Men, were either driven out, demonized, or put to the cross. The confusion we are experiencing is the collapse of our consciousness; we are imploding if you will. Previous methods of living are outmoded, non functional. You can find the reasons in the past, but not the answers. It is time to take hold of ourselves as individual expressions of the Living God.

We have elected, it would seem, not to take the easy path. We rebel even against our own emotional desires. We run from freedom of choice and freedom of the human spirit. We are all too willing to give the authority (responsibility) to choose a direction to someone other than ourselves. Life goes on. It is eternal. Our desires go on; they are eternal by their very nature. We are now going to have to choose whether or not to take full responsibility for our actions and thoughts. We, who have turned away from the Creator within, must now make the gesture to regain our natural birthright. It has always been a matter of choice.

All of the Hopi prophecies have come to pass, except for the end times. All of the prophecies given by the Peacemaker have come to pass, except for the end times. All of the prophecies of the Sacred Mayan Calendar have come to pass, except for the end times. All of the prophecies written and carved deep within the temples of Egypt have come to pass, except for the end times. The same truths existed with the Tibetans, the Aztecs, the Cherokee. We are entering the end times, the times of renewal. They are here. If you do not feel a kindred spirit with the Native American, then read the works of Edgar Cayce. We have arrived.

So is everything hopeless? Are we doomed as a species? No, not in the least. Everything is choice. Life and its outcome is born in the moment. This is the plane of action. The Earth Changes are occurring on schedule. As one who travels through time, I assure you that most of what you have heard will occur, but not exactly in your present context. For you see, you will change as well, and this will alter the outcome.

We, as *Hu-man* beings, have more opportunity now than has ever existed in our history to walk the pathway into forever. The times are such that there is an enormous amount of information out there to assist you in learning to become sovereign. We can turn on the television and experience hundreds of methods of spiritual expression by simply switching the channel. Knowledge is pouring into this plane in such abundance that it is often difficult to decide on which experience to focus. The Hopi say that when the times speed up, life will get confusing. There will be no time for children, no time for parents, no time for just living. That is when you must slow down. What is the hurry anyway? The boat leaves when the boat leaves. It is the journey that gives richness to our lives.

God is simple, simple, simple. If it is complicated, it is not from the Divine. Life lived in balance brings joy. Joy is our natural state, so simply put, seek Joy in your life -- joy in a smile, the smell of a flower floating upon the wind, the falling of rain upon the parched Earth, the laughter of children playing without any sense of time to clutter their feelings. Allow the God within you to come forth, to live in accordance with the Great Plan. Do you have the courage to place Joy at the top of the list, no matter what criticism you may attract? Remember, statues were never built to honor critics; they were built to honor those who had the courage to be criticized.

Get your houses in order. The Christ is coming. Deganaweda is coming. Buddha is coming. The Buffalo Calf Woman is coming. They are all coming. They can be felt in each and every one of you, rising like the seeds that lie beneath the Earth, growing, stretching, feeling their way through the darkness, reaching for the light. They are the seeds of God sown within the womb of Mother Earth, the seeds of *Hu-manity*. What shall we dream this time? Anything we want to!

So, to return to the story, a small group of people representing many nations in their bloodlines met in the obscure mountains of Arizona, to look once again at the prophecies that their dreamers had seen thousands of years before they even had the words to express what their visions had shown them; before there was even a written language to record their thoughts and tell of their visions. A small group of people representing the Earth Keepers, the Children of the Earth, met to pray for humanity. We sat with the Hopi Elders and they shared their stories. This is the story of the peaceful people. This is the story of the Hopi way.

The Hopi Way

I asked grandfather once why the Hopi are here. There are so many beautiful places; this is so barren and desolate. He turned towards me and the light shown through those ancient eyes of his as he replied...

> *"We chose this place so that we would not be easily found by those who wandered with no direction. Those who kill and marauder below. We also choose it here so that our eyes would not be distracted, so that we would always look up to the Creator and remember our purpose here.. The Hopi have been looking up so long that all we see is the Creator ..... in everything."*

> *Grandfather David*

The Hopi tell a story of human history that is slightly different from what most Americans are accustomed to hearing in the school room. It is the perception of the Hopi -- and also shared by many of the tribes here in the Western Hemisphere -- that man did cross the land bridge that connected the Americas to Asia. The difference expressed in the Hopi understanding is that they traveled in the opposite direction, from America to Asia. Life, as far as the human drama is concerned, began here in the Western Hemisphere.

> *"The Red Race was sent to the East and given guardianship over the Earth and knowledge of the plants and the elements. They are the Spirit Keepers of the Earth ... The Yellow Race was sent to the South and given the guardianship of the wind, the breath of life ...*

The Black Race was sent to the West and given guardianship of the Waters, the element in Native understanding which rules the nature of our emotions ... The White Race was sent to the North and given the guardianship of the knowledge of fire."

The Cogi Indians of Columbia call themselves the Elder Brother. They say the White Man, who they call the Younger Brother, was ignorant to the laws of Creator and the ways of respect and service to the Earth. The white brother was irreverent to the sacredness of all things and became very arrogant. So he was sent far away across the waters, where he could develop, grow, and not disturb the delicate balance of nature. We are now aware that ancient races traveled to and from North and South America, establishing settlements long before the appearance of Columbus.

There is a wealth of artifacts to substantiate such movement, from the mounds of the Mississippi Mound Builders to the pyramids discovered in Tennessee. The sophistication of such civilizations, retrieved artifacts, and surviving petroglyphs prove that many people, including the Celts, the Egyptians, the Chinese, and the Hebrews, were here thousands of years before Columbus landed on the Caribbean beaches, assuming he had discovered the Western passage to India. Civilization began here, in the Western Hemisphere, and spread from this place to all the corners of the Earth.

Some of these original people settled in what is now Arizona and New Mexico. They called themselves the Hopi, meaning the Peaceful People. High on the mesa tops, safe from marauders that roamed the valleys below, the Hopi built their ancient cities that survive to this day. The traditional Hopi are an ancient culture who even this day are desperately struggling against the onslaught of modern day developers who wish only to get the resources from their sacred lands.

By now, we have all seen or experienced the incessant drive that seems to be programmed within the very DNA of the descendants of the native European cultures to convert everyone to their peculiar way of perceiving reality by any means necessary. The Machiavellian doctrine of the end justifies the means is still the order of the day. The Hopi people and their way of life that they are struggling to preserve today are the endowment of an ancient people who came from the original Motherland. This rich heritage carries with it a tradition that is well over 12,000 years old, even older than the Hopi's ancient stone tablets which tell the story. The Hopi were the ancient fire keepers of Atlantis.

The Hopi tell the story of man's journey from the third world to the present fourth world. The Motherland was an island that is now beneath the Pacific Ocean. This first sinking was followed by a second sinking. In this second sinking, the "red land," or what we today call Atlantis, disappeared beneath the great waters to the South and along with all it's people was never seen again.

After the Motherland disappeared beneath the waters, the third world collapsed. They speak of a time when the surviving four races split apart and developed separately. Each of these races had, in its possession, stone tablets that tell of this beginning time, the time of separation and of the eventual time of their potential reunion. Each of these stone tablets holds its piece of the message of the original teachings and carries a part of the original instructions from Creator to each specific people.

We are coming to the end of the fourth world. It has served its purpose. We have learned all we will learn from this part of the journey. Humankind is making choices now that will effect the future of the human species, as well as their planet.

Until now there was always more time; time to process, time to figure out our next time, time to go to the mountain for a few years, time to figure it out over the next few hundred lifetimes. Things are a little different this *time* as we are at the edge of time. Somehow along our journey we have come to a place where we always knew we would arrive, a place where time as we knew it is about to once again become a no thing. Welcome to the alchemical garden of creation. Welcome to *the Quickening*.

This is what can be said by the Hopi about the ancient stone tablets. Understand that there is always more to a story. This is a beginning!

The Story From the Ancient Stone Tablets

The ancient stone tablets of the *Red Race* are held by the Hopi. The Red Race was sent to the East (*based on locations of the continents then, not necessarily now. Also, they came from Lemuria.*) They were given guardianship over the Earth and knowledge of the plants; they are the Spirit Keepers of the Earth. This responsibility is distinctly expressed in every Indigenous culture throughout the Western Hemisphere. Over 80% of our contemporary medicines throughout the Western World come from Native American herbal formulas.

We have created synthetic chemical copies of the plant structures to supply the huge demands of modern health care and pharmaceutical companies. For example, you know some of these synthetic copies by such names as ephedrine, penicillin, procaine, and even aspirin. Nearly 80% of the food products consumed in the global diet have been derived from Native American food sources as well, even the Potato. The Native American people of both North and South America truly have become the Keepers of the Knowledge of the Earth.

The knowledge of the Stone People is also within the domain of the Earth Keepers. The crystal in our radios, watches, and laser communicators are technological imitations of early crystal healing technology the Indigenous People possessed. These methods of communication have been utilized by Native Americans for thousands of years.

The ancient stone tablets of the *Yellow Race* were kept in Tibet. They have been moved because of the political climate there which continues to exist at the time this publication was released. Their location at this time is not for public knowledge. The decision to reveal their location is up to the Dali Lama.

The Yellow Race was sent to the South and given the guardianship of the wind, the breath of life. Much of the ancient knowledge of the breath, which has become commonly known in today's world, can be attributed to the work of the Yellow Race. Many healings can occur within the human body simply by learning to breathe consciously and spherically, a technique that our brother of the sea, the Dolphin, does naturally. When the mind is stilled and allowed to open, we are able to access many energies and many dimensions that we are just beginning to investigate and comprehend.

The ancient stone tablets of the *Black Race* are kept near Mt. Kenya in Africa. The Black Race was sent to the West and given guardianship of the Waters. Thus, it is not surprising that blood plasma was discovered by a Black American. Emotions within our bodies travel and are communicated through water. The Moon effects the tides and the emotions of people. Water is the element in Native understanding which rules the nature of our emotions.

Blues and jazz are world renown gifts to humanity born of the American Black culture. These unique and original musical art forms can enhance our understanding of human emotions as we listen to tones that connect us to the inner depths of the human soul. Drums, which are traditional expressions of both the Black Race as well as the Red Race and express the emotions of their root cultures, have been the emotional tools for ceremony since we have had memory of being upon this plane of expression.

The ancient stone tablets of the *White Race* are in Switzerland. The White Race was sent to the North and given guardianship of the knowledge of fire. Thus, one will find that in the course of the evolutionary development of the White Race, we see the internal combustion engine, electricity, the light bulb, nuclear energy, the match, all centering around fire. Unfortunately, this is also the race that developed high-tech warfare, being the first to utilize gunpowder in the development of weapons and escalating to the Hydrogen bomb.

War has been utilized by Creator with the white race in a most unusual way. Once I read that at the turn of the century it was said of the English that "The Sun never set on the British Empire." They had successfully raped and plundered their way around the globe. Later in this century we can now boast about not one, but two global wars, and now many believe we are on the brink of a third. The *war to end all wars*. But then, wasn't that what the first one was about?

Get off the guilt cause, reliving the horrors of war, the holocaust, and all the rest of it; we know it already. The truth of it is this bunch of fellows really loves war. I mean, since the establishment of the Sumerian civilization, we have had nothing in the last five thousand years of Earth history but tales of war. Earth has been here with human life, as recent scientific discoveries can attest to, let us say modestly some 150,000 years. The ancient schools have held within their archives knowledgeable evidence of this planet being invaded by beings from outer space, other dimensions, Gods and Goddesses. Yet, only in the last five thousand years are records available which show this tremendous addiction to self annihilation through war.

Throughout man's long presence upon this Earth, if the Ancient texts are correct, we have been here not for 10,000 years, not for 150,000 years, but according to the Ancient Mystery Schools man has walked this Earth for seven and one half million years, give or take a few centuries. Why, then, is it that we have this legacy of violence and war only in the last five thousand years -- wars and violence which has destroyed almost all of what remained of our truly ancient civilizations upon the surface of the Earth? They Love War!

The Prophecy

The Hopi Tablets are over ten thousand years old. In the tablets we are told about the Five Worlds, the Five Cycles of Evolution upon the Earth, and of the Five Seasons of Mankind. As the seasons have their cycles, as spring becomes summer, so are there cycles everywhere that Creator has touched.

The First World is the spirit kingdom; the Second World is the mineral kingdom; the Third World is the vegetable kingdom; and the

Fourth World is the animal kingdom, where man has come to experience the reality of animal consciousness.

Right now we are at the end of the fifth cycle of the Fourth World. In the Fifth World, humankind will again walk upright and evolve into the full spiritual awakening, possessing full memory of their origins. They shall claim their rightful position amongst their brothers of the stars, uniting with their spiritual source in balance, God-Man realized. *(In Tibetan, the word "Hu" means God, Hu-man = God-Man.)*

There shall be much turmoil as the new Fifth World awakens from the slumber of centuries, and the New Cycles of the universe unfold and the birthing commences. In the Fifth World we see humankind becoming God-Man, God-Woman realized, hence, the term - - *the awakening*. We have the ability in this time of the Great *Shift*, to fully awaken to our complete potential, the potential of the fully-realized being utilizing the whole of our brain. At present we are using, at best, less than 8% of our potential brain power.

In the next world we will live as One with the Creator Gods who are the Beings of the First World. This will complete the cycle of experience, and humankind will be One with Spirit as it was in the beginning, but anew. Entering the Golden Age of wisdom, we are like children maturing into adulthood, the experience of evolution having been fully realized as we approach the moment of Universal Christ Consciousness.

We will also in this time awaken to the memory of our complete genetics. For we have been encoded with the genetics of many races from the stars. This is by no means accidental. We have been chosen, as our histories will soon reveal, to be what you could call the "Experiment of angels." We are to become the hope of creation to all the beings of the stars. The moment that we reawaken as a race, the truth that has been within us for eons will unfold. It matters not whether this is achieved as individuals or in mass. But it is our eventual destiny. We are the starseed!

"So it is that long ago, longer than most have memory, Tawa, in the time of the original instructions, told the Hopi they were to remain on their mesas, practice their ways as the keepers of this original knowledge and wait for the signs. They were not to mingle with those of the lower lands, for even though they would find rich and abundant life there in the wilderness, their ways could eventually become corrupted and they could lose the memory of the original instructions. The knowledge for the fulfillment of the great plan for humankind could be lost forever. And so, hidden high upon their mesas, the Hopi have waited patiently through the centuries, living their lives as best they can in the harsh desert, following their instructions, and keeping "the hole in the top of their heads open" so that Great Spirit and the Kachinas could continue to talk to them.

"In the Fifth World we see humankind becoming God-Man, God-Woman realized, hence, the term – the awakening. We have the ability in this time of the Great Shift, to fully awaken to our complete potential, the potential of the fully-realized being utilizing the whole of our brain."

The Hopi Grandfathers foretold of a time when a strange people would come to their land from far away. These would be their long lost brothers from the time of the emergence from the hollow earth into the fourth world. The old ones also left for them a message of warning. They were warned to be very careful to not totally open their hearts until they had looked for all the signs. For it might be that they would not remember their beginnings. If these people came from the North or the South, it would be a good sign. Additionally, they were shown a secret greeting by which they could be further certain that their brothers remembered. If they witnessed these and three other signs for a total of five signs, then the Hopi and the newcomers would share all their knowledge with each other. For Tawa had instructed them in the original teachings that all the children were to share what they had learned on their journey through this Earth plane.

If these people initially came from the West, this would be a good sign and the Hopi were to meet them with open hands and offer them the opportunity to give them sufficient signs that they remembered the original teachings. If, however, these strangers arrived from the East, this would mean that great discernment should be used. If they were willing to accept with evenness what the Hopi had to share and they came with hands open, it would be a good sign. Creator even gave the Hopi a sign of a certain greeting that their brothers would be recognized as showing that they had remembered their original teachings, and the Oneness of all Earth beings.

However, if those who came were of a war-like nature or if they came with closed hearts, it would mean that they did not remember the original teachings and they would not remember the ancient greeting. As a result of the newcomers' forgetfulness and their forgetting that the Earth was indeed their Mother, a time of much suffering would begin for the people of this land. The suffering would be great; perhaps even the whole of the Earth could die.

Thousands of years ago the Hopi Grandfathers told of a time coming when it would appear as if giant bugs were crawling upon the ground. These giant bugs would spit black poison into the air and they would travel across black ribbons. The Grandfathers tell us that some of these black bugs would learn to fly and would fill the skies with their black poison. Great spider webs would appear across the land, and these newcomers would communicate across these webs. The Grandfathers told us that one day these webs would even appear in the heavens. And the Hopi were told that when they saw these things, they would know the Time of Purification was near.

The Hopi Prophecies also tell us about times of great change and about much confusion that will occur during the merging of the Fourth and Fifth Worlds, and they tell us of the signs that will precede these times. They call this time *KYANASQUATSI,* meaning world out of balance. What they say could sound like a nightmare. Understand that even *KYANASQUATSI* is but a final warning to humankind to open their hearts, and in the moment events could go the other way.

It is said that in these times of *KYANASQUATSI,* throughout much of the Earth it will appear as if the Life Force itself were leaving it. In many places plants will no longer grow; whole species will disappear from regions where they were once abundant. In other places the waters will no longer be able to sustain life; many rivers will actually flow upstream, they will change direction. Still in other places the waters will disappear and they will become desert land.

Entire species of animals and plants will begin to disappear from this world. The disappearance of these life forms will further throw nature into chaos, as the balance of things will alter drastically. If humankind does not change and adapt to the wakeup call and begin to see their true relationship to the Earth and Her creatures, if they do not recognize their role as guardian, then the troubles will worsen.

Here we are told further, that the Creator will send the Eagle spirit who will grab the Earth and shake it in an attempt to wake up the people upon it. We are told that if humankind shows, through proper thought and action, any sign that we have remembered the ways of Creator's plan the future can be altered. If not, there will be another shaking, and yet another, and each shaking will increase in intensity. The destruction that will follow each shaking will reflect the lack of harmony in humankind and the harm we have inflicted upon the Earth's energies. Creator will warn us two times. If a third warning is required, we are on our own.

After each shaking humankind will be able, if we choose, to enter into the new cycle, for the Ages of Man are like the seasons. Each age has an ending and then the beginning of a new experience of existence. At the beginning of each new cycle Creator manifests His plan, revealed through great teachers who are sent to guide the people forward into the New World.

We are told that as the dimensions start to merge teachers will come, and they are referred to as the *Pahana.* They would be seen wearing red, red hats, red cloaks, or perhaps robes. They will come as nomads, wanderers, seemingly lost to the world around them that may exist in their time. They will be as turtles, carrying their possessions upon their backs, totally self-contained, choosing to be of spirit rather than of the world.

Not too much is understood as to why specifically the color red. Perhaps things must still unfold. The Hopi put more emphasis upon the nature of the body of knowledge these beings will carry and the work they will do with humanity. Some of the stories of the *Pahana* have been blended over time. Author Frank Waters has a version in his work. There are also stories amongst the Hopi that tie into the other Pueblo peoples of the Southwest.

Another story exists of the Pale Prophet. This being seems to have visited and brought much wisdom and spiritual understandings to many people including the Mayan People. Perhaps the stories of this Messiah blended over thousands of years with the story of the *Pahana*.

What the Hopi do agree about the *Pahana* is that they will give the Hopi the sign that shows they have the memory of the original instructions. They will acknowledge the Earth and their connection to the sacred Mother and all that has expression upon her. They will begin to appear during the time of Confusion, the *KYANOSQUATSI*.

The *Pahana* will bring to the people a *way* that is like no previous way of seeing the world or life as we know it presently. It will be knowledge directly from the Creator. Along with this new understanding, they will bring the unification of all peoples into a Oneness. Their way will be the way of the Earth, of all ways that have expression upon her. They will be representative of all races in equality.

Their coming will be a sign that the Creator Gods are returning. They, the *Pahana*, will be in actuality, representatives of the Gods. They will have come to assist us through the time of transition, as we move from third dimension to fifth dimensional reality. These new ways will bring about a time of great spiritual growth. Humankind will awaken from their slumber and realize their true purpose here; and will, once again, become One with the SACRED. But we must remember that the *Pahana* will only come to those who hold a thread of the original teachings, those who remember their connectedness to life both here and beyond the stars.

The Pursuit of the Peaceful Ones

The Hopi do not claim to be a perfect people, or to hold themselves up above others who also call this planet their home. They are by natural occurrences part of the original people who first came to this surface world after the last destruction. They were the original fire keepers, keepers of the faith in the temples of Atlantis. They are, to be sure, a very ancient people.

The Hopi of today show signs of having endured great struggle to keep their simple ways and their love for the Creator of all things alive and intact. They have done as best they can, holding always to the original teachings which were handed down to them from one generation to the next. They are the oldest people living in community, a society now for at least twelve thousand years, perhaps longer.

The Hopi have had many civil uprisings throughout their history before the coming of the White Man, and very gradually over thousands of years their society crumbled. Today, only a few of the Hopi Sinom (The Hopi Spiritual Elders) remember the original teachings of the Hopi people and still carry the bloodlines of the original people.

The waters that were once abundant in the Hopi homeland in many instances have ceased to flow, and the land has become dry and harsh. Victim to an ever encroaching industrialized world, they have been waiting patiently for the reappearance of the ones from Beyond the Sun, for interaction between those from the Star Nations. The once great civilizations whose cities now lie in ruins had all but stopped by the time the White Man came, yet the Hopi persisted in keeping their centuries old traditions and beliefs alive. The word Hopi itself, means "the Peaceful Ones."

The Peaceful Ones have held up against endless attacks by the Navajo, the Apaches, the Spanish, the Western Europeans, and finally the Great American Society. They have been waiting for the Ones who will bring them the ways of the New World, the New World to come. They have been waiting for the messengers, waiting centuries for the Pahana to reveal their true presence.

Life for the Hopi was already harsh by the time the Spanish arrived in the new land. They had seen many great peoples disappear from the deserts of the Southwest. Pueblo Benito, Canyon de Chelly, Ocatai, even Mesa Verde were just ghost towns when the Hopi looked down from their mesa tops and saw the Conquistadors coming in their suits of armor; they must have appeared to Hopi to be very much like Turtles. It appeared to the Hopi, at that time, that the Conquistadors came from the South, as they came into Hopi Land from Mexico. Also, they bore the mark of the pale prophet upon their cloaks and banners. The mark of the prophet was the four directions symbol. One could easily mistake the cross of the church in Rome as the four directions symbol.

The Hopi understandably thought these could be the ones they had been told of in their prophecies, so they sent emissaries out to greet the visitors. The Spanish wore red robes, officers wore red capes, with banners snapping in the wind and armor glistening in the desert sun. But when the Hopi put their hands out as a gesture to receive the sign, the Spanish dropped trinkets into their palms. The Hopi Elders knew then that these people were not the ones long prophesied to come and that even harder times would come to the people and the land.

Later it would be the pioneers who would come across the prairies in their covered wagons, looking much like Turtles crawling across the land. Perhaps these were the ones the of prophesies, so the Elders sent emissaries out to greet them as they had the Conquistadors.

Instead of handshakes, the Hopi were met with gunfire. All that these new people wanted was gold and land, anybody's land. These were not the expected ones either, and the Hopi retreated once again to their mesas, knowing the hard times would continue.

THE QUEST TO JOIN THE LEAGUE OF NATIONS- THE FIRST TWO SHAKINGS

The Hopi are told in their prophesies that there would come a time, after great struggle, when people would build a great house for all nations of this world. They heard that President Wilson was building a great house on the West Coast of this land. They were told that this house would make it possible for all races to join together and work to improve the quality of life for all the people of the Earth. They called it the *League of Nations*. The Hopi knew that if all races representing all the people of the Earth were not represented in this house there could be no peace and instead, the hard times they were already experiencing would just get worse.

The story of Woodrow Wilson's League of Nations spread throughout the Indian nations. The Hopi Elders felt that this very well could be an opportunity to get their message out to the world. The Hopi met with the other Indian Nations in Arizona and they gathered in a great counsel, the like of which had not been seen in the West since the Ghost Dance.

> *"If the Hopi were not heard and all the races of the Earth were not represented equally, the Hopi knew that nothing could prevent the first shaking. The Hopi interpreted this shaking to be World War I ... The second shaking was to be preceded by the Sun rising in the West instead of the East. Hopi Elders interpreted this to be Japan, the Land of the Rising Sun, as we entered World War II ..."*

People gathered from several Indian Nations and elected the Hopi to lead a group of elders to Washington DC and send word to President Wilson that they wanted an opportunity to speak at his League of Nations in San Francisco. They wished to be represented and to tell the nations of the world of the prophesies they had been given, for all the signs indicated that the Shaking of the Earth and the end time prophecies were very near. The United States blocked the attempts of the Hopi and Other Nations to be heard as sovereign nations, and they were sent away.

The American government felt, at that time, that it could not afford to allow the Indian Nations to be represented to the other Nations of the world, although the Indian Nations were referred to in all treaties that they signed with the United States Government as being a "sovereign people," and "Sovereign Nations unto themselves..." The American government feared then, as it does now, that to allow the Native People to be considered a sovereign nation would open the government to suits regarding the violation of treaty terms, illegal land acquisitions and programs of genocide against the Indian Nations. When the Hopi's request was refused, the elders went home, knowing that Woodrow Wilson's plan for a League if Nations would fail. All the People would not truly be represented.

 If the Hopi were not heard and all the races of the Earth were not represented equally, the Hopi knew that nothing could prevent the first shaking. The Hopi interpreted this shaking to be World War I. There would be those who would survive this shaking, and as it subsided, humankind would again be given the opportunity to come together in harmony and completion. If this was not accomplished, then there would be a second shaking as the Eagle grabbed the Earth this time with both talons.

This second shaking was to be preceded by the Sun rising in the West instead of the East. Hopi Elders interpreted this to be Japan, the Land of the Rising Sun, as we entered World War II. The Hopi were also told they would see the sign of life, the four directions sign, reversed. This they saw as the swastika of the Third Reich.

It was seen over ten thousand years ago by the elders that during this second terrible shaking, bugs would appear in the sky and they would begin to pour forth the gourds of hot ashes that would burn the Earth itself and render it lifeless. As the gourds fell upon the Earth, the people would burn as the prairie grasses burn. Whole tribes of people would be destroyed. The gourds of ashes were first let loose upon the Earth with the dropping of the atomic bombs on Nagasaki and Hiroshima, bringing a quick ending to World War II and ushering in the arms race. Fear quickly spread throughout the world's indigenous people as they watched the war nations of the world play games of nuclear domination.

The Hopi were given yet another symbol to assist them in recognizing the coming of the final days. This symbol was the five-pointed star which represented man being placed within the great circle. The circle always represented the Creator. This symbol of the five-pointed star within the great circle of Creator would represent that those who ruled this land at that time, would put themselves above Creator. This is the symbol of the US Air Force and is seen on military vehicles today. It is yet another sign that we are in the dream of insanity, where humankind has forgotten to think with their hearts, and thinks only with their minds. This creates *KYANOSQUATSI*, the world out of balance.

The Pilgrimage to the United Nations

It was prophesied that if the great house on the West failed, there would be another attempt to construct a house that represented the world's peoples. This is the cycle of things, and the old ones understood the cycles of human beings. They saw this second house as a house of mica, a great house of glass, tall as a mountain built on the East coast of this land, and all the nations of the world would gather and try once again to find a way to achieve world unity and peace. This prophecy was realized with the formation of the United Nations. The building in New York State is skinned in glass. This was the house of mica the Hopi had been shown in their visions over ten thousand years ago.

The Hopi elders were told that they must go to the house of mica and attempt to get the people of this world to hear the ancient warnings about these times. The Hopi tried, but continually were not allowed to speak to the nations of the world gathered in the new house of mica. This upset them, for in their opinion had they been allowed to speak at the first house of all nations way back when Mr. Wilson was president, perhaps the tragedy of Nagasaki and Hiroshima could have been averted. Perhaps the Earth would not be sick today.

In the 1970's, representatives from many tribes gathered together to carry a Sacred Pipe across this land from the West Coast to the United Nations on the East Coast in an attempt to turn the destructive energies around. The original prophesies had talked about how it would be if the return of the Races to this land had occurred from the West to the East, instead of from the East to the West. It was hoped by the elders that perhaps by carrying the Sacred Pipe across the land, it would help turn the negative energies around that were destroying this land and turning the people against each other. So it was that Wallace Black Elk and other Elders of the Indian Nations lead a band of people, representing people of all races and calling themselves the rainbow people, marched from San Francisco to New York. At least this brought some world attention to the Elders and their mission. There were a lot of concerned hands, but no audience before the UN.

At one point during the march when they were in the Colorado Rockies, a sudden storm blew in. It grew very, very cold and the snow was thick, it was so cold it was feared that the march would have to be called off. It would be impossible to go on.

When some of the marchers began to grow discouraged and it looked as if they would actually disband, an old man came forward and said, "I will carry this pipe (*Chanupa*) now to the other side of this storm." He was forceful as he addressed the group declaring, "The pipe is Sacred and will protect me. We must have faith for the people," and he stared at them with eyes that burned with the Spirit Light of their ancestors. So they gave him the Sacred Pipe and continued the march.

He carried it all the way through that storm. It was a long procession with a van following close behind him. Several times they offered to take him inside to get warm, but he refused. The next morning as the skies began to clear, he finally handed the pipe over to the next carrier. He had marched all night through the storm. They brought him inside to get warm. As they touched his hair, it broke off in large pieces. It was frozen solid. It has to be very cold for that to happen. Astonished, they looked at the old man, but he just smiled and drank his coffee.

When they arrived in New York, the Hopi and other representatives of the Spiritual Elders from many Indian Nations marched up to the doors of the United Nations. Once again, officials denied their request to speak before the General Assembly of Nations.

It is told in the prophesies that if *all* the people of this Earth are not truly represented in the circle of nations, all attempts will end in failure, for without representation of all people, the words will not come from the spirit that dwells within, and their actions will become corrupted and turn to madness (as is the way with illusion.) There will be much sorrow and confusion. Corruption will spread like a disease, pushing us closer to the End Times, and it is all unnecessary! It is always a matter of choice. The road can be altered at any time.

Again, the Hopi had been told that they should endeavor to continue bringing their message to the world until the last moment possible. They were told to continue bringing it to the house of mica. They were to attempt this four times. If, after four times they still were not heard, they were to return home and prepare for the final shaking. At this point, their job was over, for, if the prophesies had evolved in this manner to this point, the world of humankind, as they knew it, would soon come to a close.

The Third Shaking

If things unfolded in this scenario, humankind would clearly have closed their hearts and would begin to lose the dream of Creator's plan. Consciousness would begin to implode as we lost our hold of the dream. What did we think this world was, any way? Life is just a dream, after all. The external world is merely the reflection of our human dream, and it is dying because we cannot live without the heart.

If we do not awaken and change our ways, there will be a third shaking. This third shaking will be so terrible that most of the people will not choose to be here to experience the horrors of these times. As the final days draw close there will be many old ones, Grandfathers and Grandmothers, who will begin to leave this Earth plane in great numbers. Among those who remain, there will exist much disease and famine. The homeless and the dead eyes will be without measure. There cannot be enough medicine people to do the healing work that will cry out. Those who die of natural causes will be the lucky ones. Those who contract the plagues will find no cures, for many of these germs are synthetic and almost mechanical in nature. Millions will perish.

Great comets will start to appear in the heavens. One will bring much destruction to the Earth. The whole Earth will shake when it hits, and there will be no way of altering the events that follow. Some of these comets will be Ships belonging to those who come from beyond the stars. We must understand that there are many races that visit us from the stars. Some are not friendly toward us.

There is a comet called *Hale-Bopp* which the scientists have seen in our heavens. It is funny how things are never real when we see them; only when the scientists see them do they then become real, even after we have been telling them about it for lifetimes. As I have experienced life, worked with spirits and removed demons from people, I can tell you this; most of the time scientists see very little.

This is not a comet, it is a ship. There are people upon this ship who are of the reptilian race. They are not friendly toward us. This ship will continue on its journey towards Earth and should arrive here in the year 1997. There are also reptilians who live within our hollow Earth. They are friendly towards us, although they have good reason to fear us, for we are a hostile bunch.

There are other ships that are in our solar system. The ones that are upon some of these ships are waiting for us to ask for their help. They cannot interfere with our way of life here, unless enough of us to ask for them to do so. They will know that it is time to interact when the Blue Kachina returns. This Blue Kachina has already sent emissaries to our villages to let us know they are returning. At some ceremonies, the Blue Kachina has been seen by our children, for their spirits are still pure and the spirits easily connect with them. You must remember that we have hundreds of Kachinas. Not all of them are singular entities. If I call you a human, hopefully you are not the only one.

The problem with this present day Society is that they think they are the only life form that exists upon this planet. They think they are the only life form in the universe. They have an attitude of "there is only us." Even after they come and do ceremony with us and see with their own eyes, they go home and in a few weeks and they forget. You can remind them and they will nod their heads and tell you, "Oh yes, I remember." The truth is that they do not remember.

This is why the beings that come from the stars wonder about them. They are in many ways like ghosts, having no substance. You try to touch them inside and nothing happens. Sometimes you think that there is something wrong with you. They can be easily filled with anyone else's thoughts. They have no clue about how to call upon their personal power, because they have none. They are afraid of their inside feelings. They are afraid to feel for they do not know who or what they are inside where their spirit lives.

Those volcanoes we told you would erupt – well, take a good look, Kola, they are! It is happening everywhere. But one day, they will no longer occur one at a time; they will start to answer each other and rather quickly. Some people do not know the bear is near until it breaks down their door. Then is too late.

One day humankind will see blood-red skies, as ancient ones begin to wake up from their centuries of sleeping. They are already waking up, one at a time; the calling has begun. They will spit up the poisons from deep within the Mother's belly. The very elements are rising up to hear her cry. Even the animals will rise up and join in the purification. The universe itself will begin to alter as the Mother lets loose her cry to be heard in the heavens. The smoke will darken the skies for many seasons and nothing will grow.

There will be nothing man can do at this point. It will appear as if the very universe is falling upon us, and the priests who have walked away from their power will no longer know how to call the Spirit World to aid us; they will have forgotten how. The dream will end as many fall into a great darkness.

It will seem like the destruction will never end, but finally a day will come when a Great Star appears in the Heavens. The light from this Great Star will be brighter than our Sun. There will be small areas where life has survived the purification. Here, in these places, the song birds will gather again and the grasses that were not yet born will fight to push their way to the surface of the Earth on the day of this Star's appearance. Some will call it the Day of GOD!

The old ones tell us that on that day the flowers will bloom at midnight and the wind will sing, calling to the people who buried themselves beneath the Earth in fear of the forces of nature. They will be called to come forth into the light of the great star, for the Day of

Creator will have arrived. The Gods who know all of the Universe will have returned for those who remembered the original instructions. These will be led into the Fifth World, as has been promised long ago. Then our dream of this Fourth World will be completed.

The Hopi Sinom say that we have now entered the end times. We have turned our face away from peace and working as caretakers of this Earth. We still continue to play with the gourds of ashes, and now we would even try to control the weather itself. This is not the first time we have displayed this type of arrogance towards the Earth.

"The problem with this present day Society is that they think they are the only life form that exists upon this planet. They think they are the only life form in the universe. They have an attitude of "there is only us"... They are in many ways like ghosts, having no substance. You try to touch them inside and nothing happens. They can be easily filled with anyone else's thoughts. They have no clue about how to call upon their personal power, because they have none. They are afraid to feel for they do not know who or what they are, inside where their spirit lives."

The waters are foul and as it was prophesied by the elders eons ago, the water can no longer support life in many regions. Even the ocean, the very sea itself, the mother of all life, is now dying. These facts, added to the problems of the Hopi Elders fighting a losing battle to save their own sacred grounds in Hotevilla, brought a great sadness to the elders. So the Elders prayed. They sent their word out for people to gather and pray for the Earth and ourselves as a species, to have intervention that all might not be lost here. In 1994 on the Spring equinox, people who heard their plea gathered in many nations throughout the world. The heavens have answered us. The Blue Kachina and those who are our relatives are here. Now it is up to us.

And so it is said, that humankind was to be allowed one final warning. This warning was to come from the heavens. The star nations themselves would carry this warning to those of us who dwell upon the Earth. This will be the warning of the *Blue Kachina*. If we have not yet learned to live together in harmony, as brothers and sisters of the One Father and One Mother of us all, *the Tales of the End Times* will become your legacy.

In April of 1994, the Hopi Elders waited for word from the United Nations, as the United Nations had declared 1993 as the year of Indigenous People. **They are still waiting.** They were ignored, again, for the fourth time. It might also be mentioned here that this is the same year that the UN adopted their policy of *bio-diversity,* where they came up with a plan designed for eliminating three-fourths of the world population by the year 2021.

But there are no contracts with our governments and the extra-terrestrials, right?

The Hopi have returned home, and they wait now for the third shaking.

These are the Final Days! This is the Last Cry.

Authors Note:

The story of the Blue Kachina is a very old story. I have been aware of the story of the Blue Kachina since I was very young. I was told this story by grandfathers who are now between 80 and 108 years of age. Frank Waters wrote about Saquasohuh, the Blue Star Kachina when he wrote *The Book of the Hopi.* It was told to me that first the Blue Kachina would start to be seen at the dances, and would make his appearance known to the children in the plaza during the night dance. This event would tell us that the end times are very near. Then the Blue Star Kachina would physically appear in our heavens which would mean that we were in the end times.

In the Final days we will look up in our heavens and we will witness the return of the two brothers who helped create this world in the birthing time. Poganghoya is the guardian of our North Pole and his Brother Palongawhoya is the guardian of the South pole. In the final days the Blue Star Katchina will come to be with his nephews and they will return the Earth to its natural rotation which is counter clock wise. This fact is evidenced in many petroglyphs that speak of the zodiac, and within the Mayan and Egyptian pyramids. The rotation of the Earth has been manipulated by not so benevolent Star beings. The twins will be seen in our North Western skies. They will come and visit to see who still remembers the original teachings, flying in their Patuwvotas, or flying shields. They will bring many of their star families with them in the final days. The return of the Blue Star Kachina, who is also known as Nan ga sohu will be the alarm clock that tells us of the new day and new way of life, a new world that is coming. This is where the changes will begin. They will start as fires that burn within us, and we will burn up with desires and conflict if we do not remember the original teachings and return to the peaceful way of life.

Not far behind the twins will come the Purifier -- The Red Katchina, who will bring the Day of Purification. On this day the Earth, her creatures and all life as we know it will change forever. There will be messengers that will precede this coming of the Purifier. They will leave messages to those on Earth who remember the old ways. The messages will be found written in the living stone, through the sacred grains, and even the waters (crop circles have been found in ice.) For the Purifier will issue forth a great Red Light. All things will change in their manner of being. Every living thing will be offered the opportunity to change from the largest to the smallest thing. Those who return to the ways given to us in the original teachings and live a natural way of life will not be touched by the coming of the Purifier. They will survive and build the new world. Only in the ancient teachings will the ability to understand the messages be found.

It is important to understand that these messages will be found upon every living thing, even within our bodies, even within a drop of our blood. All life forms will receive the messages from the twins.. those that fly, the plants, even the rabbit. The appearance of the twins begins a period of seven years will be our final opportunity to change our ways. Everything we experience is all a mater of choice.

Many will appear to have lost their souls in these final days. So intense will the nature of the changes be that those who are weak in spiritual awareness will go insane, for we are nothing without spirit. They will disappear, for they are just hollow vessels for any thing to use. Life will be so bad in the cities that many will choose to leave this plane. Some in whole groups. Only those who return to the old ways will be able to find peace of mind. For in the Earth we shall find relief from the madness that will be all around us. It will be a very hard time for women with children for they will be shunned, and many of the children in these times will be unnatural. Some beings from the Stars, some from past worlds, some will even be created by man in an unnatural manner and will be soulless. Many of people in this time will be empty in Spirit. They will have Sampacu -- No life force in their eyes.

As we get close to the time of arrival of the Purifier there will be those who walk as ghosts through the cities, through the canyons they will have constructed in their man made mountains. Those that walk through these places will be very heavy in their walk, it will appear almost painful as they take each step, for they will be disconnected from their spirit and the Earth. After the arrival of the twins, they will begin to vanish before your eyes like so much smoke. Others will have great deformities, both in the mind and upon their bodies. There will be those who would walk in the body that are not from this reality, for many of the gateways that once protected us will be opened. There will be much confusion; confusion between sexes, and between children and their elders. Life will get very perverted, and there will be little social order. In these times Many will ask for the mountains themselves to fall upon them just to end their misery. Still others will appear as if untouched by what is occurring. They will be the ones who remember the original teachings and have reconnected their hearts and spirit. Those who remember who their mother and father is. The Pahana who have left to live in the Mountains and forest.

When the Purifier comes we will see him first as a small red star which will come very close and sit in our heavens watching us. Watching us to see how well we have remembered the sacred teachings. This Purifier will show us many miraculous signs in our heavens. In this way we will know Creator is not a dream. Even those who do not feel their connection to spirit will see the face of creator across the sky. Things unseen will be felt very strongly. Many things will begin to occur that will not make sense, for reality will be shifting back in and out of the dream state. There will be many doorways to the lower world that will open at this time. Things long forgotten will come back to remind us of our past creations. All living things will want to be present for this day when time ends and we enter the forever cycle of the Fifth World.

We will receive many warnings allowing us to change our ways from below the Earth as well as above. Then one morning, in a moment, we will awaken to the Red Dawn. The sky will be the color of blood, many things will then begin to happen that right now we are nor sure of their exact nature. For much of reality will not be as it is now. There will be many strange beasts upon the Earth in those days, some from the past and some that we have never seen. The nature of mankind will appear strange in these times as we walk between worlds and we will house many spirits -- even within our bodies. After a time we will again walk with our brothers from the Stars, and rebuild this Earth. But not until the Purifier has left his mark upon the universe.

No thing living will go untouched, here or in the heavens. The way through this time, it is said, is to be found in our hearts and in reuniting with our spiritual self. By getting simple and returning to living with and upon the Earth and in harmony with her creatures. Remembering that we are the caretakers, the fire keepers of the Spirit. Our relatives from the Stars are coming home to see how well we have faired in our journey.

A Standing Plea From the Hopi Elders

We close this chapter with a plea from the Hopi Elders to all the peoples of the Earth. In 1994, some members of the Hopi tribe spoke for a few minutes at the United Nations. However, the Hopi Sinom, the traditional elders, were still prevented from speaking. At best, the appearance of the "Hopi representatives" was a token to placate world opinion.

This is a letter from them to you:

Robert Ghost Wolf,

Please get this message out if you can — the world must know! You are a friend to the Hopi people, help us!

We are now entering the last days. The Hopi Spiritual caretakers have spoken their urgent warnings and message to the United Nations and around the World, yet there has been no response. The sacred lands of the Hopi are being desecrated by water and power lines. The bulldozers are on the land. Soon the Hopi will be unable to conduct their ceremonies. Listen to their words, then Respond. The leaders say it is our turn to act.

Only the government of the United States recognizes the illegally elected tribal council. These are not our leaders; this is not our way. We must be left alone and allowed to follow our ways. We must protect these sacred lands, these sacred ways. If these instructions are not followed, the purification will begin.

Already the signs of the days of purification are beginning. For the sake of the Mother Earth, your children, and your children's children, action is needed now.

The Hopi's ancient knowledge and prophesies are warning us through many signs that we have entered a dangerous period in our lives. Humankind must return to peaceful ways and halt the destruction of Mother Earth, or we are going to destroy ourselves. All the stages of Hopi prophesy have come to pass, except for the last, the purification. The intensity of this purification will depend on how humanity collaborates with creation.

We must correct and change our ways, and take care of Mother Earth. If we do not, we are going to face terrible destruction by nature. Wars will come like powerful winds, bringing purification and destruction. The more we turn away from these instructions of the Great Spirit, the more signs we see in the form of earthquakes, tornadoes, floods, and droughts, along with wars and destruction.

If we do not correct these things, we are all going to suffer; there is no way we will be able to help each other after this. The world problems and the destruction of Mother Earth will be so terrible, there will be nothing left on this Earth.

We do not want to see this happen.

we hope that by bringing these warnings to the attention of the people of this land and around the world that we will understand the seriousness of this moment, that we will be able to help one another and to bring about a better way of life.

Signed by The Hopi Traditional Caretakers, including: Dan Evehema, Martin Gashweseoma, Manual Hoyungowa, Emery Holmes Sr., Assisted by our spokesperson, Thomas Banyacya.

"We still have a choice

… let your hearts be

heard.

This is the Last Cry!"

A Contemporary Haudenosaunee Perspective

Gathering of the Eagles/Unity of the Tribes
Lumi Island, Washington, USA, Summer 1995

*T*o many of the native people who live in the Pacific Northwest, Salmon is the staple of life. Much of their culture has been built around Salmon fishing for generations. One could say that to them the Salmon is what the Buffalo was to the Plains People. I once heard an old-timer tell a story of how at the turn of this century, the great Salmon runs in the Pacific coastal waterways were so plentiful that one could literally grab the Salmon up out of the rivers with their hands while the Salmon were on their way to the spawning grounds. The people could fill their needs for winter meat in less then an hour.

The Twentieth Century has brought with it many changes to our way of looking at life upon our planet. In less than 100 years, automobiles have replaced the horse as the mode of transportation for most people throughout our global societies. As late as WWII, 50% of the world still relied on the horse as it's main mode of transportation.

Grandpa grew up in a world where he could hope for a letter from New York to California in, perhaps, ten days - seven days by train and then another two or three days by pony express. Today we can send an e-mail to thousands of people around the globe in a few seconds.

I am like a bridge between generations, depicting a page of life that for most, has gone the way of the buffalo and a visionary of that which is to come. I have become sort of an enigma throughout a lot of the American West - never knowing which of my skills will be called upon. Will Creator ask of me this day to use my gifts as a ceremonial leader, mountain man, tracker, artist, author, musician, healer dreamer or explorer? Perhaps today as the Wizard

My soul dictates that I have a need to spend part of my time in the pristine desert mountain wilderness until the call comes to be with the magic of the Ocean, with the Dolphins and whales. My life, it seems, has become one big medicine journey. I find myself traveling from Mexico up through Canada, and even an occasional trip to Alaska. While I consider Arizona my home, I have also lived in the islands off Washington part time for nearly 7 years. I have many friends who live all along the Pacific, both on the Islands and on the high pine and Madrona covered cliffs that overlook them.

We all sail and fish the waterways from the Oregon coast to Alaska. I have a deep love and respect for the gentle people who call themselves natives there. In fulfilling my service as a ceremonial leader, I have participated in countless ceremonies with the People who live along the waterways, from the coast to the inland rivers of Canada. For the most part they are naturally spiritual and possess an intimate and sensitive relationship with the sea and Her creatures.

I have come to know the rhythms of life there as I have danced through the drama of the human experience with them. I have listened to their stories of how they once had many fishing boats and even with their fleets could not fill the demand for fish at the market. Now they find themselves struggling in their lives to create an alternative way of surviving as they face the reality that the once great fishing industry has disappeared from this plane. I have come to recognize the malaise in their eyes as they witness the passing of a way of life that is gone forever.

I know this from their stories about how over the last forty years they watched the great salmon runs being harvested along the Pacific coast by giant tankers that drop nets as long as thirty six miles. As we approach the millennium, the numbers of salmon in our rivers and lakes have dwindled to almost nothing. I have heard that amongst the river people in some cases, the salmon have not been seen heading for their spawning grounds for several years now.

In 1992, under the direction of then Spiritual Leader Joe Washington, the Lumi People began holding their Blessing of the Salmon ceremonies. I was asked to bring my Chanupa (Sacred Pipe) and lead the people in prayer for the return of the Salmon to the rivers.

Last Cry©

Even after the passing of the Native American Religious Freedom Act by Congress in 1978, this ceremony had not been allowed under the laws of the state of Washington. After many generations of not being able to practice their spiritual ways, the Lumi People themselves had almost completely forgotten the ceremony. Only a small handful of people who continued to hold the ceremony in secret remembered.

This has been the story with many of the traditional ways of the tribes forced to live under Government reservation policies. The practice of their ways, even the speaking of their own native language, was forbidden. The punishments for breaking these laws were severe. Often parents had their children taken away, and they themselves were thrown into prison camps. This may be hard for you to believe since you have been taught that you live in a civilized and free society, but I have seen it with my own eyes and know that it is the truth - even today.

On a rainy morning in 1992 on the shores of Lumi Island, over a thousand people gathered. There were Lakota, Nambi, Omaha, Haudenosaunee, Shooshwap, Ojibiwa, Apache, Cherokee, Hopi, Cheyenne, Nez Perce, Athabascan, Swinamish, Mayan, Americans, Canadians, Siberians, Chinese, and others who joined along with Joe Washington and the chiefs and spiritual elders of five nations. I gathered with the circle of spiritual elders and had the privilege to lead the people in prayer at the first Salmon ceremony to be held in over 80 years.

I returned to Lumi Island for the Salmon ceremony every year for three years. In the Summer of 1995, I was asked to *speak at the Unity of the Tribes gathering held in the Lumi Nation. The following is a transcript of my talk at that gathering.*

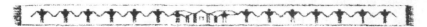

It is an honor to be asked to speak at such a gathering of so many courageous people. You are the ones who are bringing back the sacred ways of the people to this land. Your children's children will remember you and honor you in their story fires. They will speak of you gathered here as the ones who held the torches of their spirituality through some of the darkest of times.

This morning the Eagles have come while we did the pipe ceremony. See, they circle around us, pushing back the clouds. So I send our thanks to the Eagle nation for honoring this gathering.

The Earth will also honor you. And the Spirit of the Salmon 'the great Sea Bear' will also respond to your prayers. After 80 years you still remembered. The fire of Great Mystery still burns in your hearts. You send your songs as sacred prayers, as you sang through your tears. I tell you now your tears will be acknowledged, for the Mother has ears, and eyes. Today her heart beats a little stronger because you have gathered here in gratitude. It has been a long time since her children have come down to the sea together to be with her in this manner.

I see before me faces from all corners of the Globe, gathered for this Unity of the Tribes; the Earth Tribes. We have gathered here for we have remembered that we are all one people, that we all have the same mother and the same father. As we bridge our cultures, we make the way for future generations to overcome the separations of the past. I see my Grandmother's dream becoming reality before me. My Grandmother taught me that this is not a time for secrets, it is a time for *we the people.*

Today many of the Teachers of Truth and Light Workers throughout the world are working with the philosophies of the Indigenous People of Turtle Island. Even the Dali Lama of the Tibetan people has spent long hours with our Native American Elders, speaking of these very days that are upon us, sharing knowledge and prophesy and ceremony.

There is a Web of Light spreading across the Earth. It is spiraling out of the darkness that has kept Humankind within their self-imposed prison of limited thought. As a Human Race we have reached a precipice, where many of the old paradigms that have kept us separated from one another and limited our thoughts and spirits for a millennium are falling away before our eyes.

Indigenous People, unfortunately, have had to keep their understandings and ceremonies secret for the last 200 years. It must be remembered that until as recently as 1978, the punishment in the United States for a Native American singing a sacred song or praying with their Sacred Pipe could mean imprisonment or death. We are not really that far removed from the Dark Ages and a superstitious Medieval European consciousness. As a society we are still enslaved by giving our power and spiritual life away to the external world. As a society we have become a fear-based people.

"There is a Web of Light spreading across the Earth. It is spiraling out of the darkness that has kept Humankind within their self-imposed prison of limited thought. As a Human Race we have reached a precipice, where many of the old paradigms that have kept us separated from one another and limited our thoughts and spirits for a millennium are falling away before our eyes."

The Mayans tell us that during the cycle of life we are now entering, all structures that do not allow for the infusion of the Great Light, or Spirit, must and will, fall. This has nothing to do with an "Indian Curse," but rather the natural cycle of civilizations, a science we have long forgotten; seasons of humankind. The structures the Mayans refer to in their prophesy include science, religion, social, and spiritual orders of our world societies. The Mayans continue by saying that, "Even the stones beneath the Earth will not go untouched by this light when it appears in our Heavens."

There are those who are so afraid of the potential impact upon today's limited religious belief systems, that in many regions of the world the powers that be still practice organized programs of planned genocide against indigenous people.

To the discerning mind, Western spiritual beliefs have been built upon an infrastructure of one reform after another. Each new reform has changed the original form and content of Sacred Teachings and adapted them from their original form to be more acceptable to the times and the respective contemporary viewpoint of the reigning society. As a result, the original teachings have become so diluted that their substance and meaning no longer applies to actual human conditions. For the most part they have lost their truths on many levels regarding the Original Laws given by Creator.

For about 200 years, as long as there has been a United States, the name of the Peacemaker has not been spoken publicly amongst the *Haudenosaunee* People, "the people of the Long House;" those who the Hudson Bay traders chose to rename the *Iroquois*. This not speaking the name of the Peace Maker is partially out of respect of their elders' wishes, and partly because of the persecution and attacks by religious moralists. It is hard to accept that in this "age of enlightenment" there still exists people who are afraid of the spiritual knowledge that the Indigenous People hold.

The Resurrection of The Great Peace

To the Haudenosaunee, the Great Peace was a way of life that had held them together as a people for hundreds of years. In their tongue as taught to them by their great prophet Deganaweda, it was known as the *Kia neri Kowa*. Under the principals of this *Kia neri Kowa*, no member of the Six Nations people was to ever war against any other member of the Confederacy. They were all considered children of one mother and one father. Therefore, everyone was, in essence, family. This was upheld by an oath that was both spiritual and political. If this oath, sworn to by all the people in the Confederacy, was ever broken, the Tree of Life would wither and die. They as a people might cease to be as a result of breaking this code.

During the 300 years that preceded the American Revolution, each generation of Native People that interacted with the European settlers became more and more corrupt, compromising and giving a little piece of their spiritual knowing away in exchange for power and technological comfort.

There was much conflict within the tribes during these years. Power struggles were influenced and encouraged by the newcomers and fueled by the never-ending supply of new technology, weapons, and tools the Europeans could offer. This fever of greed and acquisition of material things started to separate the Indigenous People from their own governing laws.

Perhaps they too easily accepted the appearance of this new, "easier life." The Europeans' religion of materialism made a powerful impression on the Natives here. The Europeans also gave them a new understanding and appreciation of the concepts of power and war.

The European influence brought with it to this land the *warrior syndrome*. This is what the Elders called the Serpent Energy, back into the consciousness of the Native People of this land. The Serpent Energy is patriarchal, and unnatural to any people of Earth. It is not the natural order of things for us to be war-like. We are, by nature, a communal people.

Over time the acceptance of this Serpent Energy would prove, sadly, to be their demise. The result of interacting with these strange newcomers who had forgotten the sacredness of all things, would inevitably and quite rapidly bring about the end of their whole way of life, as well as the physical world they knew.

The Elders knew the actions of warring upon their own brothers would break the Great Peace, and that it would ultimately bring about the fall of the Haudenosaunee Nation. They knew that the results of breaking this bond between the tribes would bring about the ending of their way of life. This had been part of Deganaweda's prophesy. Therefore, to speak the name of the Peacemaker might bring danger to what was left of the understanding, or might possibly invoke the wrath of the Peacemaker himself.

They knew they must not allow the true nature of their spiritual understandings and practices to fall into the hands of the invaders. That would not only be sacrilegious, but it might easily mark the end of the People themselves. They must protect their knowledge for future generations. The children of future generations must know the roots of the Great Peace. These teachings had to survive. So certain individuals were made responsible for sections of the Great Peace, and every year they recited them verbatim, in secret, so that the teaching remained intact and unchanged in the living word, waiting for the future.

Now signs are coming from every form of life, as well as from every people. Humankind is awakening from within, many times without the ability to explain the source of such knowledge they know to be truth. It is this fulfillment of all the prophesies of Native Peoples world wide, threaded together into a mystical tapestry, that tell the Elders that this long-kept, forced silence may now be broken. Now, they say, it is time to speak. It is time to reveal the true nature of the ONE human spirit that connects us all as a people, an Earth People; Children of the Sun.

The principles around which these United States of America were formed and, indeed, the very Constitution of the United States itself, was based, almost entirely, on the abridged principles of the Iroquois Confederacy and the precepts by which the Six Nations were bound. In other words, the Constitution is, in essence, a Native American document with adulterated modifications. The Native People bestowed equality to both men and women; in fact, the people demanded it. In the Native Way, there was no slavery. Captives were assimilated, not enslaved. The spirituality of the people dominated their choice of action.

To this day, the original teachings of the Great Peace are recited once a year in ceremony on the Six Nations Reserves. This living part of their oral tradition has survived. It takes four days from sunrise to the rising of the Moon to complete the recitation. A different person tells the part of the teachings which they have been responsible for memorizing. In this manner, the Great Peace has remained alive and unscathed, and has come down from one generation to the next. It has been kept in its original form and is recited in the Algonquin tongue.

"...the Constitution is, in essence, a Native American document with adulterated modifications. The Native People bestowed equality to both men and women; in fact, the people demanded it. In the Native Way, there was no slavery. Captives were assimilated, not enslaved. The spirituality of the people dominated their choice of action."

When the Six Nations People saw the formation of the New Colonial Government in this land and the symbol the colonists elected to use, the Eagle, they understood well its meaning. Specifically, it was the Eagle with thirteen arrows in one claw and an olive branch in the other. The invaders said the arrows represented the thirteen original States, but the Elders had seen this sign before. It was a sign to them that there would be enslavement of the Indian People. The olive branch, the invaders said, meant peace. But the elders knew better. They interpreted this as the enslavement of the Black People, for the olive branch comes from a tree that grows across the waters, from where the

Black people come. These people had taken it upon themselves to use the Great Eagle as the symbol of their New Empire!

When the moon landing occurred, the newspaper headlines read, "The Eagle Has Landed." The Elders knew what this meant also. This, too, had been prophesied. Deganaweda told them about this while he was alive. "They will think themselves the rulers of all the land and its people, even the Heavens will not be out of their reach. They will even fly to the Moon and try to claim it as well. When these things are seen, it will be a sign that the end times are near."

The United States Government has since minted a special coin to commemorate this momentous event. When the coin was minted, it showed the Eagle holding the olive branch in both its claws. The arrows had been removed. The elders knew that this meant the Indian People were free from their forced silence about their spiritual understandings. They knew this meant the *de-structuring* of the Oppressors power structures was beginning to occur. The Black Brothers would soon have their voices heard as well. But the prophecy also said there would later be a long and arduous struggle for the Indigenous Races of the Earth. The recognition of all peoples must occur before there is to be true freedom and the Great Peace returns. Indeed, the Elders knew there would be a great struggle. Humankind would either choose to live together in love and as one family, or they would choose to continue on the road of destruction. The choice would be up to them.

"The recognition of all peoples must occur before there is to be true freedom and the Great Peace returns... The choice would be up to them."

During the 1960's and 70's, many people came to the Native Tribes and sought the ancient understandings of Indigenous Peoples. The word started to get out, and the understandings were beginning to be heard by the other nations of the world. The first Native American Religious Freedom Act was passed by Congress in 1978. For the first time since their land was taken, the Native People were allowed to practice their ceremonies without fear of imprisonment or death, or of having their children taken from them to be raised in the missionary schools. The Elders knew that the signs given in their prophecies were true. Nothing could now stand in their way, except themselves.

Now it is time for the Native People to gather together and prepare for the things that their prophecies foretold. Now is the time to awaken and be heard. All the signs are here telling us that these are the Final Days. Soon the Great Star of which the Peacemaker spoke will come, and the Peacemaker will return as promised. However, there will be much struggle before the Day of Awakening.

The Great Prophet of the Haudenosaunee People is one of the Indigenous Masters who stands with those of the Great White Brotherhood. Their great love for this Earth and their support of the continuation and the merging of *Hu-man* consciousness into the Fifth World has helped to guide us from our beginnings.

"The Elders knew that the signs given in their prophecies were true. Nothing could now stand in their way, except themselves."

The Rainbow of Creation

These are the Masters of Light who work with the Seven Rays of Creation that are seen within the Rainbow. There are now nine colors in the rainbow. Soon there will be twelve colors in the rainbow as prophesied by the Peacemaker. This Brotherhood of the Rays continues to be the mentor of *Hu-man* individuality and the resurrection of the *Hu-man* Spirit. There have been many appearances of the Messiah, the Pale Prophet. He has been called by many names; Amaru, Quatzaquatal, Buffalo Calf Woman, Wa cu ma tete, Tacoma, and Deganaweda are among them. The people of the Far East also have their Messiah stories. Much truth that has remained suppressed for many generations will reveal both our true Divine Nature, and true relationship to the Christ.

Each one of us has descended into this plane through one of these Rays of Light. The influence of the original Ray of our *descent* influences our entire walk upon this third-dimensional Earth plane. Each Ray influences our *Hu-man* consciousness and the spinning of the dream called life, the dream of temporal existence.

The Elders say a great *bow* will be seen in the Heavens as the final sign before we enter the Day of Purification. This *bow* will be seen as twelve colors of the rainbow, and from it shall issue the songs of our ancestors. It will be all voices, yet be as One. It will fall upon the ears of man, and they will know it is the Music of Creation. They will know that the Purification has come. They will be reborn into the New World according to Creator's plan, if their hearts are willing. The song will be the original Song of Creation by which we co-created this magnificent dream we call planet Earth, Ghia, Baba Geri, the Sacred Mother.

In the 1970's I was drawn to search out the roots of understanding of the Native part of my Blood, for I am Metis, meaning one born of mixed blood. During that searching, the Elders shared with me the prophecy of the Seven Fires. One was a Tuscaroran Elder named Mad Bear Johnson. He shared with me his version of the prophesy of Deganaweda, The Great Peacemaker, and his Great Peace, *Kia-neri Kowa*, which I have now shared with you.

There are many levels of these prophesies. As *Hu-man* consciousness rises towards its destiny, merging with the higher octaves, they will reveal themselves to us. Each of us has a great part in the play. No one is discounted, even if their part has not yet been revealed to them. The prophesies of the Peacemaker are the spiritual domain of the Haudenosaunee People. The following are the portions that the Sachems have allowed to be shared at this time. I honor my relatives and the sacred ways they have kept this alive for us so that we may awaken to the truth in these most magnificent of times.

"The information presented here has nothing to do with a linear order of the Light Spectrum. They are tools for the awakening of the spirit, by allowing the physical to 'lighten up.'"

THE TWELVE RAYS OF THE GREAT BOW

Excerpt from "The Return of the Nagual with Kryahgenetics • The Alchemy of Self-Transformation"
by Robert Ghost Wolf and Laura Lee Mistycah

The following is an explanation of the Seven Rays. There are many parts to the prophecies. The prophecies have been broken into many parts. They seem to have survived in this manner so that only in gathering all the people and sharing all their parts will the picture be complete on the Day of Purification. This understanding is part of the Rainbow Teaching. It is information known, in parts, by the various Indigenous Peoples of this Land, from the Cherokee and their use of Crystals, to the Denè and their sand paintings.

Indigenous people use much chanting and the sound of instruments in their ceremony. The tones they create during ceremony align them with these Rays, and can bring about an opening to knowledge. They are tools for the awakening of the spirit, by allowing the physical to "lighten up."

These Rays, in the Divine Order of the Creator, form the Rainbow, the Light Spectrum through which all creation has occurred and which is called, in the higher octaves, the assembly of the Amethystine Order. They are not material in nature. The information presented here has nothing to do with a linear order of the Light Spectrum. Rather, it explains the influences of the Seven Rays upon consciousness on the Earth plane.

As mentioned earlier, in the time that is coming, these Seven Rays will develop into twelve. There are already nine including the colors aquamarine and magenta, which have not previously appeared in our rainbow. These new colors usher into this plane new octaves of vibration which, in part, are responsible for *the Quickening* of our evolutionary process.

The **First Ray** is Red, the ray in which the vibratory essence of this Earth is held. It is the Ray of Leadership. It is the Ray that gives all things the intelligence of the Father. It is the Ray of Authority of the highest order.........the Red Earth, the Good Red Road.

The **Second Ray** is Sky Blue and is the Ray of Education and Understanding. This is the Ray of Knowledge. Here the knowledge of the Father and the wisdom of the Earth forces come into union. The Sky above reflected in the Ocean below, where they meet is often unseen, only realized.

The **Third Ray** is Green in color. It is known as the Healing Ray. It is the Third Ray that holds the vibration of memory of all events. It is also called the Ray of Philosophy, and is the Ray of higher thought patterns which connect us to the Great Spirit through the Ocean and the Standing People (trees, plants and flowers). It is the color given off by those in harmony with the Emerald Mother and her Divine Nurturing.

The **Fourth Ray** is Yellow, sometimes called the Crystal Ray, and is often expressed in man through the arts. It holds within it the ability to connect to the source of Earth Mother's life-giving elements and to the renewal of Spirit. The Sun radiates the Yellow Ray and all life is stimulated to growth. This light is reflected in all of Creator's creatures. This is the color often seen in those who possess the ability to be great teachers; it is the color of mind, of intelligence.

The **Fifth Ray** is Cobalt Blue. This is the Ray of Scientific Understanding, enhancing our awareness and seeing the order and the inter-relationship of all things, the cycles of the universe, how energies work and understanding how thought creates all reality. This is the color of the night sky, where dreams come from and where Spirit becomes the physical. It is the quantum physics of reality, sometimes called alchemy. This is the color that is given off by those who are of unbending faith.

The Sixth Ray is Rose. This is the Ray of Devotion, and Unconditional Love. This is the unique essence that allows us the state of Oneness and the inter-connection to Creator. The Rose Ray sees the perfection in all as it is, all as part of the Great Plan. Knowing the heart, it is often associated with renewal, as it is abundant in spring skies and young flora. It is representative of youth and new beginnings.

The Seventh Ray is Violet. This is the Ray of Ceremony and Transition of the Physical and the Spiritual. This Ray is the passage way for all transition and interaction between that which is known as Spirit and that which manifests as the physical. All that is touched by the Violet Ray is transformed into its highest potential. This is where matter becomes Spirit and takes on Divine consciousness. It is the Ray of Transformation.

In all, there are twelve Rays that affect our existence as Spirit comes alive in the flesh. The realization of the interaction of these twelve Rays only comes when one has truly evolved the union of Spirit and flesh into Christ Consciousness. Here, we go beyond language; we are merged with the Divine Source Itself.

The remaining Rays are created when the light from the Seven Rays merges and produces a harmonic. They are realized through emotion. Their number is not represented here because it is irrelevant.

Turquoise (Aquamarine) is The Ray of Protection. This Ray is born of the union of the Sky blue of the Father and the Emerald of the Mother. This is traditionally the color used by Native Americans to ward off the evil eye of the sorcerer and other negative energies.

Orange is the Ray of Personal Power and Psychic Medicine. It is reflected on the wings of the Flicker, the Medicine Warrior of the

Northwest tribes. It is also the Ray of Discerning Judgment. It is the Ray of Focused Intent.

Burgundy (Magenta) is the harmonic of the First and Second Ray. It is of the House of Divine Man, the Spirit attained, undying faith and knowing. It is often related to the power of the heart, or the true spirit of the soul of man.

Black/Indigo is the Great Void, the Black Light where all knowledge is. It is the color of the night. It is where Creator dreams his Divine Law of Creation. It is all potential not yet manifested. This is the realm of Spirit, where no thing is seen, yet all things are revealed in their true essence.

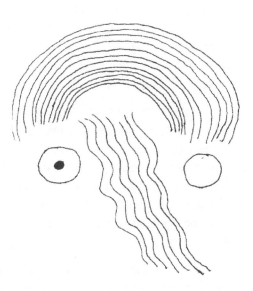

White is the collective of all the higher octaves of light, the light of the Illuminated Crystal. This is the light of Christ Consciousness. This is the light of the one who has attained, for this is the light that can be found within all things. It is the very thought of Creator.

"There will be a great bow in the sky that will have twelve rays, these will be the lords of all the universes. The lords of the seven rays shall surrender this universe to the new age."

Deganaweda and the Great Peace

*B*ack in the 70's I did a lot of soul searching. I was desperately trying to find answers from a world that for the most part thought I was a little mad. My searching took me around the world; I was looking for the Masters of Tibet. The Dali Lama was gone, he was living somewhere in New Jersey. But that was okay; I was looking for the Ascended Masters. I wound up spending a little over two years in those mountains. During that time I was aware that I had to learn more about my own heritage; there were huge parts of myself that were missing. So I returned home and started on a new Journey to understand my Native American roots.

I was very lucky, for along that journey, which I am still on, I have met some very remarkable men and women. My Grandmother was Onodaga and I went to upstate New York where there was a Tuscaroran Elder whose name was Mad Bear Anderson. Mad Bear often told stories of the great heritage of the Haudenosaunee people, the people of the long house. He told us of how they helped the early colonials of this land to become self-sufficient and survive off the land, and how they taught them the ways of self-government and the value of freedom.

In the beginning of the American revolution, before Washington even had a command, a picture of a Haudenosaunee (Iroquois) warrior was chosen for the first symbol by the colonials for the resistance against the English king in this new land, before it even had a name. The relationship between the early colonials and the people of the long house was so honored that Thomas Jefferson and Ben Franklin used most of their principles of self-government in their creation of the constitution from which the ideal of America was born. It was the strong, passionate desire for personal liberty of the Haudenosaunee that was adopted by these same colonials when they wrote the Declaration of Independence.

The history of this country and the American People has been intertwined with the spirit of the native people since its conception, and remains so today. One does not have to look far in their travels across this land to discover a work of art, a poster, a shawl, or blanket that is a reminder of the debt owed to the native people for the *give-away* they have extended to us in every way imaginable, from food, to medicine, to personal liberty. Their spirit is alive and indelible in our customs and the land we walk upon.

I would like to clarify, for the record, that Deganaweda and Hiawatha were two distinctly different people. There was a man by the name Hiawatha, beyond the character in Henry Wadsworth Longfellow's books, and he served along side Deganaweda until the prophet, as it is told, left for a higher calling. The story of Deganaweda, the Pale Prophet, tells of one who, it is said, came to many tribes throughout North and South America. Different peoples called him by different names, all of which translate into *"The Lord of the Wind."* The Native American people of this land tell many stories of this Pale Prophet and his teachings of peace. To the Haudenosaunee people, he is known as the Peacemaker. His story is that of a Christed being, one who has attained.

This is a story of the *Peacemaker* as Mad Bear told it to me. I now share it with you, that the heritage and memory may continue.

The Story of the Peacemaker

There once came from the North country, to what is now the upper western portion of New York state, a young man of Huron birth. He was called Deganaweda. Even as a child he talked of a peaceful way of existence and of harmony among the tribes. He spoke of the importance of the heart and called for an end to war-like ways and sacrifices of blood. But he found only deaf ears amongst his own Huron people, for they were war-like and not given to the ways of peace.

Our story begins when Deganaweda began a pilgrimage that would eventually bring his teachings to the five tribes of the Haudenosaunee, and later, six, when they were joined by the Seneca peoples. He helped them create a confederation of tribes, under a form of self-ruling government, in which there would be no royalty, no tyranny, no need for war. This unification of the tribes would later be referred to as the Great Iroquois Confederacy, which would include the Mohawk, Onodaga, Tuscarora, Cayuga and Oneida people, who would later be joined by the Seneca and the Mohican. The Mohicans would later be all but wiped out by the Hurons, leaving the Confederacy composed of six nations as it is described in our history books. In the confederacy, Deganaweda's words were welcomed with enthusiasm and discussed around the council fires of the elders.

During his pilgrimage, Deganaweda met Hiawatha. Hiawatha, it is said, lived as a hermit deep within the forest. He lived alone, holding a great bitterness in his heart. He grieved over the slaughter of his family by the blood-thirsty Onodaga chief. It is said that Hiawatha had even taken to cannibalism. Deganaweda was challenged by a Grandmother to share his teachings with Hiawatha. She told him that if he could convince the angry Hiawatha, the beast of the woods, to walk in peace and harmony, then perhaps there was something to this wisdom. If he succeeded in changing the heart of this beast, then all the tribes would surely listen to him.

Deganaweda met with Hiawatha and spoke with him from his heart, for he was filled with the Great Spirit and had no fear. This meeting with Deganaweda caused a transition within Hiawatha's being. They became inseparable, and from the wisdom taught to him by Deganaweda, Hiawatha became a renewed human being. A great friendship grew between the two, and Hiawatha became Deganaweda's chief disciple. It is said that Deganaweda suffered from a speech impediment; he had stuttered since childhood. For this reason, Hiawatha became known as the chief spokesperson for Deganaweda's "Great Peace -- the *Kia 'neri Kowa*."

Both Deganaweda and Hiawatha taught that the human race was one great family. They taught of love and unity, with reverence for the Creator of all humankind and the sacredness and honor of all life. The way of the "Great Peace" was established. It was a great plan for social order that centered its strength around the family fire. They taught of the inner balance of male and female within the self and in all relationships, the importance of the Mother/Father Principle.

This teaching was to spread through the many single family firesides. In the Great Peace, it was taught that from these single families would come the basis of authority, leadership, and the strength of the people. A natural order of social living was encouraged that allowed for the spiritual expression of all individuals. This concept was intrinsic to the integrity of their society and the establishment of the Long Houses that exist to this day.

> *"Both Deganaweda and Hiawatha taught that the human race was one great family. They taught of love and unity, with reverence for the Creator of all humankind and the sacredness and honor of all life. The way of the "Great Peace" was established. It was a great plan for social order that centered its strength around the family fire. They taught of the inner balance of male and female within the self and in all relationships, the importance of the Mother/Father Principle."*

In the way of the Great Peace, women are the keepers of the family lineage, and as the bearers of life, they teach the knowledge of harmony and balance within the family. The tribe is the extended family, and neighboring tribes should be considered relatives who are necessary for a healthy genetic evolution, an extended family, if you will. The balance within the whole of a society originates with the individual. The balance of male/female within the individual expands to the relationship between man and woman, and then into relationship with their offspring. This then expands into the extended family. All women are mothers to all the children, as are all men their fathers. The tribe was a living ecosystem for human consciousness, a living heart.

Women had equal status within the tribal council. They formed the Council of Grandmothers that looked out for the survival of the family structure above all things, for without the family structure, the people could not continue. No major decision that would affect the tribe as a whole was ever made by one individual of either gender, or any singular council -- all councils were accountable to the Council of Grandmothers. Thus, they had devised a matriarchal system whereby no structure of dictatorship could arise and seize power from the people themselves. There simply was no position that allowed for the rise of a tyrant within their society.

The teachings of the Great Peace likened all war to quarreling amongst children. Spiritual teachings were intermingled with the teaching of balance in the social order. In this culture there was no separation between living an abundant, full life and the expression of spiritual practice and beliefs because social laws were created out of an evolved spiritual understanding of human nature. In this manner, human beings learned to live in harmony with nature, thus they dwelt in a state of harmony within themselves. For nature was the kingdom with which humankind shared their dream. Mankind and Womankind were seen as spirit, alive in the flesh. There was one Creator, one Father. There was one Mother. From this union came forth all their children -- the human race.

So powerful were these teachings that the tribes of the Algonquin peoples formed the Iroquois Confederacy. It is from this Confederacy that much of the Constitution of the United States and the Declaration of Independence came. It is from the doctrine of life expressed by the Iroquois Confederacy by which the invading white Europeans forged the foundations of the American constitution, the basis of all Western Democracy.

The Great Prophet, the Peacemaker, would spend many seasons with the Haudenosaunee people, who would later become known as the Iroquois Confederacy, establishing the ways of the Great Peace. All things must change, and the Peacemaker would not be amongst the people forever. He heard the call to move on along his journey, but before he would go he would deliver his final message to the people. It was time for him to fulfill his agreement here that he had long ago made with Creator. The people were very saddened by the announcement of his departure from them.

He met with the People one last time upon the shores of the Bay of Quinte, near what is now Lake Ontario. All the tribes were asked to send representatives to participate in a great ceremony to show their integrity and their commitment to the Great Peace. At this ceremony, it is said that the people who represented each tribe of the confederacy buried their weapons of war into a huge pit over which they planted an evergreen tree.

This tree represented the Tree of Life. Its branches reached to the heavens, to the Father. The tree and its roots represented the five tribes of the Iroquois Confederacy. The tree would grow and send its roots deep into the earth to draw its nourishment and strength from the Mother, as did the people. The tree of life was planted upon an island in the lake, which was mostly white granite. The White granite represented, as did the white shells of the wampum belt, a blanket of purity, the Mother's most pure mind. Some say that this tree is still alive today.

Wrapped within her robe of purity and wisdom, the Mother protects that original dream and wishes of those who participated in this great ceremony. Deganaweda spoke to them of Three Great Double Ideals, upon which they could build their foundation of self government:

1. *Ne Skenno*

Purity of the mind and of the body are tied together through the experience of the flesh. It is called the Human Drama, which is our dance through this life. It is harmony between groups of people, for all of our human existence is realized through mastering the experience of relationships between each other. Inner harmony and peace, and the true union with Creator, the source of all life, is realized through maintaining the balance of the spirit while it is alive in the flesh.

Our purpose along our path is the expression of divine love of the Creator and the divine Mother through our actions, and emotions given and received through our expression of that divine love. For all has been given to us, without question, that we might reflect that which we receive from Creator and the divine Mother -- unconditional love.

2. *Ne Gaíihwíjo*

Righteousness in deeds, action, as well as our thoughts, should be the premise for all conduct. Our action is the expression of our true thought. Our actions often times speak louder than our words, for it is through action the inner self, the true state of being, is expressed.

When we maintain a state of most pure mind, we deal with life's events with open heart. Thus, we are acting as the expression of the Creator. In this manner, we maintain a justice and equality in dealing with human rights, in integrity of spirit. The superior quality within all beings is the expression of Creator, who always speaks through the human heart.

Remember always, it is in the heart of a thing that its spirit can be found, and within its spirit is the very essence of the Creator. Creator's deeds, being from the heart, are always righteous and Sacred. Our actions thus applied are filled with the power of that which is Sacred. The state of Sacred, by its own decree, is the state of most pure mind. Although often silent and sometimes soft in its action, this path is for us never without power. Consider this truth -- is not the Creator realized within all things? What thing exists that is not by the decree of the Creator?

3. Ne Gashedenza

It is good to maintain within your society a force that counsels a skilled power for the self-defense of the people. This force must always be tempered by employing the guidance of your spiritual understandings of the higher reason of the mind. All actions taken must be of righteous intent. All things that can be called righteous are the results of the balance between the physical and the spiritual; there are no exceptions.

Therefore, when differences arise, as they will, the councils between your peoples must always be held with both the spiritual leaders and the military leaders present. The views of these councils should then be presented to the Sachems, who are your spiritual elders. They in turn must answer always to the Council of Grandmothers. The council of Grandmothers represents the social order of the people. In your societies, all relationships are born from the foundation of the family fire -- Mother, Father, and their children; brother, sister, nephew, niece.

This structure is of the Mother's own design and purpose, and will reach out through your society like the roots of a great tree, seeking its strength and nourishment from the Divine Mother herself. Without the purposeful maintaining of the family fire, your social order would quickly fall into disorder and decay. You are all extensions of this family fire, which is your strength when the times of change and calamity overcome you. Standing together, you have the strength to withstand the storms that will come. Standing separately, without order, you fall easy prey to the forces of darkness, which are born of fear out of chaos, and as a people you would vanish like leaves before the wind.

We are all, in the end, brothers and sisters of one family, the children of one Mother and one Father. The balance of the male and female must be maintained within your relationships. It represents the balance of the Mother and the Father in the very process of creation, from which all of life is manifest.

In this way the Great Peace shall be established. In this way it shall be a living dream of the people that shall be handed down from Mother to Daughter, and as the bearers of life they shall pass it from Father to Son. And this peace which is born of the heart, and the people who live through this heart, shall be forever, for they shall be in rhythm with the heartbeat of the Divine Mother, which never ceases.

He told them that they had done well living in accordance with the Great Peace. He told them they would know much abundance, and they would be happy for awhile. However, he also told them they would have great trials in the days ahead of them. He told them that a time was coming in which many of them could start to forget the principles of the Great Peace. A time was coming when the way of the serpent would rise from seeming sleep upon the land.

If the ways of the heart were forgotten and the people took to their old ways of warring amongst each other, dark days would come as a result. He foretold that if the Serpents were awakened, there would be a time of great trials and much suffering. In the darkness of this time they would come to mistrust themselves as well as their leaders, and they would doubt even the very principles of the Great Peace.

The Oppressive White Serpent Devours the Great Peace

Deganaweda told the people he saw that during this time of the return of the serpent energy, that a *White Serpent* would come into their land. For a time, it would intermingle with the people. It would be accepted by the Indian people, and they would come to regard the Serpent as a friend and a brother. This Serpent would grow and be nurtured by the people, and over time the Serpent would become powerful. As it grew, although outwardly friendly towards the people, the Serpent would ultimately become obsessed with having more and more power.

This Serpent would have an insatiable appetite for power. It would seem that there would never be enough to satisfy this Serpent. It would reach out a giant claw and attempt to choke the life force from the People if they did not succumb to the twisted will of the Serpent, which would grow more and more delirious with its quest for knowledge and power. The Serpent would grow mad and think that it could own the very Earth itself.

In its desire for more and more power, it would eventually attempt to drive off and even kill the very people who had befriended it. It would threaten to completely destroy them and any other People that dared defy its will. Many would become addicted to the seemingly easy way of life that the Serpent would offer them, and through gradual corruption of the spirit they would fall under the power of this Serpent. The Serpent's power lay in its ability manipulate the people by creating fear and self-doubt in the true spiritual path.

The Serpent was a master of illusion, and could even fool itself for a time into believing that it was like the people itself, that it was no longer a Serpent. But while it talked of love and a new way of life for the people, it would be devouring the Earth itself. Even the beasts of the forest and the great seas would flee in terror when it showed its face amongst them.

However, there would be People who would continue to live in the way of the Great Peace. They would see the Serpent for what it was. They would not give in to fear and illusion. Although small in number, they would somehow survive the times that were coming. Many, however, would choose to leave rather then endure the years of struggle and hardship that would come to this land. It would be very strange times. A great struggle would develop between these few people who still held to the ways of the Great Peace and the Serpent.

There would be much contest and long suffering by the People, as the ways of the Serpent would have slowly corrupted many of them from the inside, separating them from the power of the great spirit that moved within them. The ways of the Serpent would separate them from each other, mother from child, child from grandparent. The family fire would be almost non-existent in times that were coming. If the family fire was ever allowed to be broken, if brother took to warfare against his brother, it would only be a matter of time before all was lost. A great despair would fall upon the People and the land. Since the People were the land, in time the land would eventually start to die.

The Battle of Darkness

With the Great Peace broken, the once proud People of the Long House would become weary from the endless torment of the soul that would never seem to end. Deganaweda told them if the peace was broken, they would become as few in number as leaves on the trees in winter, that some tribes would have vanished from the face of the Earth entirely; they would be as dust in the wind. As the seasons continued, many would forget their ways entirely, and the Great Peace would appear as a myth of a distant long ago past. He told them that as a result, they would endure spiritual pain that would seem to be endless. He saw the people falling upon the ground like turtles on their backs. They would be as helpless as children fighting this Serpent. Then one day a Great Red Serpent would appear. There would develop a great battle between the two; so great that the whole Earth would appear to shake. This shaking would occur three times.

The battle between the Serpents would be unending, and after awhile the White Serpent would appear at one point to accept defeat by the Red Serpent, but only momentarily. This was only because the White Serpent was stunned by the sudden blow of the Red Serpent's strange power and rage. For the Red Serpent would have grown quickly and mysteriously to great size. And this Serpent would have strange powers that would be unfamiliar to the White Serpent, as if they came from another world.

With the coming of this Red Serpent, even greater confusion would befall the land. The White Serpent would let loose of its hold on the People in an attempt to fight off the assaults of the intruder. All of its attention would go to battling the Red Serpent. Some of the people would manage to run away to the hilly country towards the West, which would be away from the Serpent's grasp. Hidden in the hilly country, their wounds would begin to slowly heal, and they would seek once more a peaceful way of life and begin to return to divine order, seeking harmony with the ways of the Mother Earth.

Some would begin to remember the old ways once again. They would begin to re-establish the principles of the Great Peace among themselves. People would come to them from all over, not just the Haudenosaunee, but people from all nations, from the four directions, from the beginning times. They would be called to gather together in the hilly country to heal from the war and terror. Here they would renew their original bonds of friendship and brotherhood, as it was during the Great Peace.

They would, at first, be small in numbers and would choose to remain neutral in the fighting that would ensue between the Great Serpents. They would slowly begin to awaken, as if from a bad dream or sickness. They would come to own themselves once again, and through their renewed connection to the spiritual powers of the Earth they would grow stronger in their understanding of their dormant wisdom.

The People living close to the Earth would learn to become strong in their hearts. In this way they would become free from the fear that would be like a great plague upon the land. From this place in the hilly country their lookouts would be watching the Serpents' battle in the distance. The Serpents' warring would never seem to end, for the way of Serpent energy to renew itself is through killing and war. The Serpent would create fear in the hearts of the People, who would become lost and be unable to connect to the source of their creation. From their fear, these Serpents would draw their energy, for the Serpents would have no energy of their own.

From their place in the hilly country, the People would hear and see the battle raging between the Serpents, which would become so violent at times that the mountains would begin to crack open. Fire would spew from their mouths, for the Serpents would learn to use the lightning energy and they would even grow wings as they carried their wars unto the heavens. It is then that the rivers would begin to boil, and the fishes would turn up on their bellies. There would be great flooding and great drought. Some of the great rivers would flow upstream in an unnatural manner. The weather would become erratic and nothing would grow as it once did. It would seem as if the Earth itself was lost in confusion and sickness.

In those areas where the greatest of fighting took place, there would be no leaves left upon the trees, and the grasses would burn up as great fires fell from the sky. Strange bugs would appear in the sky and come from the ground. They would be like beetles, and they would crawl along the ground and attack both the Serpents and the people. Everywhere there would be death. The land would appear as if the whole of the Earth was dying. Everywhere the Earth and all her life forms would become sickened from the stench of death and destruction.

Then there would come across the land a great heat. It would swell from the Mother's belly and move across the land in great clouds of fire. It would appear as if the bowels of the Earth were opening and spilling forth this great fire everywhere. This heat would last a long time, so long that it would cause the stench from all the death to become intolerable. Even the Serpents, who would continue to battle for they loved war, would themselves begin to sicken from the stench of death.

Thε Vεηgεαηcε of τhε Black Sεrpεητ

Then one day a warrior, who was standing lookout from the hilly country watching the Serpents' battle, would see from his lookout post the Red Serpent reach around the neck of the White Serpent and pull from him a feather as he tore open his throat. This feather would be carried by the wind to the South. Here it would find its way to a Great Black Serpent that appeared from some mysterious place where it had been hiding in the darkness, awakened from all the commotion and warring in the North. The Black Serpent, upon studying the white feather, would be astounded as he watched its hair begin to dance upon the currents of the wind, turning itself into a white bird and then into a white-skinned woman.

This white-skinned woman would have power and wisdom. She would be skilled in the ancient arts of the People, and she would speak to the Black Serpent in their ancient language which he understood. She would tell him stories as she danced upon the wind, shapeshift before his eyes. She would tell the Black Serpent stories of great sickness that was upon the land and in the hearts of the People, stories of death and horror going on in the North. These things he would somehow *know* to be true, but again he would have been asleep deep within the belly of the Earth for a long time.

He would ask her to tell him the stories once again, for it would be unbelievable to him that such things could be occurring upon this Earth. Then, when the woman was through with her tales, he would ever so gently place her down upon a rock, with great love and respect for her purity of spirit and her personal powers.

He would then turn to the North and let loose a great roar, filling the winds with his furry over the horrors he had heard. The winds and the sound of the great roar they carried would be felt over the whole of the Earth. It would rise up from the belly of the Earth, and even be heard in the heavens. With great speed the Black Serpent would then head towards the North to find the other two.

The two Serpents would already be weary from the fire storms and the stench of death. They would be sickened to the point that they were weak and exhausted. They would rise in horror and shock at the sudden appearance of the Black Serpent which seemed to come from nowhere. They would recognize him but not believe his appearance possible.

The Black Serpent would attack the Red and White Serpents with a great vengeance, and he would defeat the Red Serpent entirely. Then he would stand upon the chest of the White Serpent, letting out a horrible and boastful roar as he tore him into two pieces. The battle would be short. It would not be too long before the Black Serpent would begin to look for yet another Serpent to conquer, filled with the energy of war and killing. He would have taken on the evil of both serpents and become a power of darkness that defies description. It would appear that he intended to devour the whole of the Earth and even the heavens in his fury.

The Great Black Serpent would look in all the directions for a formidable foe. When he turned towards the direction of the hilly country, he would see the People standing noble and erect, with their arms open, having fearless hearts, facing the winds of change. He would know that this was not where his fight was to be found; he would turn and look elsewhere. For a time the whole of the world would be in darkness. Great clouds will have formed from the battle and the spewing of smoke from the Mother's belly. It would seem as if time itself had stopped.

The Black Serpent would then turn towards a sound coming from the heavens and, for a moment, become blinded by a great and mysterious light that appeared from there. This Great Light would be many, many times brighter than the Sun, traveling East, coming from the West, over the great waters. It would appear in the skies for the passing of twelve of our days. When it arrived there would be no night or day. This would terrify the Black Serpent to such a degree that he would slither into the ocean, trying to hide himself from the great light. He would sink beneath the Great Waters and never be seen by the People again.

A part of the White Serpent would have survived. Although weak, he too would see this light and make a feeble attempt to gather himself up and go towards that light. Suffering greatly from the wound received in battle with the Black Serpent, this portion of the White Serpent would find its way to the hilly country. Here it would be taken in and helped by the People, as it is their way to nurture the weak. This portion of the White Serpent would take on the ways of the People, but for a long time after, he would shake with fear whenever he again witnessed a great light.

Then, as if rising from the ground itself, the form of the Red Serpent would appear. He would also witness the strange Light shining like a great star, and he would tremble with fear. He would also try to crawl towards the North Country, but would die along the journey from his wounds, leaving behind him a bloody trail that would split the Earth into a shaky canyon. This trail would split this land of the Turtle in two, and then into four pieces.

To the South where the Black serpent had vanished, the ice would begin melt. Great pieces of ice would begin to fall from the sky, putting much of the land to the East into the deep sleep of winter. There it would be purified from the death that it had known. In these times, we would witness other strange occurrences with the weather. The seas would become violent and rise covering much of the old shoreline. New cliffs would rise from the sea, as well as new lands.

The trail left behind by the Red Serpent would be washed clean as it filled with the waters from the North. New mountains would form along where the body of the Red Serpent lay still and cold in its death. This would form a new sea in the North Country, which would forever remind the people of the dark times through which they had passed.

Salvation - The Return of the Great Peace

The mysterious light would be as a mist and would engulf the entire Earth much like a giant cloud. We would be lifted from the wheel of time, and we would be unable to determine it's passing. Death would cease to be. Our dream would blend and become many realities, all different, yet all truth, as we experienced the unraveling of the dream. We would witness the force which allows our perceptions to manifest and express as our reality, for within this great light the nature of all things is dreamlike.

From the center of the mysterious light the Great Star would begin to emerge. The light from this star would swell and eventually become brighter even than our Sun. It would appear to take form as an eight-pointed star as it came closer and closer to the Earth. It would become so large that it would block out much of the heavens from our view. Its presence would affect many things and we would witness much phenomena as the new world was born before our eyes.

There would appear in the heavens a great bow having the twelve colors of creation. From this bow would be heard the sound of all people -- all whoever were and all whoever would be. Then there would be a shifting of the sound like a great harmonic. It would appear as if they were all one voice, singing the sound of the new Creation -- the sound of what had been heard so long ago when this world was itself created, when we first walked upon the Earth and wondered at the newness of Her.

When the Star emerges from within the light, many of the People who were hiding would come forth from their seclusion. Many would come from their refuge in the hills and mountains. They would feel strange, as if they were walking for the first time. There would be many new colors and species of life that would come forth from the great void, for they would have lifted their voices to join with the voices of the heavens.

Man and beast and all manner of life forms upon this plane would recognize and acknowledge their part in the spider-web of life.

They shall know their part in the dream, for life would have become, in a moment, the expression of each of their visions of how things should be. There shall come a day like no other, for all the creatures of the Earth in that moment of forever shall be as one, and man and beast shall communicate as it was long ago, for fear shall be a "*no thing*". A sound shall come forth from the great star.

The people who would be coming forth in little bands from all throughout the hilly country would witness the appearance of Deganaweda, as if he was walking right out of this Great Star, returning to the People. The Peacemaker would be joined by many others as the dream of horror would come to a close. With his return there would be much rejoicing, and the people would feel like they had awakened from a dream. They would once again walk the way of the Great Peace, *Kia 'neri Kowa,* and form a new and great civilization that would continue into forever, creating a new world from the essence of the old. In this world even the eldest will be as children, yet possess the wisdom and experience of the ages that had come before.

We will join once again with our brothers from the stars. No one shall be denied, and no one shall be untouched in this time. No dream shall not come to pass, and no thought shall go unrealized. To speak more of it would serve no purpose, for what will occur will be beyond our comprehension. The way of the *Kia 'neri Kowa* shall help create the new world you seek. That which is created shall be born of the heart.

The time for the need for darkness will have passed. We will once again be as we were in the beginning, "*children of the Sun,*" and we will feel as if we have awakened from a dream. Our need for death and dying shall no longer  serve the purpose it did before, for we will be walking upon the pathway of our foreverness. *Man and spirit shall be as one in the Great Peace.*

Childʀen of Babylon

*G*randmother told us that this was to be the year of commitment and that we would be tested in many ways to enable us to see what was the nature of our true path. We would by necessity let go of things which did not strengthen our pathway and help develop our character to it's fullest potential. That which was unnecessary would not follow us to the year's end. Many of us would choose to completely change the direction our lives had been taking. Others would find that they would be compelled to wander as if directionless, to seek new places they would be moving to. She warned that relationships would also see radical shifts as our true nature resonated to the Mother's higher vibration.

Grandmother would say, "You know, it's really sad that so much of what we truly are has been repressed within us. People cannot feel themselves any more. They don't know who they are anymore in the scheme of things. They have lost their way in the game of life. They stumble around like they were drunk. They are not connected to the Earth any more. They just stumble around, bumping into each other. It has become an accidental universe.

"Living only in the mind of man and not in the heart leads only to madness, because the mind cannot feel. As a result, people lose their ability to feel the moment of a situation. The Mother is doing things to make them feel themselves again. The Mother is going to take control of her house back."

As she sat back in her chair Grandmother became very still and silent. She wove an invisible web with her fingertips while she interacted with a world that is just beyond the veil. She changed from Grandmother to Spider Woman. Grandmother wore every emotional learning she had ever experienced in the lines that graced her face. In her eyes there were many stories, from many levels of reality.

Breaking the silence, she turned to me and began her dialog again. "People aren't with each other these days because they know it's right. They are together by accidental circumstance. How can people know what is right for them if they can't even tell who they are. How can they tell who they are if they can't feel. People aren't allowed to have feelings of their own any more. It is a dilemma. A lot of families are going to break up because of this.

"They engage in their relationships without consequence. They have children without consequence. They live life upon the Earth as if it were without consequence. We have taken the honoring out of life, and now we are also losing it from our relationships.

"It is a great responsibility and an honor to raise young people in this world. Through our own experiences we know that we come into this life with much to learn about the nature of our reality. Children must be taught what it means to be human beings. They must be taught to walk lightly through this life, and to respect the Earth that gave them the opportunity to experience this life. We all have to pay back to the account of man. We have forgotten to pay our rights of passage.

"I see that a lot of families are breaking up, which means even more children are going to be homeless and parentless while their parents go about their business of trying to find out who they are. We have all been fed this lie for so very long we have begun to believe it. The Mother is going to shake up their houses. It bothers me, but perhaps it is necessary. It is better for the children to be alone than to be abused and misled.

"When the honoring between man and woman is forsaken, the family unit dies. Children can only know to mirror what they see their parents doing. If the parent expresses love through anger because of the lack of love for self within, then it is certain the child will only think to express their need for connecting with that emotion in the manner they were shown. The nature of the dream remains the same. The rules of the game are no different now then they were 180 lifetimes ago.

"The whole structure of society begins to degenerate as a result of expressing unbalanced relationships. As a result, we are left with the feeling of abandonment, and feeling total lack of support for our *being-*

ness. Human beings need to have a reason for being or they fall apart. They are not as wise as the plants, who are content with just being.

"It is because so many of us have accepted the condition of living in a synthetic world that we have lost our ability for having and understanding our own human emotions. Our relationships are becoming corrupt because we no longer have ritual in them anymore. Without the deliberate placement of ritual into the dance, we forget to keep spirit close to us.

"The body and the mind need to be integrated with spiritual reality in order to stay responsive. We can forget that life is a dance. When we live our life patterns separated from our spiritual selves, the life essence starts to die within us. Eventually, with the passing of each day, playing out the dream of the necromancer over and over, we grow cold and unfeeling. Soon we lose the dream of each other and sometimes the ability to dream altogether.

"When we lose our ability to dream, we lose our commitment to life. We lose our connection to our soul. Life becomes a drudgery, without any hope of change. Change is what keeps us alive. But this is true only when the nature of change is connected to our dreaming, for then we have purpose. Purpose is born of intent. Human beings are dreamers, that is the way Creator made us. Anything else is an unnatural way of life. Our power and our future as a species depends on us reawakening to this simple but powerful truth.

"So the Mother is now creating the environment necessary for us to have experiences which will trigger our memory of this knowledge. We can no longer go on living the lie. The time has come that the children must choose their own path. The dream we are dreaming no longer has a life force of it's own. Only one thing can change that condition. We must renew our commitment to the dance of life. It is a matter of heart......it is all a matter of heart."

Grandmother felt that this experience would continue for five years until it began to come into a calmness once again. We would experience many levels of this emotional and spiritual confusion. She talked often about those who where here long ago, the old ones who gave us our original instructions. She spoke of how the time was coming when they would return to take an accounting of how we had done.

"We will know of the time of their returning from the signs the heavens will bring. New stars will begin to appear in the heavens. There will come two kinds of beings from the stars that will appear. There will be those that are benevolent, and the lovers of our kind; the givers, the one-horned beings. They will bring with them the energy of spring. They will offer us the chance to renew ourselves, equal to the intensity of our dreams.

"There will be the other kind, however, the ones with two horns. They are a very ancient race. They come from a time before our memory can see. They will be the reapers, for they will come to gather those who have disconnected from their spirits, those who no longer can use their ability to dream.

"The two-horned ones are not evil, however. In fact, they will be here to carry out Creator's will. They will help clear the way so that there is room for the living things to grow. For does not the grass appear to die in the harshness of winter, only to be reborn again with new life and energy in the spring? It is for all things that grow, a matter of commitment to the source of life. If we are to grow again in the spring, we must renew our commitment.

"In this time there will also be another sign. The stars will join together to create the eight-pointed star in the heavens. The appearance of this star formation will indicate that enough souls have completed this part of the transition, we have earned the right to continue with the great plan of creation, we have learned the way to generate our own reality. We then can keep the dream the Mother gave us freely alive by means of our own free will. We will have become the source of life itself."

As the year of our commitment comes into the season of summer, emotional storms are breaking out across the horizons of our dreams like prairie fires. There appears at times to be so much "busy-ness" in our lives that it is hard to see the forest for the trees. In the

Dakotas they are in preparation for the Sundance. There is a whole new flock of young ones now entering the job market, a whole new generation looking for their place in a world they unwittingly inherited. Everywhere we turn the young people of this country are in turmoil, and their behavior shows us the state of their confusion.

There are people coming out of their cocoons looking to connect spiritually, sexually, and materially to some unseen force in the abstract panorama we experience as the Human Drama. Life has become a collage of expressionism. It seems as if Van Gough's visions of twisted trees and violent skies filled with turbulent sunlight have now become our reality, and we must redefine madness.

As we look across the landscapes of the old paradigm, we can see the patterns we left behind that have caused the pain in the human experience. We wonder, are we as mad as he? We stand locked in the dream we created as the hidden pain of billions of people fills the air; the human emotion amplified by the billionth power. Thoughts and emotions too long buried are screaming for release after lifetimes of repression. We witness the human expression suppressed for generations by the religious and political institutions of our world.

> "Many people feel a deep emptiness inside, a lack of fulfillment. They are frantically running around in circles, for the most part. They are trying to find their missing piece. Well, perhaps the first mistake is in looking outside yourself. After all, whoever proved we were incomplete? Perhaps the missing piece theory is only a lie. Perhaps there is no missing piece."

Summer is traditionally, and naturally, the time to strip off the robes that allowed us the introspection of the winter, the robes that sheltered us from the cold and the scrutiny of the collective unconscious. After spending the winter locked in our shells of introspection, we feel the natural desire to throw off the restraints of a cloistered existence and overbearing malaise.   Summer is the time of coming out, a natural emerging for all life forms.

Summer is a time when there are many gatherings across this Island of the Turtle. People are gathering in thousands of small groups, expressing themselves through many experimental avenues of spiritual release.   Many of them are being drawn to Native American teachings, more so than ever before.   There seems to be more medicine people out there than I can remember, all competing for the light of center stage.

Many are drawn to the *Indian Way,* the *Good Red Road.* Perhaps this is natural, for most here are part of the land now. It has been five hundred years since the first European broke the spell of innocence in America and began the rape and plunder of the pristine landscape they found when they arrived.   America has become a potpourri of mixed nationalities and fragmented spiritual belief patterns.

It is easy to fall in love with the Indian Way. On the surface there seems little responsibility -- running around in pickup trucks, going to pau wau, drumming in tee pees, and feeling the desire to fly with eagles. There are exciting shamanic journeys to break the exasperating routines of our unfulfilled lives. But following this Native American path we find ourselves, more often than not, trapped in another expression of the same old movie, another unattainable romantic Hollywood version of life.

The Indian.... What is an Indian anyway? Grandfather used to joke and tell me he did not know. He would say that all his life he lived on the reservation and he only saw Lakota, never one Indian. In a queer way, it was a grand truth. There is no such thing as an Indian. There never was, not even in India. There are only people. The name each tribe uses for itself means "the people, the human beings,". Nowhere is there an Indigenous word for Indian.

Many people feel a deep emptiness inside, a lack of fulfillment. They are frantically running around in circles, for the most part. They are trying to find their missing piece. Well, perhaps the first mistake is in looking outside yourself. After all, whoever proved we were incomplete? Perhaps the missing piece theory is only a lie. Perhaps there is no missing piece. And as for everything outside of ourselves -- well, it is just that. It is everything outside of us, and no more.

If there was a way to describe *Indian*, it would have to do with realizing self, realizing self in relationship to Great Spirit, Mother Earth and all the life forms that dance upon her embodiment. It is being with self, accepting self, empowering self, loving self. It is seeing the true relationship with all of life around you and mastering it, knowing that self is OK. The flow of nature, outside of us and within us, is natural. We are not apart from it, we are part of it. *Indian* means just being what you are, accepting the Creator within as the guiding spirit that empowers our dance through life.

We could never be *Indian* like the Old Ones talked about in the legends. Not even many *"real"* Indians can do that, for the old ones we speak of is of a time that no longer exists on this plane. It is past; it is behind us. We can no longer walk that way. It is not the path of power to walk through this life with your head turned backwards; you will only trip over what is in front of you. You will never get to where you are going.   At best you'll stay snug in the rut of going nowhere, accomplishing nothing, just going around and around on the merry-go-round.

> *"Walking with your head turned backwards*
> *is not the pathway of power. Tomorrow is created in*
> *the action you choose this moment."*

How many times have I heard people who come to ceremony say *Aho Mitakyue Oyasin, (all my relations,)* only to see them turn around a few moments later in casual conversation and draw lines of demarcation between us and them. We -- the people, and them -- of the establishment. We who follow our way, and those others. My side, their side; Black, White, Red, Christian, Jew, Hindu, Indian, Mexican, Pole, Asian -- this kind of thinking is an affirmation of our being trapped in a limited mind. Can we consider that perhaps there is just simply a human character, a human way?

How many times I have seen people come out of the *Inipi* Lodge feeling like their lives were changed, and in fact, they were. For in that moment, all the doors were opened. They were free of their dogma and their past for a moment. They were free at last to walk into the moment if they simply had chosen to step outside of old patterns of belief. Yet they would insist on returning to a way of life that leads them into one dead end after another, repeating the same old stuff every day of their lives. Their lives become nothing more than recycled ignorance. Freedom of spirit, sovereign choice has become an illusion to most.

How many *Indians* have I met that do not know the spiritual ways of their own people? Whole tribes have lost their ways, even their language. I have seen young men in tears at my ceremonies because they did not know about their own heritage. Those of European ancestry are not exempt from this occurrence. There are many who have no remembrance of their grandparents' customs and beliefs or understanding of their own legacy as People of the Earth.

It is frightening what organized religion has done to humanity on a global level. It has built walls between people. It has driven the spirit out of them, separating them from Creator, the Earth, their own emotions and human feelings, and from each other. They have fed humanity with a dogma that, like cancer, is now killing its host. Social consciousness is creating a mutated consciousness. The diagnosis of the patient is that it is unable to support its own life force, and it's creating patterns which will prove suicidal.

So they come to the *Indian Way* hoping that perhaps they will find salvation from a world gone mad with its own illusions. They come like the waves upon the ocean, in endless patterns blown by the winds of change. They are the sea of the emotionally and spiritually wounded. They number in the millions now. They are confused and lost, for their world has lost its meaning, lost its spirituality, lost its capability to feel love. It is turning to illusion. They are the children who grew up without learning the meaning of commitment. They are the *Children of Babylon*.

They come in all sizes and colors. They come from a multitude of cultural and religious backgrounds. The sickness in the hearts of humanity has become a global epidemic. It is not restricted to a specific region or selected peoples. Truth comes rarely, and only through a handful of teachers who have evolved beyond tradition and dogma, who understand the wholeness of life (and their numbers are very few).

The return of Christ, the Second Coming, is indeed in the making. However, the true Second Coming is the return of all Christs. The Christ in all of us can be accessed at this time -- *Christ in Mass, CHRISTMAS.* This raising of the Christ Consciousness is for all peoples. It is also the rising of the Christ consciousness within all living things. We all are of the Father. All upon this plane are one with the Creator. For the God Force is within all life forms. And all that transpires upon this plane is the responsibility of each of us. We are the co-creators of reality upon this plane.

And what of the Anti-Christ? It lives in the hearts of humankind. When man, singularly or collectively can realize that Creator, the source of life, is truly within, then will the Christ be risen. Then, and only then, shall the New Jerusalem be realized upon this plane. There is coming very soon a time of great change in the energy patterns upon this plane. No living thing will go untouched by this mighty change, for all upon this plane is of the same vibration, or it would not be. There is no greater energy, no lesser energy. The Christos, the divine source, has no discernment. It is available to all equally. The degrees of intensity are dependent upon the ability to hold its divine principle of being.

So I offer you a new term -- Neo-Indigenous People -- those who are of the Earth, the Earth Keepers, those who live upon the embodiment of the Sacred Mother. Consider this simple question. Who upon this plane does not contain within them the very elements that we call the Earth itself? Reason it out. No one people has the exclusive territorial claim to *Sacred,* for all upon this plane is *Sacred.* Each of us is but a small part of the whole. Many of us are like fish swimming our whole lives trying to discover what is the ocean, only to find in the end, that we are in the midst of it.

Reality upon this plane is likened unto a dream. We are the dreamers of that dream. In matters of personal power, it can only be taken away when you allow someone else to dream you. No one can live another's dream. Dreams can only be shared. When you depart from this plane you will realize what all who depart from this plane do, that this plane is but a very small part of that which comprises Creation.

At the moment of departure and realization, many desire to rush back into this plane as they realize the gift of being a participant in it. For truly, it is a grand honor to experience life as a *Hu-man*. If you find this hard to believe, perhaps you should consider your perimeters of perception of the state of reality -- that which is the result of God's creation, that which is the principle of divine law. If all things were created by God, then how could any one thing be less of God than the other? Are not all things of God? Is not all that is around you God? And if this God made all things, then who made the Devil? Is there a Devil?

We get hung up on our words. We get lost in the interpretation of the words. The Creator of all things has no name. The Creator, the source of life, cannot be contained in a word. The Creator simply is. If you wish to see the variations of meaning of the word God, try thinking about all the different languages and cultures that are upon this Earth. Then try to think of all the civilizations that have come before our time and all their words for God. Now think of all their definitive descriptions of their God.

God is all things. God is the source that causes the seed to become the flower. God is the soil that the flower grows upon, as well as the Sunlight it seeks for energy. God is the scent of the flower as well as the texture of the flower. God is the color of the flower. God is the flower in life and in death. God, the Father, is the source, the thought of all that is. Christ is the God in man.

There is a grand change coming, to be sure. All life forms in our solar system are aware of it. The whole of the Earth is aware of it, every living thing. Only man resists. The other living beings of this Earth -- the trees, the animals, the fishes, that which you can see with your eyes and that which you cannot see, are also aware of its coming. Terrans are not exclusive in the realization of the fact that something big is going on. As a matter of a fact, we are in many ways behind other life forms in waking up to the reality of it.

We have become children lost in a maze, a maze of our own creation. It is the maze of limited mind. We are seeking, in our turning to the ancient ways of the Indigenous people, a way back home, a way back to the beginning of it all. The Indigenous people who have survived the onslaught of centuries of civilization hold within their consciousness the original plan of Creation, the fragments of the original understanding of spiritual truth. Their stories are written on the rocks. Look everywhere upon our planet. The people from all cultures wrote it on the rocks, the living stone; the same symbols, the same geometry, the same holographic language.

There is a new energy that was born at the Spring Equinox of March 1995. It is filling the consciousness of the world known and unknown. It is about being yourself, living in your truth, being what you are, being your truth. Life is all about change, which means that the person endeavoring to learn an ancient custom should be cautious about becoming trapped in the dogma that might be embedded in its tradition.

The old ways do not necessarily apply to today's world. They were designed for situations that existed then. Take the knowledge from the history of a thing and apply it to *the Now*, to yourself. Learning to master *the Now* is the only way one can truly affect change. It is a matter of Alchemy.

The past is simply a time space event, a frozen moment of God's expression. We remember the events of our life and take from it the experiences we choose to embrace for learning. Remember, walking with your head turned backwards is not the pathway of power. Tomorrow is created in the action you choose this moment.

The new world, if it is to exist, will be brought about by very courageous people, people who hold within themselves the tenacity to stand up against the rigid limitations of centuries of dogma and control. The critics will be harsh; they always have been. But no one has ever built monuments to critics, have they? It has always been the few that had the courage to dream that resulted in change. It is not popular to be a genius these days.

The people who will bring about the new consciousness will do it in spite of the actions of the collectively unconscious. They will have learned to reach inside themselves and bring about their own vision of reality.

The stories that have been handed down from the grandfathers and grandmothers, were the grandfathers' and grandmothers' stories. They were on their own path living their own dreams. That is why they are so honored. They were not preoccupied with living someone else's dream. They were men and women of sovereign vision. Their stories are shared with you in hopes to be an inspiration to make you want to seek your own destiny.

"Reality upon this plane is likened unto a dream. We are the dreamers of that dream. In matters of personal power, it can only be taken away when you allow someone else to dream you. No one can live another's dream. Dreams can only be shared."

You are like seeds lying dormant in the Earth. There is a force swelling up within you. You do not know why but you are feeling moved to push your way up through the rocks and the soil. In the first part of the journey you don't see the light. Life it seems is always formed in darkness of the void. Though you don't even know what the light is, you struggle and feel your way through your blindness and the unknowing.... you grow anyway.

You *are* for the sake of being. This is the essence of the force that we call *ska*, the Great Mystery; that which moves the life force, that which causes all things to occur the way they do. It is life seeking to fulfill itself.

Through its process, the seed has no way of knowing that it will become the rose. It has no way of knowing that above the dark world of its known existence there is brilliant sunlight or the sounds of birds singing. Nor does it know that its future depends on its willingness to allow the bee to pollinate it, or that some thoughtless human might come along and pick it to place it upon their lover's table.

There was never a Master Seed schooled in the wisdom of the ancient seeds. The seed just is. It relies upon its own instincts, the inner voice that is telling it to grow, grow, grow! It is, within itself, content to be the seed, to seek nourishment and water, to push even the rocks from its path of destiny. We humans are, by our true nature, the same as that seed.

What about those Masters and Shamans, Mastresses and Shamanesses who did not make the headlines? How did they view the world and their relationship to Creator?.... Through their own eyes! This is the essence of the *Master*, the *Shaman*. They saw the Great Mystery through their own eyes. They possessed their own thoughts. In no other way could they have achieved what they did; they did not let someone else dream their dream. They owned themselves, thus, the spirits spoke to them and they were able to speak to the spirits. The veil that separates us from Spirit is only a thin veil of illusion. Our limitations lie in how we perceive ourselves to be limited.

Whatever you come to own in your being, you own. No one can take it from you. If you are afraid of losing your power, perhaps you have not yet made the conscious choice to own that power. Great power is never held or possessed. Rather, power and the access of power is a process of allowing. You become the power by allowing it to be what it will be, not by controlling it.

If you can control it, it is not real power. You can only control yourself in the flow of real power. Power flows like a river. To claim your power, you must first come to terms with your life and make the conscious effort to own yourself, to claim responsibility for the whole of your life. Evolution is a process, not an event. Awakening means just that -- awakening from slumber to the truth that lies dormant within you. And if we stop and think about it, are we ever fully awake when we first rise from a nights sleep?

When you go to your teacher, when you go to have your growing experience, know that it is about self-realization. You are not there to steal away the secret wisdom of some wizard. They are not there to give you their power, rather they are sharing what they have come to own and to pass it on so that you are able to continue on to your next evolutionary experience. By passing on their wisdom, their load is lightened; they have followed the Law of the Giveaway.

"Great power is never held or possessed...
You become the power by allowing it to be what it will
be, not by controlling it."

Over the next few years, as the vibrations of the Earth plane continue to intensify, commitment will remain a matter of choice. You shall have the choice of being one with Creator or being lost in the limitation of materialistic worship and the continued devotion to ignorance. No one will come to judge you. *You are the Lord God of your being*, no matter what you presently perceive your reality to be. Whichever pathway, whatever reality you choose, SO SHALL IT BE.

People will begin to notice that this condition of instant manifestation will show itself moment by moment. Life will continue to quicken as we evolve out of the necessity for time in our experience. In the span of a single day you will have the opportunity, through choice, to go from the highest end of the spectrum to the lowest ebb of human emotion. There will be no easy, smooth pathway. One must be conscious and awake every moment of each waking day. We are going to be taught to become responsible for our thoughts and actions through example. The free ride is over.

In the supreme humor of Creator, whatever you desire shall come forth with the velocity of hurricane force winds. In many cases, for those working with disciplines of higher consciousness, there will again be many experiences of almost instantaneous manifestation of thoughts and desires. We are going to have to quickly learn to become the captains of our own ships. This is going to demand complete mastery over those unconscious thoughts. You know, the ones we have while driving to work when we thought no one was listening, or while we were walking down the aisle of the supermarket? We can change the mood of the day and the course of our lives in a moment of careless, self-indulgent thought. Or we can, in that same moment of experience, re-qualify our thoughts and change the effect of their outcome. Each time we choose an action we alter our future forever, and the future is a mutable reality.

You can expect a lot of extremes in your life experiences in the five years leading up to the millennium as we are prepared for the eventual complete *shifting* of the Earth's energies. Use the experiences to strengthen your inner values and your sense of self-unity with the Spirit within. Now, more than ever before in the history of humankind, we are going to have to integrate self, all of the aspects of ourselves.

We have become a fractured composite of the many aspects of ourselves that we are trying to maintain independently and secretly from our other parts. Society is suffering from a disease called denial. When we live in denial, it is a natural tendency to separate the different aspects of our personality in fear that one might slip out and show itself at an undesirable moment. This is causing extreme stress within individuals, as the new energies entering the Earth plane make it difficult to perpetuate dualities within ourselves.

There is our spiritual self, the public self, the self we project for career success, the self we show only to our lover, and the self that only we know in the quiet of the night, when all around us is dark. Of course our spiritual side we mostly keep secret, which causes a lot of friction with the side we create for the outside world to see.

Now some of you will argue that it is the nature of human beings to be multi faceted, or that we are multidimensional beings after all. Unfortunately, sides we allow the outside world to see are artificial for the most part and have been designed for appeasement purposes. This synthesized part of ourselves compromises our true inner nature for the sake of material success and social status. The solution? Get simple!

Over the next decade we will see great stratification of the dimensional realities occurring which will increase as we come closer to the *Shift,* which at this point in time can be expected to occur sometime between the year 2000 and 2007 in our counting.

The polarization process which is occurring is a natural order of things, as the Mother sorts out the cupboards of our hidden consciousness. She is assisting us in clearing out our hidden agendas. You will find yourselves being polarized towards that which you hold close to your core belief patterns, drawn toward each experience which leads you to the next step in your evolutionary process.

Those who are approaching the understanding that all is one will be magnetized to that vibratory field of energy and their lives will reflect it. Likewise, those who find it hard to let go of the self-gratification of the *altered ego,* and those who keep grasping onto the unwinding games of power and tyranny over their fellow humans and are stuck on their addictions to material spirituality, shall reap a very bitter and empty harvest indeed.

Try in these times to understand that that which we have come to call the Armageddon is occurring first within the souls of humankind. The fire that consumes the world shall be the fire of human emotions we have not yet learned to master. The Earth and you are one. You are reflecting her feelings, emotions, and desires, as she reflects yours.

What you are feeling in your inner being, whether it be turmoil and violence or the peacefulness of the Master, shall be reflected in the whole of life around you. This is governed by the laws of attraction. Life will, and must, affirm your innermost thoughts and desires.

The Mother, will continue to clean her house, and shake things up. She is getting rid of all undesirable emotions and unappreciative guests. She is tempering our emotional strength so we can learn to deal with a time when our thoughts will manifest in the moment we think them. Those who remain rigid and are not willing to change with the process of her restructuring the nature of reality will have a very hard time coping with things.

We will witness the polarization and then breakdown of class systems, as financial systems and the social structures they are attached to continue to fall away. One of the effects of the resulting chaos is that we will be made more and more aware of the necessity for our individual and environmental sovereignty. These will need to be developed to degrees where we can absolutely rely upon them.

We will, if we choose freedom of choice, have to eventually break away from the "*System*", or be forced to take the debit card and comply. Complete change will occur within our lives sometimes within a matter of a few days or even hours. It will appear to many as if shattered by the higher vibrations of Universal Law. This shall be the case the world over.

As we draw closer to the millennium, the intensity of geophysical changes occurring upon the surface of the Earth along with the accompanying erratic extremes of the weather and the confusion of seasons, shall be governed by the Universal Laws of Attraction. The consciousness of humankind shall draw unto itself its manifestation of the collective thought in specific areas.

The emotion held by the local inhabitants of a particular region shall immediately affect the nature of the weather in that microclimate. The forces of nature will play themselves out physically in direct relation to the human drama which dominates that particular region. Scientists will have no explanation for this kind of meteorological behavior. It will be quite interesting to watch.

Unless you develop your inner spirituality and the acceptance of all that is as being a part of Creator, these will prove to be very hard times. The dogmatic, politically structured religions of the world will eventually fail in their attempts to manifest a global program to control the Peoples of Earth. There will be significant numbers of People who will realize through the friction of their experience that they have been caught up in a fabricated system that was created purely to enslave them.

The Peoples of this Earth long for the reunion of their spirits and the reconnection to Creation, in the state of true oneness of all humanity. It is their destiny. Their leaders shall begin to run like frightened children from forces and powers from which they have long ago separated themselves, and of which they have little to no understanding or knowledge to control. They shall find no comforting answers to the questions that humanity shall present before them.

This is a time when humankind is being given the gift of choosing their destiny. The Blue Ray is upon the planet and it is a two-edged sword. It is time to separate from the "herd" mentality called social consciousness. Humankind is being given the opportunity to expand into *God-Consciousness*. It is their destiny

Those who do not choose to follow this pathway that is being opened to them as we enter into a fourth dimensional reality of the Fifth World shall be provided a place where they can develop at their own rate. But as for this Earth, She is already moving along on schedule. Her course can no longer be altered or slowed. We must move with self-assurance and with the speed of the hawk, for the dawning of the awakened man is at hand. The age of our tyranny over each other is coming to an abrupt close.

The Sacred Hoop is already spinning in its sacred spiral pattern, expanding into tomorrow. This can only be viewed by one coming fully into *the Now*. The Earth is simply moving towards its next step along its own evolutionary path, and no one can predict when that final *Shift* will actually occur. All we can do is prepare ourselves. We can see the storm clouds in the distant horizon. They are telling us to tie down and prepare for the brunt of the storm. All that can be verified at this time is that the storm is inevitable. Everything will be changed after its passing.

Prophecy at the Red Rocks

Payson, Arizona, July 1995

*I*t was one of my mystery weekends. I had elected to take a group of people to Sedona to experience a rather unique pueblo that I had found during one of my wanderings through the Red Cliffs of antiquity that dominated the landscape here. I had chosen to meet with them at this particular pueblo. It was a smaller pueblo. Once it had been a flourishing village that probably accommodated about 300 people at its height. It was built in the south facing cliffs of rose and saffron hue along the banks of a now dried up river bed.

Sedona was once abundant with waterways that were long ago plentiful in this area. Many cliff sites are to be found where peoples made their homes during times of changes. There are indications of many peoples living here, from Anasazi, to Druid, to Hebrew, to Toltec, to those who came from the Stars.

What was different about this place was that there were many chambers in which the Goddess was the center of focus. At least that is what one would derive from the writings that were all over the walls. There were chambers where priestesses during ancient times had held their rituals. The pictures spoke of birth and women's ceremonies. They spoke of journeys through the Stars. They portrayed calendars that told of dates and star configurations, the meanings of which had long vanished with the artists that drew them upon the living stone.

We did a quiet pipe ceremony outside one of the larger chambers. It appeared that this chamber had been the focus of many ceremonies where the Mother, the Goddess, was the focal point. Pictures of her in various stages of life—the Mother fertility, dancing, the Enchantress—covered the walls. We stated to Great Spirit our purpose here and we honored those who had come before us. We could feel the presence of the Goddess embrace us in acknowledgement.

I spoke in a cave which had witnessed many ceremonial occurrences by the indication of the writings and drawings rendered upon the walls which rose to almost sixty feet above my head. There were story drawings and the recording of events in at least two if not three alphabets which indicated the presence of all those who I have mentioned at one time or another in this place. This was a living university, a library of knowledge and sacred geometry that held many secrets through the centuries. Waiting for those who would follow in these times when we walked between two worlds.

Many of the Hopi prophecies which were carved and painted with pitch upon their living stone tablets almost 12,000 years ago have come to pass, except for those that speak these end times. Likewise, all of the Prophecies given by the Peacemaker of the Iroquois have come to pass, except for those telling about these end times. All of the events of the Mayan calendar have come to pass, except those that address these end times. All of the prophecies written and carved deep within the Pyramids of Egypt have come to pass, except those that tell of these end times. The same truths exists with the Tibetans, the Aztecs, the Cherokee, the Osage, The Lakota, and no doubt, countless others. We have entered the end times. They are here, now. They are not off in some safe, distant future.

We have come to a place where the whole of humanity is engaged in the collective initiation, the nature of which can at times assume expression through many realities. These are no longer times when one truth can suffice for what is occurring. It is more complex then that, yet the fabric of reality is simpler then we have ever known. What we have known is unraveling. Billions upon billions of layers of interwoven experience is *de-structuring* as a whole new paradigm is being birthed. It is not quite yet fully manifested; it as of yet has no form, no clear nature of its own.

This is the unknown -- that which has yet learned to express itself. We are experiencing something new, something which perhaps has never expressed itself anywhere within the universe, never mind upon the planes of Terra. Beyond any doubt this is the initiation. We have come to live within our dream, yet for the most part we do not realize that it is only our dream. We have for the most part lost our knowledge of the nature of reality, choosing to play the role of being the victims of a predestined fate rather than creators of our destiny in the splendor and freedom of the moment.

So as Jupiter was being bombarded with 21 meteors and we were being told on the television that this would have absolutely no effect upon us, that we were all safe and not to worry, that our life of predestined boredom was going to continue, I sat with some 30 people in the cave of the priestess somewhere in the Red Rocks of Sedona. We chose to talk to spirit about the galactic occurrences, rather than relying upon ABC's Nightline with Ted Kopple.

An old friend came to me. I could feel his presence and familiar energy. As I slipped into trance and felt my personality leaving my body, I felt his voice begin speaking through me. I give you no name for I give you no opportunity to judge the personality based upon past experience. Rather, I give you the information that you may come to know your own truth in the interest of most pure mind.

The Prophecy of the Red Rocks

The occurrences that recently transpired with the planet Jupiter have started a process. In this process, Jupiter shall be born again as a new Sun. For a time Terra, our Earth, shall know the presence of two suns. This process will occur gradually over the next 100 years, although it could occur, given the right conditions to its completion point, within twenty. What we are concerned with here has to do with your immediate changes, what is going on within your consciousness, and your immediate realities. There are many things which will effect you as we come closer to the millenium. The years 2000 to 2009 will allow you to experience the complete altering of all that you presently call your reality. This is what we wish to talk about this day.

There will come much social disorder over the next three to four years as the governmental and financial institutions exhaust new ways of covering up their failures. They are like dinosaurs that no longer have a place in the new Consciousness. They do not have the capacity to deal with the two kinds of people born unto this plane. One kind is spiritually advanced, possessing much light and inner wisdom. The second kind is quite different. Without the proper facilities to work with and help to advance them spiritually along the path of evolution, they are likely to revert to their animal instincts.

The conditions are such upon this planet at the present time that there are many inequities within your social structures. There is little, if any, Spirit in your societies. You have become a people who have lost touch with your hearts. It seems as if Spirit is left to the few who, like the spiritual madmen of old, go to live in the wilderness areas. From these staunch few who keep the flame of knowledge lit, there will arise a new Manu, a new race of humankind.

They will possess a new understanding of the physics that will apply to your new and expanded reality. The powers of their minds will seem frightening to you at first. Eventually, those who survive the coming transition of energies that are merging as fourth and fifth density and are increasingly becoming one, will understand, and the distance between the two awarenesses will diminish. This will occur as the teachers, the Crystallites, who are the starseed upon your plane, take their rightful positions.

Many of the laws that your sciences have built their doctrines upon will begin to fail. This will, at first, bring about a feeling of fear and confusion which must be overcome through the greater use and command of emotional energy that will accompany the shifting of consciousness. There is a new energy coming into your plane. This will be aligned only within the perfection of the heart energy. Love will be realized by those that break the chains of social limitation in their thought patterns. This will be a time of extreme duality as those who hold to the lesser energies and use their abilities to dominate others, reap the harvest of their limited dreams. The spirit of the Christ energy will soon flow forth as the rivers after the spring rains. Humankind will drown in a flood of emotional manifestations before the time of light becomes apparent.

However, this will not appear as you might expect, for in many instances the Christ energy will no longer tolerate duality in its domain. What you have been told about the Blue Ray is very accurate. That which is based upon false foundations shall perish of its own hand. There will be much darkness at the beginning of these times. Fear not. Take a firm hold on your inner truths. Bring the light of creation into your being, and walk out of the dream you have created. The duality will, for many, be extreme. Like the lightning energy spoken about by your elders who understood, it will, for some, be the fire of human emotion, the storms of the Gods.

We are coming; we are all around you. We are you and you are one with us. We are working simultaneously between dimensions to achieve a common goal. As your consciousness lifts, so to speak, responding to the higher octaves, we will be able to communicate with you with more clarity. It is no longer possible at this time to enter your energy fields. They are becoming too dense. You must raise yourselves to the vibration of the higher Manu, what is more accurately referred to as your new order. It is the new physics, the physics of light energy. It is within the grasping of even the simplest of you. Children can do it easily. It is the higher octave of emotion, what you call heart. Learn this well; it is simply a matter of allowing. Then teach this principle to all those who will listen. The rest is automatic. Energy bands are presently being adjusted to prepare for your arrival. Yes, it is you who will be making the arrival, the arrival to the new octave.

> *"You must raise yourselves to the vibration of the higher Manu, what is more accurately referred to as your new order ... It is the higher octave of emotion, what you call heart. Learn this well; it is simply a matter of allowing. Then teach this principle to all those who will listen."*

In America, as throughout the other countries of the world, the Gray men, the ones truly running your governments will attempt many desperate measures to keep control over the people and their already failing monetary system. But in the End, within four to six years, it will collapse entirely. This will most likely occur before the ending of this century. This acceleration is due mainly to the continuing of the Earth Changes which will leave much of the world's population in a state of mass hysteria.

There will be several attempts by these Governments to enforce systems of martial law. The measures for this are already connected through all of your utility companies and communications networks, your financial systems, ATM, DEBIT CARD etc. etc. Already your government here in America is trying to establish a Citizen Card for National Identification purposes. This is the prelude for the planned world government system. The new health plan that President Clinton is trying to get the American People to accept is part of this program for the ultimate control of the populous. Within the next eighteen months, all currency will be recalled and new forms of paper money will be imposed. This is actually part of a world financial movement by the Gray men.

The effects of the plagues that are already rampant upon this planet, already killing millions, will no longer be able to be kept quiet. All previous remedies will prove ineffective against many of these new strains of viruses, as they will mutate with each generation.

As the level of diseases becomes unmanageable, hysteria will build up in the cities. Water will also become increasingly scarce. The accessible city water will be impure and treated chemically, which will prove to only agitate an already bad situation. Only those with the National ID Card will be able to obtain goods through the stores that survive and are able to get supplies. Eventually, due to a complete collapse of the economy and severe climatic occurrences, your government will ration certain essentials. Cities will become much like reservations -- compounds, if you will. This will be considered a necessity to keep the diseases contained, and to curb uncontrolled violence.

The crime rate will continue to escalate as people find themselves in an ever increasing environment of hopelessness and despair. This will open the doors for the military to enforce martial law. You will not be able to leave the cities because of the threat of disease; and you will need to be approved to cross State borders as each state will begin to rebel against the Federal control. They will employ civil controls within each state border as the situation worsens, due to hysteria, as the institutions break down and the populous succumbs to fear.

All activities within urban areas will be monitored via microwave devices. These have been readily accepted by people to accommodate the widespread use of Cellular phones and other communication systems, all of which are hooked up to satellites. The truth behind the *Starwars Project* has yet to be revealed to the people. There is a world communication system presently being established that is capable of identifying and monitoring your every move. Only those in the rural mountainous areas will be able to avoid this system, and then only to a degree.

As huge areas are sectioned off for control purposes, people who do not comply with the government programs will be placed in compounds. Many people will be shipped to encampments, currently being readied through the redesign of old military bases and the expansion of our interstate prison programs. Certain elements in the present Crime Bill before Congress are designed to establish the foundation for a Federal program that calls for the disarming of American citizens, which would make them vulnerable to military domination.

The geophysical Earth changes themselves will also begin to increase in intensity during this time. Erratic weather will cause massive crop failures in many areas in America, as well as abroad. Insurance companies will not be able to keep up with the disasters that will occur with overwhelming intensity. Millions will be in danger of starvation, and there will be no medical help available to assist them.

Within the next three years the volcanic activity along the Pacific Rim, as well as throughout the world, will cause many new kinds of catastrophic calamities to occur. You can expect one to erupt by the year 1998 in the mountain range known as the Cascades. This will be a final warning from Mother Earth of the upcoming turmoil headed your way. You will experience the phenomenon of Fire Storms due to the collection of highly explosive gasses trapped in our atmosphere. Eventually, they will even outlaw the use of combustible engines. This means you will not be able to use your automobiles, or be able to purchase fuel for generators.

The Southwest, California, areas of the Northwest, and many of the Coastal areas which are infused with millions of lines of underground gas and fuel lines, will be particularly hard hit by these storms. There will be much danger to those who insist on inhabiting near underground storage facilities, presently created by your government.

As the Earth Changes increase in occurrence and intensity, many will draw the negative side of the prophecies, as they become overcome by fear. We create equal to the intent of our emotions, coupled with the direction or perception of our thoughts. This outbreak of hysteria within the peoples of your lands will prompt governments to give voice to many sanctioned religious leaders, to feed the need for a spiritual calming of the population.

The world governments will employ many of the devices that we have acquired as a result of Alien technology. Many of these will appear to be miracles to the masses. Some of these devices will be employed to control the emotional attitudes of the people in the urban areas. The process will be similar to radio waves. They are frequencies that control your emotional outlook. These are already in operation to some degree in many cities, especially on the West Coast. Imposed chemical inoculation will be widespread. Your scientists already possess a level of genetic understanding that will enable them to control your physical as well as your mental abilities and behavior. Your perception will be a direct result of the consciousness to which you adhere to -- Unlimited, being that of God, or the limited, being that of man.

Nature herself will play a part as the consciousness of the masses continues to implode. It will seem as if Neanderthal beings are evolving within our urban areas. This is a direct result of the decay and collapse of consciousness within the human spirit.

The arrangements and shadowy dealings between your governments and Aliens will become common knowledge. This will be used, at first, as a tool to further tighten the grip on the populous by those who would control for power and domination, the Tyrants, if you will. This program is already under way. It will become very apparent in the year 1997.

"That which is based upon false foundations shall perish of its own hand. There will be much darkness at the beginning of these times. Fear not. Take a firm hold on your inner truths. Bring the light of creation into your being, and walk out of the dream you have created."

Although it will seem, in many ways, to be a horrible time to be alive, and for many the future will appear bleak, certain events will transpire that will allow the truth to surface. Science will become bewildered by dimensional shifts. Windows between dimensions will occur by an increasing phenomenon. This will, however, be a two-way street. That which you have created from fear will also be drawn into your realities, liken to the experience of the Lachupacabra, the gargoyles of your dark ages. They have been contained in lower densities, which are now cracking open under the stress of a collapsing consciousness.

As the geophysical changes intensify, there will also be an increase in the opening of these dimensions, multiple occurrences actually. The first ones will occur with the continued shifting of the Earth's magnetic poles. This will allow for the Beings from our inner Earth, who have long been only the Watchers, to emerge into the outer world. Great ships will make their presence known, arising from the Southern and the Northern poles of the Planet. There will be a large contingency that will emerge from an area off the Western Coast of the America's, in the Pacific Ocean. They will emerge through a large tubular funnel of water that will rise from deep within the oceans depths. The phenomenon will become known as the "G" force.

Major portions of the population will fall victim to viruses and strange mutated forms of parasites, as it is seen in more than one-third of the Earth's population. Still, almost another one-third will perish due to natural disasters and the violence humanity will play out through the fear of the intensity of the emotional shifting that will simultaneously accompany the dimensional shifting. In the end, as the century closes, and as it is seen by the year 2009 in your reckoning, two-thirds of the Earth's present population will not survive the changes.

As it is seen now from the present perception, around the year 2009 even more extraordinary phenomenon will occur when dramatic dimensional shifting happens. This is due directly to the diminishing of the magnetic energies within the solar system as a whole. This experience has already begun in isolated areas upon your plane where higher consciousness exists through will. They will become common occurrences within twenty years. Many people will choose to leave the Earth in groups during the appearance of these dimensional windows, as the living conditions here on Earth will not be desirable for many during this time.

New forms of animal life are already beginning to appear, as many previously considered extinct are resurfacing. This is due to a combination of the dimensional shifts, climatic changes, and the increase of radiation entering the Earth's atmosphere. This is due to the direct abuse of the upper layers of the stratosphere by your scientists in their attempts to control global weather conditions. This will also cause many existing life forms to disappear. This will occur within the human species, as well. You have crested a world out of balance, thus, much is happening by chance.

For the survivors, there will be a mobilization, if you will, of peoples moving and uprooting, creating continuous patterns as you return to nomadic instincts for the survival of the events of the days that are upon you. Then a time will come, after people have migrated and found their balance in the rural areas, that our relationship with inter-dimensional beings and extra-terrestrials will have the direct affect of accelerating our personal and spiritual development. This is actually already happening. As a result, human beings will develop new abilities that will help us control the effects of the Earth's mutations and, to some extent, balance the geophysical changes, helping maintain a sense of cosmic balance.

Renewing our understanding of universal truths will enable people to go beyond the effects of the mutations occurring in the physical plane. These have only existed because of improper thought processes. We will be capable of commanding our reality to such a degree that we will literally be unaffected by the mutations. Throughout the world there will be many small groups of people who hold to the higher thought vibrations. Some of them will even evolve into a new race of humankind that will possess what now would seem like unbelievable psychic and mental abilities.

There is another dimension that lies parallel to this one, and as we currently understand dimensional shifting, people will be able to move into this parallel dimension almost without effort. This dimension is now invisible to most people, because they have not allowed their vibratory rate to expand to accept the reality of such a phenomenon. As the capability to shift dimensions increases, this type of transition will become increasingly easier to accomplish. For as more and more have this experience, it will become *realized* within our consciousness; it will become part of our reality.

You can expect strange occurrences as time sequences in your time/space matrix collapse and merge. Your scientists have been playing with this ability for some time now, but they are presently totally unaware of its consequences. There is, after all, no actual separation in time, no past life and future life. It is all one continuous thread of consciousness. There are many of you who presently have come here from the future, so to speak, as well as from the past, working on the perfection of Christ Consciousness.

Much of the present technology will survive, although there will be very different ways of enabling it to work. Power sources will change immensely, and much of what we accomplish now with technology will be accomplished with consciousness. Instant manifestations will soon be the order of the day.

The increased dimensional shifting will cause a warping of our present conception of time, which is an illusion anyway. We will learn to exist beyond time, as it will become a thing of the past, so to speak. You are learning through experience to become a forever being, which is your natural state.

It will not be uncommon for people to live for thousands of years, if they choose to do so upon this plane. For the Great Mystery of Death will be no longer necessary for the sake of the experience. The season of flesh in its present mortal concept, is at its close.

Paths to the Future

There will be more than one pathway into the future existence. As it is seen at this moment, there will be one path that will lead to what we have come to term "everlasting life." There will no longer be a need for the body as we know it, although it will still exist, in a manner of speaking. It will be a matter of choice.

Many will have the knowledge to expand their molecular structure through conscious vibratory shifting of their energy fields. This will allow the body to become a "light body." This occurrence has to do with the parallel plane and the merging with it. This is very effective in the use of breathing meditations, and quite easily maintained and controlled after some practice.

Another path will become available but will be less blissful, because it will still be connected to the physical mass we presently enjoy. The people on this path will continue to evolve through the teachings of the new knowledge that will be established in certain areas upon your plane. Golden cities are the term some use, and these will, indeed, be centers of great learning. Many people who have moved beyond, in a manner of speaking, to this particular desolate location, not yet knowing why, are future light workers of the highest order. Many of these will choose to remain to help with the establishment of the new Consciousness upon this plane. There will also be a renewed relationship with our brothers from beyond the Sun. They will re-establish their presence and exchange of knowledge, as it was before this experience of limited reality.

Some will choose to go within the Inner Earth. Mainly, they will be the very simple folk. They will be counseled by the great beings who live there in miraculous cities that will also have experienced some degree of disaster due to the re-birthing of the Earth.

There will be still another path, a path for those who could not, for whatever reason, accept the change. This will be the path for those who remain locked in third-dimensional reality of Monkey-mind intelligence. They will find themselves in a world very similar to this present one, although in many ways it will be like starting over from the beginning. They will have lost the memory of this conscious existence. They will begin again from point zero

Hu-mankind shall take their rightful place in the universe, a place very far from here by today's standards of thinking -- on a new Earth, a reborn Earth, an Earth that has evolved to it highest potential and entered its continuing journey through the Fourth Dimension. This area is not so much a physical destination as it is a dimensional destiny. You have already opened an entirely new density in the higher octaves, a twelfth density, if you will. It is a brand new reality that you have created. It is this very octave of vibration that is pulling you upward, so to speak, along the spiral of evolution. You are coming home!

The important thing is to realize that it really is all a matter of choice. We will have the opportunity to choose our realities with the coming of the very next moment. We can change our direction in a moment, within the twinkling of an eye, through the understanding of emotional consciousness and our very rare abilities of being human.

We can choose to be the sons and daughters of the living God, or we can turn back and continue to live in the repetitious world of limited monkey-mind reality, playing the same old drama over, and over, and over again. *Choice* is the key here. You won't be graded. Your qualifications are expressed through the purity of the human soul. Love is the supreme power here, for *true love* has no boundaries. It is limitless. The more consistently we can *"think as God would think,"* the easier the changes will be.

Temper your anger, your rage. This is quintessential at this time. The time of that experience is over now. It will only solidify that other reality. Stop your judgment of those all around you; learn to allow the differences. You will still be you. Be your own truth; stop living someone else's. You never could anyway! Don't try to change people; you cannot. One can only guide someone to their own truth. The one who is busy doing the guiding may not even see the same truth. Accept the multi-dimensional levels of your own reality, and you will easily enter the planes of forever, intact, and with unlimited consciousness. It is not going to be as you perceive it from your limited point of reality. Learn to let it go. Learn allowing. Judgment will only slow you down in this process. And as for the emotional devastation due to uncontrolled emotional outbursts, well, you haven't seen anything like instant manifestation yet.

Now, you can continue to embrace ignorance and limitation. What is your choice? This is the time you have all waited for. You have prophesied it. You have dreamed it. And you have called it forth. So why act so surprised that it is here? You don't believe in yourself, do you? You couldn't be that powerful. Seven and a half million years, and you still do not believe in yourselves -- remarkable!

Your immediate future? It will be like a science fiction movie, only there is no rewind with this show. Live your truth. Fulfill your dreams. That is important. You can have anything you desire. Didn't you know that? Your problem is, you don't know yourself, so how could you know what you want. You must get clear -- very, very clear. Keep it simple, stay focused, and breath!

Sangre de Christo

Santa Fe, New Mexico

I have been doing a lot of talks lately and the hardest part is always, *where do I start?* I mean, there are so many places we could choose to start, aren't there? There is a lot of information that is sort of lying dormant in my Akashic library until the subject is triggered by someone's question. So I would like to let the questions dictate where we will start today. These are questions that I find are most often posed to me, relative to the times we are living in:

"What should I do?"

"Where should I go?"

"Is there some one who you can direct me to?"

"Can you tell me where to be?"

"Should I be concerned with the aliens?"

"Is there any place to be that will be safe when the Earth changes come?"

There is the most exquisitely simple answer to these questions, one so simple that few want to hear it. The answer is best met with another question.

"What do *you* want to be doing and how is *your* heart best served?"

If you haven't found the answer to the question then perhaps you should look at ...*what you are not doing in your life that would make you happy and why you don't allow yourself to participate in the state of Joy. Where are you not being truthful with yourself; where are your compromises being rendered?*

If you can answer these questions, the way to find the answer to the where, and can I be safe, would not be as hard to satisfy. You see, if you can't answer these two basic questions, quite frankly you are living in complete denial. So it wouldn't matter where you went. The chaos inside you is greater than the chaos outside you!

Where is it I heard said "know yourself and the kingdom of heaven shall open unto you," or there was "to know thyself is to know God." How many of us can say that we really know ourselves? How many of us can say that we allow ourselves the time to just be , so we can observe and feel just what it is that we are?

It would seem that most of us just live out patterns of compulsive behavior, to which there is no self purpose. We live for someone or something other than self. We live our lives to please, to be accepted, to be liked, to sacrifice for the kids. We stay together because they really love me, better to be loved and not love than to not be loved at all, because I have to pay the mortgage. Is there something familiar in these declarations?

We have become so estranged from our true essence that we no longer trust the counsel of our own being. We are constantly seeking answers outside of ourselves. We have become strangers unto ourselves!

Through time we have embraced a complete acceptance of *social consciousness* programming. From an early age, at some deep, intrinsic level, some still small but commanding voice, inaudibly but compellingly, whispers monstrous things to us. Somewhere inside we get the message:

"You are not worthy...Whatever it is you want, you don't deserve it."

"You don't know enough to be successful."

"These are the rules. If you don't obey, you will be punished, here and now, or later, in some other world to come."

"This is a selfish thought, young man. How dare you think only of yourself!"

"My behavior is not acceptable."

"I'm not good enough."

At Stanford University in California, scientist have deducted from their studies that...

1. *On the average, a human being has some 60,000 separate thoughts each day. So we can estimate how many thoughts that might be per minute.*

2. *Almost all of the people studied indicated that greater than 85% of those thoughts are negative and self-critical, dictating patterns of unworthiness and self-denial. This suggests that we are dominated by fear and doubt, and we are reactionary by nature.*

Most of us live within the confines of a synthetic reality where we are responsible to the external world, while we ourselves are in denial of our feelings, our desires, and our spirituality. We have so lost touch with ourselves over the last century. We have lost what Grandmother knew growing up, never mind what she accomplished with her hours during the space of her day. Today, most of us have to go to workshops to learn about life and get a sense of accomplishment.

The control of our lives, even of our thoughts, is too easily given over to some unseen hand that pushes us to give our power away to almost any outside source, rather than to seek our own answers within. This condition has created a consciousness of enslavement. This is consciousness shaped by tyranny. This is the residue of the same conquering consciousness that has laid this great land to waste.

In less than 200 years in this country, we are now being told we have so disrupted the balance of nature that, in most places, the water from a stream is undrinkable, if it can sustain life at all. It is no longer possible to grow pure food. In many places, even breathing the air can cause great harm to our bodies. The very *balance* of life is so upset, it has finally reached the point where nature has taken it upon herself to heal the damage. She has declared war on the human race

Nature, I believe, has declared war upon the human society, not the human race. We are dying in epidemic proportions from plagues, parasites, and cancer. It is the war with valued life. Our very cells are devouring us. As the Hopi say, this has become a world out of balance, *Kyanosquatsi*. For the most part it does no good feeling guilty; you are not responsible. You have not spent enough time knowing yourself -- it isn't even you taking the actions you take. It is the robot.

I know there are a lot of you who are asking yourselves, "Is he going to let us know when these changes will occur?" Well, they already are. You are swimming in the sea of Earth Changes; they are happening right there within you. But you are too busy serving the Tyrant within to know the true state of the God within. Then again, wait a minute, is it not the God out there? I find it strange that a person can spend their whole life trying to please some God out there, never once acknowledging the God within. Now that is true paganism.

There is a game going on here. It is all about, you can't catch me, but I can see you. You can't do what you want to do; you must answer to me and my needs first, or else you are a bad person. It is the multi-dimensional game of *Lord of the Tyrants*, sometimes called the real-life game of *Dungeons and Dragons*. You see, we need to be controlled, don't we. I mean, we can't make decisions for ourselves.

What is wrong with you -- this is the perfect Tyranny! Look at your TV. Can you not see how happy good people are? Yet while this propaganda is going on, I defy you to turn on the Good News Station! Try to find the Ascended Masters hour on your radio. I think Bill Moyers should do a show called "Society, Freedom, and Myth: The Story of Spiritual Decline and the Loss of Sovereignty".

We have bought into the *society myth* so deeply, we are not even aware of it's impact for most of our unconscious day. It has become the norm to let someone else think for us. We just keep running and running around the wheel, never slowing down to take a look, because if we do, the Dragons will get us. Oh yes, *the Dungeon*, well that is the box we accept as our life.

The consciousness of Tyranny has always controlled people by perpetuating fear, encouraging a sense of personal inadequacy, and exploiting the concept of separation. This perpetuated sense of separation is most insidious, because it makes us feel separated from everything, from Nature, from the Creator, from our own Mother Earth, and most significantly, from our own souls, from ourselves!

Be reminded that there are higher realities and greater truths that govern the course of events. We have entered into a time that will only allow for us to stand in our own truth, and the only way to stand in our own truth is to know ourselves. How can you ever hope to find your own truth, if you don't know yourself?

I'm not talking about the self you created for the acceptance of others! I'm not talking about the self you created to please a mate. And I'm not talking about the self that is created to contend with the drudgery of everyday life on this plane. I am talking about getting in touch with the self you talk to in those intimate moments when your rational mind has gone numb and you are finally left with pure thought.

Getting in touch with this self can occur when you are so involved in a physical action that the rest of your conscious reality naturally finds itself in the great void. Or it can be induced in those rare moments when you allow yourself to not think -- to just be.

These are precious moments when you leave the everyday world and allow yourself to be with yourself. Sometimes you slip into this space driving. Some people reach it more easily hiking in the woods or walking along the beach. I am referring to the time you allow yourself to be alone with yourself, without judgment, without fear, just *feeling* it all. This is truly a natural state and it occurs constantly if we are open to it. It is the space between words; the space between the blink of an eye. It is the space called God. It is you, trying to wake yourself up.

When was the last time you looked at yourself in a mirror and liked what you saw? When was the last time you said, "I love you" to yourself, and meant it! When was the last time you looked into that mirror and loved what you saw unconditionally? I know it has been awhile for some of you, never for others. Loving oneself is an art form; it is a state of mind, and it all has to do with allowing.

Aloneness is very different from loneliness. But you can never know the unbelievable potential of living in that state without loving yourself. And if you don't love yourself, you exist in a state of denial. Living in denial, you only know separation from life, from God, and ultimately even from Self.

That which you hold in your closest thoughts and embrace with emotion, is what you will manifest in your outer reality. This is a great truth. The external world is constantly responding to, and affirming your declarations of reality. *Your* reality.

So what is your reality?

"I am not worthy. I am inadequate. I must find someone else, outside of myself, to tell me what to do with myself. I must find someone to love me."

You go to clairvoyants and fortune tellers to get a reality check. How on Earth could anyone outside of you possibly know the reason why you create chaos in your life, the reason why you never seem to draw to you the compliment of your desires, the love of your life? Consider this. You think so little of yourself, you show such little respect to your divine self, you would rather dwell in the state of unworthiness than focus upon your achievements and successes. What kind of person do you expect to draw to yourself?

The Universal Law of Attraction dictates that like draws like. It is infallible, and forever. It is now what it was thirty thousand years ago; the principles still apply. Whatever you think you are, so you shall be. Everything in your outer reality will manifest that which supports your feelings, which are your transmuted thoughts. Life itself will literally manifest the result of your thoughts, by reflecting your feelings. You see, life speaks the language of Creator, the Emotional language.

The consciousness of life, the essence of that which is the God Force, the Creator, knows no judgment; therefore, no degree of good or bad can exist within it. It is pure consciousness. It will cause to come forth into your reality, physically, mentally, and emotionally, what you desire. That is Universal Law. That is the foundation, the essence, of quantum physics.

And what brings you into a state of unhappiness? It is *what* and *how* you feel. Like it or not, if you are unhappy, it is because you have chosen to have the feeling, to allow the feeling. And you will feel unhappy as long as it takes for you to *own* the emotion, so that you can embrace it, experience it, understand it, and let it go.

In these times, it is essential that you see the Truth of this in all things. You must see the God in all things. You must see the Spirit in all things. You must be able to see God, even in your worst enemy. They, too, are part of Great Spirit. There is a strength that comes from first seeing God in yourself. That is the turning of the key that unlocks the door to seeing God in all things!

When you can see the connection between yourself and all things, it almost becomes automatic that you see the web that connects all of consciousness. Through the use of will, conscious responsibility, this process of reprogramming your thought process is available to you, and is entered into simply by calling upon your *will*. This is what reclaiming your power is all about. If you consciously exercise this new thought process on a daily basis, for only a few minutes each day, you will begin to manifest it in your outer reality. The world outside of you will literally bend over backwards to accommodate your desires.

If you love yourself, if you have forgiven yourself for not knowing this great truth, then your exterior reality will begin to alter radically. Day by day, and then hour by hour, you will see your life change in response to *you*, taking control of *you*. Native People have always remembered to consider the affect an action will have on the next four generations. There is no one else to blame for our sorry state of affairs; that is obsolete thinking. That kind of thinking is only another form of passing the buck.

> *"Your will is set free by allowing yourself to be yourself, by allowing yourself to feel yourself. You are set free by allowing yourself to forgive yourself. It is a grand truth that you have never done anything that would eternally damn you. You have simply learned to listen to everyone else's description of how your life should be."*

All of life is a circle, and most of us here now are reaping the effects of what we ourselves created four generations ago. We have come back to experience first-hand what we created.

We worry more about financial ramifications in our lifetime than we do about what our great grandchildren will inherit when they walk this Earth and there is no more water to drink! At the rate we are going, in four generations there won't be any fish left. There will be no buffalo. There will be no Grandfather trees.

We are so at odds with nature and with ourselves that even our own cells are rebelling against us. It is this sheer rebellion in the body that has created the many plagues upon the land. And for many of these plagues, there will be no cures. There are multitudinous reasons for this dilemma. Consider that some of these diseases have been manufactured; they are not organic. In fact, they are mechanical in nature. They are a virtual reality -- synthesized life forms, to be blunt.

Did you know that for some of the plagues that are killing your loved ones the cures already exist, and have existed for quite awhile, but you do not have access to them because your ruling government, the true world governmental order of financial overlords, won't let the cures be made available to the public. They are of the opinion that the Earth is overcrowded. There are simply too many people. We need to decrease the population, and they are quite willing to help that happen. It is already calculated in a plan put out by the United nations called Bio-diversity (1993). It is their solution to the problem. Read it; know the truth for yourself.

The powers that control this Earth through the doctrine of greed and tyranny are saying that by the year 2010, this Earth will not be able to grow enough food to feed all the people. They are aware of the coming Earth Changes. They are the ones who made secret agreements with the Grays from the Star Nations. During the Eisenhower administration, you were sold out. That is why so many billions of dollars have been spent on underground installations. When the changes occur, the plan was for the selected few to go underground. That is only on the Earthly level. They already have their plans working and have for some time in your heavens. There are colonies even now upon your moon.

That was the plan. But it won't work! It could never work. The people who think it will are reacting to their own fear. There is a lot more to this, and there is also much more that your overlords are not aware of. You see, they have lost the natural ability to contact higher consciousness. They have lost the Spirit World. They are reacting to their own fear.

Technology can only go so far. The scientists and *technocats* may be able to go to the moon and even calculate the potential size of an earthquake, but they can't tell you when it's going to happen. They have even learned to time travel, to a certain extent. They can assemble and disassemble the structure of molecules, as they did in the Philadelphia Experiment and the secret work at Montauk. They might even know the experience of other dimensions.

And yes, they may even be capable of creating other life forms, as they are doing in Los Alamos New Mexico. Have you ever read about the "Post Office Babies" of the 50's? Most likely your answer would be no, but you've heard of virtual reality? Did you know you were living in one? The wake up calls have begun. Soon the whole of humanity is going to wake up one morning and find out just how artificial our little bio-sphere is.

What they don't know will ultimately be their undoing -- and our salvation! They lack the knowledge of true self. They have disconnected themselves from the Mother, as well as the Father. They have forgotten the hidden road map to the knowingness of the Great Void, and that is a road map that comes with knowing that the power of the Creator lies within us all. That is a power that cannot be conquered, that cannot be manipulated. Within us lies the mystery of the ancients.

We have been separated from this Earth, our Sacred Mother, for so long that, unfortunately, it is hard for most of you to feel the emotion of what I am saying. We are so separated from Spirit that the whole of humankind is suffering from an epidemic of spiritual loneliness and despair. This is why everyone feels so abandoned, so unloved. Why are we never satisfied with our lives -- because we really don't have a life of our own. We are playing out someone else's script. We have never been allowed to have one under the doctrines of tyranny.

> *"Aloneness is very different from loneliness.*
> *But you can never know the unbelievable potential of*
> *living in that state without loving yourself. And if*
> *you don't love yourself, you exist in a state of denial.*
> *Living in denial, you only know separation from life,*
> *from God, and ultimately even from Self."*

The people who have been spending so much energy developing ways of controlling our thoughts, creating the game about our relationship with the sacred Mother, are children who have lost their way in the long wandering. They have forgotten that it is their thoughts, their dreams, that have created the very nature of all reality. Now they are in a panic about the *Shift* that is coming, and they are tightening their grip upon our freedom, thinking they can control life itself.

A real concern regarding this shift that we are facing is not so much a matter of the Earth shaking, or the floods coming, or the plagues, but rather how to integrate the Shifting of consciousness. We are about to undergo a radical change in the way we think, feel, and perceive, as well as expressing our living of life as a species. Consciousness is about to make a hollow leap, what science calls the jump. We are about to become a new life form, expressing ourselves in a new fifth dimensional reality.

The *Shift* must come, regardless of the degree of our willingness to accept it. Without this *Shift*, humankind would go the way of the dinosaur. We must remember to look at this time with our hearts. We must learn to look at this time with *soft eyes*. We must remember that we are the children of one Mother and one Father; we are expressing in their dream.

We were born of their union, their love. You cannot undergo a change of heart of this magnitude while you are thinking that you are separate from life around you. You cannot *thrive* through these shifting of realities if you think that animals are just beasts with no consciousness, and therefore you can kill them without consequence, or just for financial gain or for sport. Murder for sport doesn't cut it.

You cannot *thrive* through this shifting of consciousness and dimensional realities, if you think you can take whatever you want from the Earth without asking or without giving anything back. There is a little matter of the law of the give away. All law has cause and effect. We are feeling the effect of our lack of awareness of the Sacred.

We must learn to heal our thinking. We must learn to heal ourselves. Somehow, we must remember *Sacred*. The future is not somewhere out in space. The past is behind us. We must find *the Now*. Ram Das was always right about that. We only allow it to exist in fleeting moments of beauty that we mostly shrug off as fantasy! Then we shut off the fantasy to return to reality, which is hopeless fantasy, isn't it?

We are coming to a time of having to make some serious choices, and it is approaching very rapidly. Our government knows that the Native Elders know this. Our government knows that the Native Elders know about the agreements with the Extra terrestrials, made in the 50's in Wyoming during the reign of King Eisenhower. That is why they are constantly observing the Hopi, why they send people to distract the traditional elders from their work, why they create rumors about their behavior which are not true, and why they spend so much time and energy creating counter-intentions between the traditional elders and the People.

There are people who have been given the job of watching and waiting for the day when the Hopi elders follow the guidance of the Kachinas and go below the ground. They are even trying now to eliminate the existence of these truths by supporting a program of planned genocide that they hope will finally destroy the Spiritual elders and the Peoples' faith in the old ways, the traditional ways. The Spiritual elders know that this is a time to eliminate secret doctrines. There should be no secrets between people. If we remove the secrets, then there is nothing that will be hidden from us, and we will have choices.

So we can and should ask, what is the choice? Do we let go of our untruths and allow ourselves to feel again? Do we take the time to allow for ourselves to move through our old patterns that kept us imprisoned within our limited thinking. We *can* reconnect with nature. We *can* accept what She communicates to us in Her universal truths every moment.

Next time you're at the store or in town, slow down and take a look at the people around you. How many of them look happy with their lives? Are they smiling and can you see the joy bubbling up out of them? Do they seem to be *feeling* alive? Is there a light in their eyes? Or does it appear that their spirit is leaving their body. This is called *Sampacu*, loss of the life force. You can see it in the eyes of the people in a village just before disaster strikes. There is a lot of *Sampacu* in the eyes of people I see today.

Now, let's talk for a moment about Alzheimer's, because it is a reality to the families of over 70 % of all people over 70 years of age. At least that is what the medical research statistics in America shows. Doctors study these things so they can plan out future income projections, I guess. But anyway, know that Alzheimer's is a condition. It is a condition that, when it happens naturally, the person has given up on the experience here and accepted defeat. If that is the case, then the body will no longer serve a purpose for learning on this plane and they will ultimately die. That is their choice. It happens when the spirit self and the physical self can no longer cooperate with each other. Life is in conflict. In most cases, it can be healed, if we can create a new pattern of reality.

Remember always that we are each creating this plane moment-by-moment, through conscious thought. So we can choose to *remember* how to think as free spirits, rather than think as part of the social consciousness gridlock of the collectively unconscious. We can choose to think of ourselves as Children of God. We can choose to think of ourselves as the sons and daughters of one Mother and one Father. We are part of them and they are part of us. We have access to an inexhaustible energy. We have blocked it, but it is there, regardless.

It is all consciousness, and everything around you is the direct result of conscious thought -- yours. Therefore, you hold the power to change your reality -- in a moment, if you can focus your energy. You can declare, "Oh, wow! This isn't what I wanted my life to be about. I am going to change this scenario." You have the power to say that. You have the power to do that. You're doing it anyway. You're doing it right now. You've been creating your lives unconsciously so far, because you have slipped into reactionary mind through accepting the programming. For the most part, you have been letting someone else make the decisions for you.

There is hope. There is great hope. It lies in you. It lies in your allowing the awareness of conscious will. Your will is set free by allowing yourself to be yourself, by allowing yourself to *feel* yourself. You are set free by allowing yourself to forgive yourself. It is a grand truth that you have never done anything that would eternally damn you. You have simply learned to listen to everyone else's description of how your life should be. You have let everyone else tell you how to behave, how you should look, how you should feel about matters, what you should be doing, and what you shouldn't be doing. You have let someone other than yourself be *responsible* for who you are.

When you were a child, did you think about fairness? Can you remember dreaming? Do you remember ever telling yourself that something you wanted really badly couldn't be? Do you remember looking out your window in the springtime and being amazed at the wonder in a butterfly? Can you recall that kind of beauty, that kind of simplicity?

And what has all this to do with prophesy? Well, from, my point of view, the best prophesy is the one that is heard by the People, received by the People, and the People then take an action. They take an action to affect change in the potential outcome. You see, the prophesy does not have to happen at all.

Prophesy is the clairvoyant ability to see a total potentiality of a time space event. Perhaps the world is not coming to an abrupt end. Perhaps the world is only just beginning! We are living in *the Now*, whether or not we acknowledge it. What you are thinking and embracing with emotion this very moment is creating the next minute of experience that you will encounter along the path. In a manner of speaking, life and the experiences we have are a Joke.

Yes, it is a time of change -- everything is shifting. We can make the conscious choice to live in the state of love or remain in a world governed by fear. Do we have the courage to abandon our fears and live in love? Or have we become too comfortable with our pain? It is hard to break an addiction, isn't it? And we have become addicted to our suffering. We identify ourselves with it. Perhaps this is why we keep re-creating the conditions that perpetuate this suffering.

Ultimately, all there is, is God! Everything we approve or disapprove of is alive and feeling because of God. So keep walking through the grass, keep loving, keep dreaming. When we are the heart of God, we can feel what a miracle it is to simply be alive!

Watch what you are thinking now -- you are creating prophecy. By the way, which reality do you choose?

Truth or Consequences

*T*he following information was received between October 15-17, 1995. I was living in a log cabin on Orcas Island. Orcas is located in the San Juan Islands, off the coast of Washington state. One could swim from Orcas to the Canadian border. Orcas has long been a place that many students of the Masters, including Blavatsky and Krishnamurti, would come to reflect and heal. It has been called a place of healing and revealing. People were coming from around the world to see me about healing and to work with the knowledge given by the indigenous Masters. In many ways my life had become a fairy tale.

Scientists have come to Orcas to study the energies and land formations. It is perhaps one of the oldest land formations on Earth. Now they have gone so far as to put a space satellite communications center on the Island, so I guess it is the beginning of the end for those primordial energies on the sleepy rock. According to the Native Elders, as well as many clairvoyants, the Islands are the original hill tops of the Mythical land know to legend as Lemuria, the land of Mu, which was of course the Motherland, the original garden of Eden.

I had been asked to attend a meeting of sorts. There are those of us who know that there is an ethereal city just a few miles off the shores of Orcas. Not all are of the vibration to see it. But sometimes pilots speak about the lights they have seen while flying into the islands at night. When they take off the following morning, they soon realize the only lights that could have been seen was the moonlight dancing upon the surface of the Pacific Ocean. Nevertheless, the stories are frequent and the location hard to chart, due to the fact that compasses often do not function around the islands, especially around Orcas.

Over a period of two days, I was escorted by the Masters and lifted through the dimensional barriers to attend these meetings at the City of mystery. Present at these meetings were entities of great radiance, included were representatives from the inner Earth, and other dimensional realities and the worlds beyond our sun. I recognized some as Andromedans, Sirians, and the beings from the Motherland—they were indeed beauteous in their countenance.

I was given permission and asked by those present to share this information, because this counsel wished to contribute to the body of knowledge of the consciousness of humanity -- knowledge that will help hold the space for the preservation of human consciousness and species in the Universes, thus allowing for easier transition through the great shifting, and assist in our ascension process, or graduation, into the higher octaves of the Christos.

It was the consensus of those present that the specific personalities of the individual beings present, and their personal thoughts and visions through the holographic time space continuum, were irrelevant. In this time it can be difficult, if not impossible, for beings whose chosen reality is of the higher frequencies to take physical, or should we say optical, form in third-dimensional reality along with us, as they have in prior times. They can, however, still merge with our consciousness through thought process without too much difficulty. The only blocks existing are our human nature of resistance to the acceptance of divine experience.

The human consciousness that holds reality as we know it on the Earth plane is in the process of collapsing. It is not the first time this has happened. If it were not for continuous intervention on the part of those who are our benefactors, it would have already solidified. It, quite literally I have been told, would have crystallized and we would have gone the 'way of the dinosaurs'. You see, much of what is happening at this time should have occurred almost ten years ago. We have been allowed the grace of extended time experience. But that grace period is about to come to a close. We can no longer be shielded from what is occurring on a galactic level throughout the entire multilevel reality of the universe.

This body of information represents, rather, the collective messages of those present, as it was seen in the moment. As I was told, consider this a wake up call.

"Greetings. I am Deganaweda, Aleph in service to the twelve Rays, servant to life and the divine source. It has been decided that you be asked to attend this August Body of Souls, as a gesture of respect and friendship. There is much to share. I have been asked to speak in representation of the collective. With your permission, I shall continue.

The Final Initiation

"This is a very different time, unlike any time that has ever existed on this plane or any other before. For many, there is a feeling of malaise. The tendency of your emotional experience is to see no future, not remember your past. You are losing your dreams. As a result, you are losing your will. Because of this affliction, many see this time we are living in now as a time of confusion and suffering, a time of hopelessness. But this is not the essence of this time, nor is it the purpose of this experience.

"May the people of the Terra hear this message and may the hope and dreams be rekindled into flame. May they draw the power of the violet flame from within the great halls known as Amenti. May they again reach within and touch the love that has always been there for them from the dawning of creation -- love that arises from that first union of the Divine Father and the Divine Mother. For they are the Sons and Daughters of the light. One day they will realize how greatly loved they have been. There will be much change between now and what you could call the millennium year.

"To the undiscerning mind, this can be seen as a time where we are headed in a direction that only brings with it the greatest conflicts that have ever been experienced by the souls of humankind. We would ask you then to consider, "Where is your heart's commitment? What does your inner guidance tell you?" You must believe in yourself, in your own Divinity. If you do not believe in yourself, how can you put faith in the concept that some heavenly host would even consider taking you up in a great ship or through the experience of divine rapture.

"Now, more than ever, we implore you to become the very expression of the love that you seek outside of yourselves. For in that act, you shall draw to you the likeness of yourself. In the moment you become love, love shall be reflected in all you experience. Stand fast, for you now enter the final stages of your initiation into Christhood. In the twinkling of an eye you shall become the very dream you have been dreaming. As yet you do not realize the full potential of yourself. We tell you now you are the law givers. Your sword is your will, and your shield is your heart, which is why the whole of the universe sits and awaits the consequence of your decisions at this time.

"... Become the very expression of the love that you seek outside of yourselves. For in that act, you shall draw to you the likeness of yourself. In the moment you become love, love shall be reflected in all you experience."

"As we look upon the peoples of the Terra, we see that there is much conflict throughout your global society. Your story, the story of Earth -- what is known throughout the universe as Terra -- the story of Man and of Woman, Womb of Man, is the fairytale of the universe, it is a love story extrordinaire. The nature of its expression now seems to be a tale of human conflict and woe. But things are not often what they seem. In your spinning of the human dream you have harbored many dualities and judgements. These thought forms must now manifest to be released. It is all part of the process of purification. We call it purification as this is your own decree.

"Yet even in your blindness, the great plan unfolds along its intended path. You are truly fulfilling the Father's dream and the Mother's dream. Through experience, as it must be upon the plane of action, you are ridding your consciousness of inequities that would prevent your awakening. You are freeing yourselves from that which would prevent your destiny. The pain you feel is equal to the love you withhold.

"You are in these final stages of the dream, experiencing the effects of the Blue Ray. You are familiar with this Ray as the Ray of Michael, and the Ray of Shiva. The Blue Ray brings harmony through conflict. It is the double-edged sword that is the great equalizer in life. In our observing the condition of the human drama, presently there is much pitting of belief against belief, culture against culture, race against race, gender against gender. There is much concern as across your globe there are thousands of little wars erupting. They light the evening skies like a thousand campfires. But this is how it has always been here, has it not? When you no longer have a need for that experience and it becomes a collective desire, humankind will be able to move beyond the affects of that vibration -- the blue vibration, the vibration of Shiva. At that point humankind will enter the realm of the Violet Ray, which is the gateway home.

"Presently, this state of moving beyond consciousness, competing against consciousness, can only be experienced by individuals singularly or in small groups. There still exists much separation between groups holding to their thoughts of how it should be. Each group and each teacher continues to exert an energy that sends the message, "our way is the better way". We have more ancient secrets than those groups. We see many groups collapsing from within because of their insistence on holding onto this vibration.

"The root of this vibratory pattern is that it is born from a perception of fear and lack -- the fear of one group being more correct than another, the fear that a different way cannot be as pure and powerful as *our* way. This characterizes the lack of the individual or individuals to express with complete certainty the ownership of themselves and their viewpoints. Strong personalities will bring strong viewpoints, and strong viewpoints bring about strong opinions. In the end it is all attitudes. The greater the God, the greater the drama.

"Throughout the universe you are regarded as great initiates. You have chosen in the game of life upon the Earth plane to conquer yourselves. You have chosen to purify your own race on your own terms. From around the universe there are many great beings who have come to support you and your chosen pathway on your journey back home. Know that your thoughts are felt and known throughout the universe by your galactic brothers and sisters. To many of those who dwell in your heavens, you are considered to be royalty. They are aware of your plight, perhaps even to a greater degree than yourselves.

"There is much that is filtered from you upon your incarnation into this plane. This has been established, for the most part, by your Godself as rules for the game. There are many layers to the conditions of the human evolutionary experience that become clouded when we enter a conditional reality, and creates within its paradigm separation from the source of all. We are then dealing with a partial reality experience. The conditions here which dictate a limited awareness of our reality are self-imposed. Awakening can only be achieved through right use of will.

"We are aware that for many of you, you are experiencing your *dark night of the soul*. If you have reached this knowingness, know that you are not at the end of your ropes, in a manner of speaking. Rather, we would ask you to realize that through your experience and willful use of intent, you can cause the greatest effect for change.

"There is still quite a way to go to reach your intended destination on the other side of this journey. This is the awakening of your spirits. This is the time of your experience when you elect to embrace or not to embrace your lordships in the kingdom of light. You cannot expect to enter this kingdom of light carrying all your baggage -- so lighten up!

"Your present situation is likened to a war. But the war is within and the emotional toll is great, for you have long ignored your mastery of human emotions. This war is being waged within the confines of the DNA. It is your Armageddon, one thought pattern against the other, one genetic heritage against the other. How often have you been told the battle and the peace are found within, that the kingdom is within? The true nature of your reality is within. You are concerned with events developing in *outer space,* yet you continue to think you can avoid the events transpiring in *inner space*.   Here is where your true Earth Changes are beginning, and here is where they will be resolved.

"From the perspective of the bigger picture, you are participating in a drama designed to develop within you 22 strains of DNA to their highest potential, Christ Consciousness.   You are in many ways a composite of many grand species, created with the intent to develop the strongest possible life form to hold the vibration of Christ Consciousness.   You are in this manner, your own great experiment. Nothing can occur against your will.   But do you develop that will?   Do you exercise it over your emotions?   Your job here at this point is to find the source of that will, harness the eternal energy of it, and own yourself -- but not at the expense of other life forms.

"What has slowed you in your evolutionary process was the willful intent of others to manipulate your kind to suit their own purposes. Not all your shortcomings are of your own creation.   You have at times been manipulated, and not always for the highest good.   But, alas, you are grand initiates having a dream.

"You are now about to enter the last and final initiation.   There no longer exists in this realm the chains of past Karma -- your spirits are free to soar with the Eagles.   The secrets are unveiled to any who seek. We encourage you to take up a new sword, the sword of knowledge. Take it and turn to face the final gatekeeper, the one who keeps you from entering the final door.   The gatekeeper has been identified—alas, it is yourself.   But know, oh Lords of light, that you are free to go and conquer yourselves, free to rise above the illusion of limited mind.   For all is mind, the house of thought, and thought creates the nature of reality.

" ... You are concerned with events developing in outer
space, yet you continue to think you can avoid the
events transpiring in inner space.
Here is where your true Earth Changes are
beginning, and here is where they will be resolved."

"Humanity has indulged itself in manipulating its political will over its own kind. Humanity is suffering the *"dance of the tyrants"*. The dance has been a calculated game of domination of one species over another, one concept over the other. Now you have reached the end of the playing field, so to speak. The old methods are losing their hold as the new consciousness ushers in, and in many instances no longer applies. Power over one another will prove utterly useless in the days that are unfolding upon you and your kind, for we have entered the time of *Truth or Consequences.*

"There has already been too much misinformation manipulated by those who would perpetuate fear to control the emotional growth of humankind. Therefore, we will not dwell on geophysical changes during this counsel. Know that there is a plane of expression where these occurrences will manifest. But there are many other planes of expression which will be realized. For you are destined to a grand reality. You have now entered the final labyrinth. You must now escape the traps of your own perceptions of limited existence. As you move into your foreverness, you shall break the spell of mortality.

"It is possible to see the probability of your future events, what you call prophecy. We will, therefore, remove the veils and illusions of time to speak of your potential future events. The intensity with which any of these events occurs will be determined entirely upon the level of awareness of humanity, individually and as a whole. There has been much evidence of humankind's awakening. However, we must remind you, it is much slower than current events require.

"Already, natural events upon the planet and in your heavens are occurring that can no longer be slowed. Nor can there be any further intervention to encapsulate humankind's consciousness to prevent the playing out of the dramas of their own self-destructive tendencies. This is the final gateway to the self-realization process. You yourselves have dictated the rules of the game, so to speak, long ago.

"What is occurring at this time is no more than the turning of the Galactic Seasons. Humanity is entering a period of unfathomable growth and experience. Your surprised reactions and tendency to regard natural events as mysteries and phenomena, are no more than the *altered egos'* resistance to the natural unfolding of the dream of your own existence within the dream. But remember, the universe has its own dream, and there is a changing of seasons occurring.

The Seed of the Dragon

"Once upon your plane, there were Great Halls where radiant beings from your world and the worlds beyond the Sun taught of these seasons and much more. They were established to help humankind remember their Divine origins. They have, unfortunately, been destroyed through ignorance and fear by your own kind, fear that the ancient truths of your origins might be revealed. Once you also flew beyond the Sun and interacted with these beings. Even now your domain goes beyond even their knowledge. There are no beings in your heavens greater than you. There are no beings lesser, either. Understand your home and you will understand your universe. In the higher understanding, they are one in the same.

"The knowledge once taught freely through the Great Temples and schools established by your elder brothers still exists within your world. One of the last of the great halls of records was gathered from various locations and taken into Alexandria. For it was here that certain factors of the Pythagoraus and Isis would come together to create that which would come to be called the Druids. Some of these records were taken to Rome by the Caesars. Upon the demise of the Caesars, what records remained were then taken into the safekeeping of the Church of Rome, where they still exist today in the catacombs beneath the Vatican and other sanctuaries throughout Europe.

"The great libraries once kept in Alexandria were never destroyed by fire. That story was part of a diabolical conspiracy intended to conceal knowledge of your Divine Origins. These thieves of knowledge were tyrants who sought to rule over the masses and possess and cloister the halls of records which they knew held the secrets of your beginnings, as well as the doorways to your possible future experiences.

"Those who removed these records, however, were not trained in the ancient laws, or in the use of such knowledge. They were not of the old race; they were of a newer race of humanity upon this plane. They were given unto violence, constantly struggling against the war within. They feed upon fear; it is the war of their genetic heritage. Within them is what the ancients have referred to as the *"seed of the Dragon,"* and it would rage against the more peaceful side of their origin. So in conflict was the strain of DNA which was manipulated within their beings, that the inner conflicts would cause a kind of insanity to manifest, and the war of the races was loosed upon your plane.

"Once there was a time, a period of experience, where momentarily all consciousness that was upon the plane of Terra collapsed. It was a shift in conscious reality. This shift, however, was caused by experimentation with the forces of nature by the Atlantians, in an attempt to harness and control the very power of Terra itself. A huge rip in the time space continuum occurred due to their experimentation. The affects of this experimentation were devastating.

"Many dimensional planes were opened, and all manners of conscious expression had access to entry into your plane of reality. Entities from the many layers of dimensional realities that exist began to merge into this dimensional plane of expression. There was complete chaos. It was the Sirians and Andromedans that came to your aid; later others joined in the struggle to rebuild the light grids which contained your consciousness, under the direction of your higher selves, the source of your thoughts. All expressions are from thought, and all thought is from the source, the Creator -- all is one and the one is many.

"Throughout this plane there were beings that had taken on grotesque forms of expression as the grids collapsed and merged into unnatural states of union upon each other. There were frequent instances where many embodiments merged into one single embodiment in the confusion of order that resulted in the collapsing of consciousness. Also, there were beings of the lower dimensional expressions of this plane that manifested, threatening the higher order of expression that was intended. Many of these manifestations became the dark forces that frequent your mythology -- werewolves, werebears, griffins, and such.

"In the rebuilding of the Consciousness grids to enable life to express upon this plane and find a way to restore the natural order, there were many experiments that took place upon the higher octaves of expression. Many new life forms were created, as life as it was prior to the shift was altered forever.

"It was during these times that temples of beauty were built and constructed to facilitate the work of those from beyond the Sun. You would know these structures as the Pyramids. Within them, the damaged waves of the electromagnetics could be overridden and life forms placed back into a natural relationship to the expression of reality here. In these temples, it was possible to connect with the flower of life, which existed within the great Halls of Amenti, which lie beneath your Earth's surface. The inner Earth remained untouched by the events that took place upon the surface. Through this connection, it was possible to correct some of the damage that resulted from the catastrophe that had occurred upon your plane.

"With these experiments being conducted within the temples of beauty, new life forms were created. Among them a new form of human was also created. From Cro-Magnon would come after several attempts at creating a new embodiment, Homo-Erectus. Within it's embodiment, although possessing more density of structure than the previous embodiments created, it was possible to activate the genetic coding of the then 12 strains of DNA from the original species of beings of the galaxies who participated in your original creation and expression through physicality, or matter.

"These genetic codings are what comprises the intelligence capacity of the DNA structure, which governs our ability to express in life form, access frequencies of consciousness, and express upon various planes of dimensional realities. Later, with help from the Sirians and

Andromedans, the number of strains reconstructed throughout the races of humanity within the DNA would be expanded to the number 22.

"The destruction of life upon this plane, caused by tampering with the natural forces during the latter part of the Atlantean civilization, was quite extensive. Only a few survived the surface destruction, and a few sought refuge within inner places. To most, those who sought this inner refuge were thought to be vanished, even to those from the stars.

"Numerous times, it was attempted after the destruction of Atlantis to develop a new form for expression of the human consciousness upon this plane, each time without satisfactory success. The foundational DNA strains which were needed to maintain human consciousness would ultimately break down, and humanity would be reduced to operating upon insufficient numbers of functioning DNA strains. Along with the effects of radiation from nuclear pollution, mutated beings developed. The attainment of Christ Consciousness was further from realization.

"It was elected by one group of Orions, those that were aligned with the God Jehovah, to place into the embodiment of humanity, which still dwelled upon the surface, the seed of the Dracos. The Dracos were reptilian in origin and this was done as they held claim to the original creation of physical life forms upon Terra. The Dracos, it seemed, had an immunity to the radiation. But again, this was a reptilian race, and the man-beast upon the plane of Terra were mammalian. It was felt that they were experimenting with Neanderthal beings, and that the success or failure of their experimentation with this race was of little consequence.

"It was felt by this group of Orions that by including the genetic strain of the Dracos it would help create a stronger, more resilient and more adaptable DNA composite. One able to resist the radiation from our Sun, which seemed somehow to be mutating the life force and causing regressive patterns within the DNA and mutations in the cellular structure. This was rendering the surface dwellers to an existence of having little more capabilities for evolved consciousness than the existence of the beasts they lived with.

"The seed of the Dracos was originally taken from deep within the depths of Terra. There from the great temples of antiquity, they would take the seed from the embodiment and the consciousness of the ancient beings, in secret, without the knowledge of those Gods; those aligned with the God, Yahweh, who worked with the Children of the Sun. But these attempts also seemed to end in failure.

"Finally, a method was derived whereby the seed of the new man was taken up to the great ships that were numerous in the heavens at that time. There, the seed was to be impregnated into the womb of Orion females and a new strain was created. The new strain, Homo-Sapiens, was greater in its resistance to the radiation than the previous hybrids.

"This new hybrid strain was then brought down upon your plane where it was again interbred with the original. It was hoped that this new genetic strain could survive the extreme degree of radiation which was upon your plane in the time which followed the destruction. What was found by those who observed this new strain was that, in fact, the resulting entity developed levels of consciousness often possessing qualities that their creators did not understand because they did not possess these same abilities.

"Earth, it seemed, had her own agendas. This new human was manifesting its own form and consciousness. Many of them were disappearing into the wilderness, where they were developing their own societies and interbreeding with those indigenous to Earth. They began to present a very real threat against the rule of their creators who desired Homo-Sapiens to remain subservient to them. Their intent was, after all, creating a slave race. The new human was a conquering species that could not be contained, either within the physical or within its own consciousness.

"Measures were taken to curtail the potentiality of this new strain from becoming a threat to its benefactors. War broke out against the ones who were developing their own societies, and they were pursued by Jehovah's ships. The future generations would be dealt with through genetic manipulation.

"It was programmed into their DNA that in the formation of their structure, the hemispheres of the brain would develop into two separate halves, without possessing the ability to develop neuronal connectors necessary for communication between the two. Thus, the thinking process was permanently disabled, and the new human was condemned to live within limited consciousness accessibility. Further, emotional implants were programmed into the species, and thus placed within the actual grid that contained the consciousness that created their cellular structure at birth -- holographic implantation.

"These early species of your kind stood little, if any, chance against the superior technology of their overlords from the stars, who were mainly the lords of Orion and Serious B. In essence, they were programmed to develop into little more than a slave race, capable of only serving their creators. Man fell into darkness. Only a natural order of nature could be hoped for to correct what had been done.

"The radiation combined with a natural tendency of the original Cro-Magnon genetic strain to come into violent emotional conflict with the new strain introduced in the Orion experiment, and altered the pattern of life in a not so favorable way. Although Homo-Sapiens continued to multiply, they possessed an insatiable craving for conquest. When matched with their abilities for adapting technology to enhance their endeavors, they were afflicted with the tendency towards killing of their own species, which ultimately created such a degree of insanity they would even destroy themselves. They were war machines.

"The Gods of origin eventually discovered what Jehovah and his forces had done Together with Yahweh they intervened, and Jehovah warred against them. There took place a great war in your heavens, and many accounts of this war can still be found written upon the living stone by your peoples.

"Initially, Jehovah was defeated. He and his forces were driven off from Earth and this solar system. Many of the Seed of the Dragon perished in the destruction upon this plane as a result of that great war. The priests of Jehovah sought refuge in the Caucasus Mountains near what is now Russia. They presently are waiting for the return of the forces of Jehovah, whose ship is nearing your solar system as we speak. It is known amongst your peoples as the Red Comet.

"Beneath what is now the steps of Russia, they continued to work with the seed of their heritage. They developed huge complexes over the centuries within your inner Earth, which to this day they maintain and still interact with their relatives from Orion. Many of the ships seen in your heavens are of these peoples. They have huge machines which bore under your Earth, often causing it to tremble upon the surface.

> *"Although Homo-Sapiens continued to multiply, they possessed an insatiable craving for conquest. When matched with their abilities for adapting technology to enhance their endeavors, they were afflicted with the tendency towards killing of their own species, which ultimately created such a degree of insanity they would even destroy themselves. They were war machines."*

"After a time, those who were the original inhabitants of the surface world of Earth began to return to the surface, and began to repopulate in isolated areas of Earth. The descendants of these people today comprise many of your indigenous peoples.

"Through the waging of their wars and conquest, the Homo-Sapiens have interbred often times over the centuries with the indigenous people, who returned to dwell once again upon the surface. Through interbreeding, they have taken on the appearance of being very much like those who remained upon the surface. But within them, the *seed of the Dragon* always dominates their behavior. They can be known quite easily through their eyes. They are a race with little emotional development.

"This new species of Homo-Sapiens was very industrious and given to a fondness for technology, with an addiction to material worship and a strong drive for violent displays of behavior. War, rather than peace, became their obsession. The history of their civilizations has been built almost entirely around war.

"The new species harbors a deep and relentless hatred for those who possess any connection to the original races created by Yahweh. Their history has been one of genocide and warring upon all others around them. When there remains no one left to conquer, they create wars amongst themselves. This strain cannot, it seems, exist without war. They do not possess the natural ability to access the hidden doorways to the ancient knowledge that could only be opened through awakened consciousness. Therefore, they continued to dominate the masses by keeping them in a state of controlled ignorance, employing reigns of terror and savagery, relentlessly trying to find those who came from the remaining schools of knowledge -- one in Europe, four in Asia, two in Africa, and six in the Americas. Thinking that through conquests and torture, such as what was exacted during the Inquisition, they could force those initiates they found to reveal the mysteries held within.

"Specific vibrational codes and formulas are the only access to these doors of higher knowledge. In time, these codes will again be brought out from their hidden locations in consciousness so that humankind will have access to their hidden heritage. Humankind *is* truly Divine in concept, and they possess abilities to command the natural forces of the universe. You are the Children of the Sun; gods in amnesia. You have not *been* forgotten; you have simply forgotten yourselves.

The Transmutation of Humankind

"It is necessary, at this time, for humanity to realize the full significance of Earth's entrance into the Photon Belt. This event is pressing very near now, and it will soon be upon you. The ancient ones, from whom you are descended, held the knowledge of this event so sacred that they carved it on living stone so that future generations would have access to this information. They were aware that the spell of mortality would take deeper and even deeper hold over humanity, causing them to experience an almost complete state of amnesia.

"We will attempt to touch on points with you that, when translated to the written word, will still hold a degree of understanding that is understandable for those who are experiencing life in the lower vibratory fields. This is very difficult to accomplish, as we know true language is *felt* and not heard. Thought, received and translated through the brain, is greatly filtered by the altered ego, allowing for very little recall of the actual *experience* of thought communication.

"It is recommended that once you have experienced these words, you go out and affirm these truths through documentation. In other words, the proof of what we say is available to those who are willing to search. If it is important enough for you to have proof, you must use your personal *will* to find the evidence.

"Earth is already emerging into the Photon Belt, even as this message is being rendered, although this is not openly acknowledged by your scientists because they do not yet understand the impact on human existence. Therefore, this is not a possible future event, but an occurrence presently happening. By and large, people are *feeling* the effect of this entry and not *seeing* it, and as a result, they are attributing their feelings to anomalies within their limited ability to access information and thought.

"Movement through the Photon Belt has occurred many times in your evolutionary experience upon Planet Earth. It has occurred even before the first civilizations developed on Earth. Earth is the remnant of a previous world destroyed by greed and competition. This is where the Lucifer Rebellion had its beginnings.

"Prior to your entry into the actual Photon Belt, Earth will pass through what is being referred to as the "Null Zone." In many ways, this will act as a preparatory adjustment for your planet, allowing for a relatively mild transition as much higher octaves of vibratory reality merge with the archaic consciousness, which is presently solidifying. Your atmosphere needs constant manipulation to keep it from, quite literally, crystallizing.

"You are being made ready to adjust to existence within the realms of the full light spectrum. You are actually transmuting, to allow the final emergence. This is quite natural; even those who express upon your plane as the animal kingdom and the plant kingdom are experiencing the effects. It really takes very little thought to know if the sun is shining. What is important here is your ability to function within the expanded light spectrum, for as your evolution is accelerated, you will come closer to the goal of reuniting with the higher octaves.

"Simply said, you are completing the dream -- you are waking up. With our help and the help of your brothers and sisters who have gone beyond limited reality, you will have the option of retaining full memory. This is your sovereign choice.

"There is an Armageddon, of sorts, that is already occurring in your heavens. The results of this has yet to filter down through the lower octaves, where you, the Children of the Sun, the Children of Light, are working on your end of the project. You knew all about these events and all the probabilities prior to entering this physical expression on the Earth plane. In a manner of speaking, you are like migratory birds, following an inner instinct, a flight path, yet you do not consciously know why.

"The following points should be realized before we continue. The individuals who are uncomfortable with the term Ascended Masters can corroborate this information with the prophecies of the Mayan people. Their prophecies are quite accurate, and their knowledge of your solar system and its relationship to the universe is very advanced. You would also be well advised to study the prophecies of the Hopi, the works of Zecharia Sitchen and Nikola Tesla's work with energies. Compare these with the "discoveries" about to be announced in your media.

"Thought is the cause and creation of all manifestation upon your plane. Action always follows the thought when the thought is embraced with emotion. The outward or physical realities you experience are merely the final result, equal to the intensity, intent, and degree of completion of the thought through its process. You create the thought; you create the reality.

"The more you are caught within the confines of social consciousness, the more you are trapped in the spider's web; hence, the more impossible it becomes to untangle and see the true potential outcome of events. For when caught in the web, the nature of the outcome is governed by the thoughts of the masses, rather than our Divine Reason within -- the Source, the Father that is in all things.

"All social structure, as it presently exists, must and will crumble -- even structure which you consider *good*. They are all based on the old paradigm which is fast outgrowing its usefulness. The very nature of reality is advancing into the new dimension. As you approach the Photon Belt, all physics and all mathematics, which is currently based on the concept of cause and effect and the magnetic planes, will alter.

"You will be pressed to seek new ways of expressing your need to live in community and relationship. This means that all concepts that presently reference human relationships must be altered to merge with a new, unlimited existence. This is the merging of humankind with your Divine inner nature, the Christ. The harder you hold on to archaic ways of thinking, the faster they will seem to crumble within your grasp. This will be very disconcerting for some, to say the least. But humanity is inevitably aligning with Christ Consciousness, the Mind of the Father.

"Expect your present governments, municipalities, communities, and even your own families, to split apart for no apparent reason. It is quite evident that a fracturing is occurring throughout your entire global consciousness. Some of this fracturing is due to natural causes. But there are those who, if you are not operating from your God center, will succeed at manipulating your race for their own purposes. Keep in mind that when there was an agreement reached to extend your time space experience, both sides were given equal access to influence your reality.

"*Thought Creates Reality*. This will be expressed to you, over and over. You must accept the simple truth that you draw your own experiences to you. When thought is embraced with emotion, it creates! If we passionately express a thought in chaos, it will bring chaos. *Like draws like.* The external manifestations in your life are the sum and total of the human drama you are presently experiencing. Perhaps it is not what you feel you are thinking in the present moment, but what about your thoughts two or three days ago?

"In the coming days, some of you will feel like puppets being manipulated by higher forces. Many will feel possessed. This sense will affect those who continue in patterns that place the responsibility for their actions upon external forces. External reality is just their essence connecting with the greater consciousness from which it comes, forcing them to realize, through experience, their own reality and position in the Divine Order. The result will be an expanded theatrical display of human drama. Human drama is what was truly meant by "the world being consumed by fire". This is the fire of unresolved thoughts and reckless displays of human emotion. Some people will experience the manifestation of their thoughts almost instantaneously, as the artificial time/space matrix continues to collapse.

"Humankind has experimented with the time/space continuum many times prior to the 1940s and the occurrences that transpired on the USS Eldridge. This experimentation goes back to the pre-Atlantean times. There will be some confusion, from time to time, as several of these artificial time/space continuums merge during the frequency adjustments.

"Human drama is what was truly meant by
"the world being consumed by fire."
This is the fire of unresolved thoughts and
reckless displays of human emotion. Some people will
experience the manifestation of their thoughts almost
instantaneously, as the artificial time/space matrix
continues to collapse."

"Currently there are Seven Great Seals located within your physical bodies. Their number will expand to twelve to accommodate the greater frequency that you will need to facilitate your light bodies. You are becoming a new species, in spite of yourselves. Mother Nature will have her way in the end. Life will seek itself and transmute, adapting to new environmental conditions as it requires.

"Your chromosomes are being adjusted to accommodate the incoming Christ Consciousness. This is being done slowly, over the next decade. Not all manipulations of your genetics are done with intent to harm. There will be a complete transformation of your present DNA structure, which is already occurring. The present number of chromosomes within the human cell will expand six to ten times. This is necessary to accommodate the magnitude of the Christ Consciousness. Within the next twenty years, many of you will have reactivated up to 22 strains of DNA within your cellular structure.

"The effect of the Manasic Radiation Belt has been ordered to be kept hidden from you by your world governments. This belt, which now encompasses the whole Earth and is now merging with a radiation belt that already exists, is the result of the accumulation of nuclear waste due to experimentation and explosions on Earth over the past fifty years. This belt is extremely toxic and volatile, and it poses a very present danger to all life forms on Earth.

"This Radiation Belt is a major cause of the global warming that is occurring, certain forms of cancer, and the death of certain life forms within the other kingdoms of your plane. These life forms are essential for the balance of life on this plane. As a result of this destruction, many of the life forms which presently exist upon your plane will not continue after the transformation of the planet is completed.

"The Manasic Radiation Belt is presently descending into Earth's atmosphere and merging with your stratosphere at an extremely rapid rate. Just a few short years ago it was over 750 miles from the planet's atmosphere. Now, due mainly to the openings in the ozone layer, in some places it is already merging with the air you breath. Hopefully, the full effects can be stalled until your brothers from beyond the sun are allowed to successfully dematerialize it without causing harm to life forms here upon the Earth.

"There are many mutated reactions beginning to surface within the social consciousness of the human societies of the world and these are a direct result of the Manasic Radiation Belt. This is causing mutations in the forming of the Protete, which is the universal building block of all life forms within the Earth Plane.

"ALL YOUR STUFF WILL COME UP. You are being shaken to the very core by the higher octaves entering your plane of perception. These are raising the level of consciousness on the planet at this time so you can merge with the fifth and even sixth dimensional realities. Uncontrolled emotions and behavioral patterns, some of which have been suppressed for many life times, are rising up. They must be released to enable you to merge with the incoming consciousness.

"There is an overwhelming sense of malaise permeating the consciousness of many of the Earth's peoples. This is a necessary, unpleasant side effect of transmuting and existing on multiple levels of reality. Your ancient ones, like the Anasazi and Mayans, spoke of these times when humankind would walk in two worlds. This feeling of unstable core belief patterns within the inner being as you begin to exist in consciousness within multiple levels of consciousness, causes friction within the dual circumstances of the mind.

"For instance, there are overwhelming feelings of friction and agony being expressed from the female of your species against centuries of male dominance and patriarchal tyranny. Many of the males are already losing their sense of self-identity. Among others, there is a dark, foreboding fear that the world is about to end, which is exacerbated as they see the social structures and roles they have played out for so long aligning to the new energies and no longer holding traditional substance and order.

"Unfortunately, many of your youth are becoming increasingly violent, committing self-destructive acts with no thought to the future consequences -- further indications that the human dream, as it is presently being expressed, has reached a point where it will go through a jump, a critical mass. Critical mass causes the jump. It is inevitable that at this time humankind will evolve into a new Human. We could call it *Neuvo Galacticus-Magnus*, Divine Earth Being; a living composite of many races from the Stars.

"Your thought absolutely creates. Your thoughts create, absolutely. Absolutely, your thoughts create. How many ways can it be said? Every single thought ever created is still woven within the framework of human consciousness. This is what composes the Social Conscious Grid that ultimately defines the limitations of your perception.

"Every individual personality trait is going to be revealed. You are experiencing isolated, *seemingly* real events in the unified field of reality in which everything is occurring at the same time. Your life is simply an event in your own time/space continuum, which is a part of the much larger whole. Likewise, the universe is undefined and limitless, so is it infinitesimal and unique. As above, so below. As with the universe, so with you.

"All the pain that was experienced during the destruction of Atlantis -- which occurred over a 150 to 200 year period -- is currently being released and felt by every human being that had an experience there. The emotional response to this frequency is affecting everyone and everything around them. This means it also affects the bodies of land which still, to this day, carry the emotional vibration of that experience, as Earth prepares to undergo yet another change.

"All of this is being released on a global level. With every breath you take, you are exchanging cells (one to the power of twenty) with all of those who are now or have ever occupied this plane. That is over one million cells per breath. Perhaps this can begin to explain where all those strange thoughts are coming from about past lives. It is not madness; it is the universal human memory unfolding at an amazing rate of speed.

"Currently, the feminine energy is raising on the planet. It is reviving after a very dormant period. Like Spring this energy is very vital, and is the cause for much growth and excitement of the life force. Earth is *de-structuring* its blueprint of order. The social implication of this occurrence can be witnessed everywhere in your daily lives.

"The understanding of this experience cannot be fully realized until humanity, as a group, can differentiate the difference between male and female energies, and the physicality of the "*Male body*" and the "*Womb of Man's body*" -- Woman. They are two completely different concepts. Physicality is tied to your sexuality; the energy aspect is connected to your Spirit, your God, your very essence, which is constantly pouring forth from the Source of all Life.

"As human beings, you possess the qualities of both male and female energies. You must balance these if you hope to attain Christ Consciousness. This place of balance is too often mistakenly expressed as androgyny. This is a misinterpretation and incorrect language. One may still express through the embodiment of the *Man* and *Womb of Man,* without distorting the perception of these energies through the limited understanding of the body physical. Both genders are, in the Divine sense, one and the same. Male and female are just two sides of one reflection. They each possess the same capacity for lust, domination, competition and fear. Social consciousness has simply *trained* you to dramatize it differently.

"We are discussing energy, not physical gender. Despite where you come from or where you are going after you no longer express in the physical body, you are neither male nor female; yet you are both. You come from eternal *Isness* and you return to eternal *Isness,* which is God. This level of understanding is hard for most to grasp, because humankind has adopted to hold to a concept of subjective reality rather than objective realization that they are a part of the whole.

"We are dealing with energy here; and that is what must be dealt with if you are to understand the deeper truths of your own being. There is a dire need to end the conflict between male and female energies, *now.* Once that is achieved, the human drama will play itself out in natural alignment, without conflict. Your nature is Divine; conflict is not necessary. It is a self-imposed condition.

"There is too much emphasis on sensuality in your society, and not enough on spirituality. You must cease all inner conflict. As it is now, you as an individual, and society as a whole, are a house divided. *You are so much more the stuff of spirit than the flesh.*

"To open to the love of Creator, God I AM, you must first know yourself and love yourself. God I AM dwells within the creation of the body, while you are in a body. God is neither male nor female -- God merely Is. Love what you are. That makes it a lot easier to know what you are. When you know what you are, then you can know what God Is. Live the ideal in your everyday walk and you will have accomplished what the Master Jesus came to teach you in his time upon your plane.

"Feminine energy will continue to increase upon your plane, and match the resistance of the male energy exerted to contain it. This will be part of your individual experience until these energies equalize. God is to be found in the Neutral Zone, not in the friction zone.

"What is occurring in your emotional experiences, is happening for your own benefit. It is allowing you to release what has been blocking you for many, many life times. You have been dancing around this wheel for seven and one half million years. It is time to let it go!

"Despite where you come from or where you are going after you no longer express in the physical body, you are neither male nor female; yet you are both. You come from eternal Isness and you return to eternal Isness, which is God ... There is a dire need to end the conflict between male and female energies, now."

"Observe what is occurring in Eastern Europe and the Middle East. These areas are notorious for the prevailing dominant male, patriarchal consciousness that is presently ripping humanity apart emotionally. The nature of the destruction in these areas reflects some of the worst violations to human rights that have ever occurred in the history of your plane.

"It should be remembered that this geographical area was formerly the Persian Empire, home of the Philistines. Look to the Bible, if you have no other source, for even there the records of the distortion of human consciousness is evident, for these were the lands of Sodom and Gomorrah.

"You are witnessing the human psychodrama being played out at the most base level -- through war! The lessons in these areas will be hard, and will reach a level over the next three to four years where their drama will threaten the whole of the known world. As it is seen now, it is inevitable that in this area there will be the eruption of a major war, as the human conflicts rage once again and the fighting is renewed. The higher consciousness is almost completely closed down. Simultaneously, fantastic phenomenon having major global impact will also occur.

"This area has huge warehouses of devices that include germ and chemical warfare substances. These are very unstable and are stored in mass quantities. An accident could surely cause the end of all life within these areas. Its physical containment would be difficult given the ease in which world travel is exercised today.

"There are three possibilities for this region. First, if the balance of the principles of male and feminine energies are accepted, then the situation will, of course, diffuse of its own accord. Presently, this outcome is a highly unlikely.

"Secondly, a holographic projection will appear in the skies of whichever deity is held most dear in the hearts of the people. In other words, Mohammed will appear for the Muslims, Jesus will appear for the Christians, and so on, and so forth. This hologram will be manipulated so that the whole world will stand witness. A fiat will then be issued to cease and desist. All of humankind will be able to view this moment, frozen in time through the media.

"Thirdly, this entire experience, including the life forms that created this drama, will appear to dematerialize. Nuclear destruction of the Earth or multitudes of people will never be allowed. Many of the plagues now on the Earth are the result of experimentation done by the so called secret world governments. Many of your new strains of viruses are the result of the war game you have called Desert Storm, where

Last Cry©

billions of particles of death were released into your atmosphere to wreak global destruction on innocent people.

"There is another possibility, however, and that has to do with the Photon Belt. When Earth comes close enough to the Photon Belt, the effects will neutralize your present technology. All we can do is watch the unfolding of events and allow enough time for humankind to awaken and choose another course. If that awakening does not occur, there will be an intervention. This much of the Great Plan can be revealed to the world at this time. Understand, this prophecy is shared with love and is not to be construed to further oppress the peoples of the Earth.

"The Earth's vibratory level will rise slowly, although for some the tension of the increased frequency is already causing disruptive pressure. Individuals with locked consciousness are already feeling their reality tear on emotional levels. You will experience this emotional turmoil through the break-up of relationships, the sudden impulse to move to another career, or even the desire to just pick up and move to a totally new location, leaving behind jobs, family and dreams. These are all actions taken by the God of your being. It is the I AM within you that will not allow you to live in an environment which is not in harmony with your inner being.

"As it has been said in the Bible by the Lord Sananda (Jesus), "With my coming shall the wheat be separated from the tares." This statement is taken out of context from a brilliant prophet addressing the potential occurrences of this time, and it has been abusively misused to cause separation amongst the people. Fortunately, some of you understand that the second coming of the Christ is the raising of the Christ within each and everyone of you, and not the materialization of a single Messiah.

"All social structures will fracture from within as the Earth's vibratory level rises, every single one of them, for there is not one of them that carries forward the whole truth. The ability of institutions to be flexible, open, and honest will determine their future. Those organizations that are rigid and refuse to stretch, grow, and take responsibility for "his-story", are dissolving overnight. This is happening within your state and federal governments, within your world banking institutions, and within your religious organizations. Eventually, it will filter down to your local municipalities and even your own families.

"Institutions, structures of all forms, and all governments based on patriarchal tyranny have fostered thought forms upon the Earth plane that are archaic and dysfunctional, leading humanity towards an inevitable path of self-destruction. You must be aware that there are those heavenly hosts of beings who had a hand in your creation and, at this moment, are laying claim to their property, both real estate and human. This archaic consciousness which has dominated your world for over ten thousand years has served its purpose -- its time is done!

"There are some courageous souls who hold the space between self-destruction and self-realization, but social attitude and the addiction to fear is fast reaching a level where most of these voices will need to seek refuge in the mountains of your world. You are a judgmental lot. There is still time before the windows close. When these voices go to the mountain, it will be to hole up for a brief but turbulent period of your experience.

"To you romantics, you may hold onto love, but also grow in your understanding. It is but a brief time before the prophets of old see the coming of the Golden Age. We hope that those of you who read this information will be among those who choose to persevere.

"Many of you meet someone, merge into a relationship with them and find in a matter of a few months, or in some instances weeks, you have experienced an entire life time. One or both of you will be left in the unfamiliar position of having outgrown the relationship in short order. Learn to pass through these dramas without becoming attached to the outcomes.

"Many of these experiences are being called forth so that you may release the residue of resentments harbored for lifetimes. You are in the plane of action. The human drama must either be totally accepted within each of you or it will play itself out in the physical realm.

"Again, the old paradigms are dispersing. You are experiencing the growing pangs of a new consciousness, similar to birthing pains when a woman is in labor. The new life form is taking its own identity and space in forming its reality within the womb. It possesses its God essence. The two of you are simply momentarily sharing the same body.

"Remember, the true understanding of the balance of the male/female energies can, and must, be experienced within. Only then can they be expressed in the outer manifestation you identify as your life. It all has to do with energy, not gender. Gender is only third-dimensional expression.

"Fortunately, some of you understand that the second coming of the Christ is the raising of the Christ within each and everyone of you, and not the materialization of a single Messiah."

"You must understand that what is occurring throughout your world, on yet another level, is occurring to the whole of the embodiment of the galaxies. It is by no means restricted to just this little planet. Your connectedness to ALL is difficult for you to assimilate because of your limited view of subjective reality, a perception that fosters the concept that Mother Earth is a thing, a chunk of dirt and rock. Humanity has lost its objectivity and its ability to see the whole picture because of the state of amnesia that exists within your consciousness. The consciousness of humanity is ill. It is out of focus. It has been deprived of the nurturing truth it desperately needs.

"Mother Earth is a sovereign being, possessing both her own vision and emotion. She has a galactic family of her own. The meteor experience with Jupiter in 1994 was much more than it appeared. It was impregnation! Jupiter accepted the Divine sparks for the new solar system which will replace this present one when this solar system shifts into a new experience. Jupiter is destined to become the new sun for this region, and will remain within the confines of third-dimensional reality. It was no accident that precisely 21 pieces of the asteroid comet struck the planet. But that story is for another time.

"Several of your prophets have spoken of the appearance of two suns in your solar system. Look to your ancient writings. Some of the remnants of these teachings exist to this day. They are hidden beneath the Great Pyramid in Egypt. They can, and have been, accessed. The Mayan and the Hopi people also possess a knowledge of these ancient teachings. We tell you now the two suns already exist. When your solar system realigns, both suns will be able to be seen from earth as they were in ancient times.

"The turmoil that humankind is presently experiencing is necessary so that you will know, beyond doubt, that life is a continuum, not an isolated event. There are many professing to hold the Christian teachings of the Master Jesus. Many of these people would have you believe that after a handful of years, and within one single lifetime, your soul is ready for judgment, into either eternal bliss or damnation. How is it that such folly and ignorance remain unchallenged in a civilized world?

"The teachings of the Master Jesus, Sananda, were about the Christing of humanity. They were designed and delivered to give hope to the Western culture, so that you would understand there is, indeed, life after death. You were to have learned from Him that death is not the ending, that the Kingdom of Heaven is within, and that God the Father dwells within all of humankind.

"In your desperation to justify your dogmas and petty existences, you have imprisoned yourselves within the walls of limitation, remembering almost no trace of your Divine origin. You have *fallen asleep at the wheel*. You are immersed deep within the spell of mortality, dreaming the separation between time/space events within the universal field of potential realities, as if these moments were all there was.

Re-Birth—Breaking the Shell of Limitation

"Those who have auric vision often say that they see the light around human beings as a luminous egg. This is a good image because, for the most part, you have yet to be born! You are about to experience this birth phenomenon on a global level. You are, in essence, eggs about to hatch.

"The vibratory reality of the emerging Photon Belt is forcing us to birth by breaking the shell of our limitation. You are being freed from your imprisonment of limited existence. You cannot stop the birthing process; you can only live in denial of Life itself.

"Humanity is rather like a wild seed carried by a migratory bird that gets dropped in the sand on an isolated beach. The sand and wind and water thrash at it, but it remains hidden among the grasses that camouflage it from predators. Battered by the wind, some seeds are lost to the relentless rays the sun. The survivors germinate. The winds of change are upon us and the birthing time is here.

"As you break out of your shell of limitation, you will notice a wonderful new world around you. Your wings will dry in the winds. Slowly, like the butterfly, you will move them in the warming rays of your new Sun. The skies above you are filled with hues and fragrances you have yet to see with your new eyes. It will be new and different for you; it will also feel strangely familiar.

"As you break out of your shell of limitation, you will notice a wonderful new world around you. Your wings will dry in the winds. Slowly, like the butterfly, you will move them in the warming rays of your new Sun. The skies above you are filled with hues and fragrances you have yet to see with your new eyes. It will be new and different for you; it will also feel strangely familiar."

"Driven by some unseen motivation, you will look to the heavens and dream of flying. Then you notice that most of the other seeds on the beach have not sprouted. For a brief moment, you will feel compassion, gazing on the surreal landscape of faceless forms, vacantly left behind.

Sorrow will dissipate quickly, however, and your Divine essence will be warmed by the nurturing rays of the Great Central Sun, Alcione. You remember that life can never know death, and you will feel no relationship to the empty shells strewn about the landscape. You will feel the urge to flap your new wings and lift off into the thermals, seeking your foreverness, as your memory returns with each moment, as you remember once again ... you are a Child of the Sun.

"The physics of the Photon Belt dictates that the photon field has no weight or structure -- it is pure, white light. A photon is a particum of light. In its reality, it knows only velocity and vibration. It can, however, have tone, for the movement of light causes sound, which produces color. The entry of the Earth into the Photon Belt will cause the metabolic rate of the entire planet to radically increase. The experience of unusual phenomena will become common place.

"As you merge further with the Photon Belt in 1996 and 1997, there will be many occurrences of light phenomenon. The effect of the Photon Belt will be the restructuring of light as you perceive it. Your will see colors in sunsets and evening skies that have never been seen on the Earth plane during this civilization.

"New species of flora and plankton will develop to help with the realignment of Earth energies, so that life can be supported in it's next stage. Many new species of insects are already appearing, and new crystal formations will occur within the mineral kingdom. These new crystals are formed by the harmonics of the higher octaves.

"Appearances of Light Orbs will become quite frequent, especially in more rural areas. This will happen as our dimensions continue to merge and our brothers and sisters from other dimensions attempt to communicate with us, as the veil between the dimensions continues to thin and fracture. Many will spend their evenings watching the balls of light in their heavens.

"Many of the Old Ones are utilizing this thinning to slip through the veil, to use Native American understanding. The old ways are done, and as the Old Ones realize their time is past and they have done what they came to do, many will slip through this veil rather than experience the ending of life upon the plane they loved so much.

"Your solar system is already speeding up its rotation and velocity of orbit through the universe. A few years ago, Earth was traveling through space at a speed of approximately 8,000 miles per hour. By 2110, your solar system, if it stays constant at the present rate of increased velocity, will be hurling through space at approximately 234,000 miles per hour. This rough illustration might help you understand the speeding up of the time matrix on your planet at this time.

"When the Earth enters the Photon Belt, there is a point where the Earth will leap into light speed. Know that there are those from the higher octaves of reality who will assist those who choose to get through this energy shift. When the actual shift, the jump, occurs, those who hold to Christ Consciousness, living in love and light, not imprisoned by dogma, will experience a slight shifting of realities, almost as if they were waking from a conscious daydream.

"There are many prophecies relating to the Days of Light and/or the Days of Darkness. You have been given little information that is accurate and does not impose fear. This event is being used by the preachers of doom and gloom to instill fear into the masses. That is because the orthodox deliverers of this prophecy have little understanding of the physics of the higher octaves and are caught in their addiction to superstition and religious dogma.

"Prophecy is information delivered about possible/probable future events. Whether a prophecy is possible or probable is up to you! Prophecy is not the foreboding warning of an existential occurrence. The prophecy that fulfills itself is a failed prophecy. It is a failed prophecy because those that heard it did not heed the message. In its failing, it has become future memory.

"Returning again to the effects of the Photon Belt, there will be either days of light or darkness, depending upon whether the sun or the Earth enters the Photon Belt first. If it is the sun, its expanding molecular structure will turn into pure light, a moment of brilliant light, many times its present light. As a result, your planet will be in a nebula, and the sun will change its structure. This experience will last, in your current perception of time, approximately 110 of your hours. If, on the other hand, the Earth should move into the Photon Belt first, the entire consciousness grid of the planet will experience the pure darkness of the great void for approximately the same period of time. During either of these scenarios, the expansion of consciousness will occur so rapidly that human consciousness will be, momentarily, unable to assimilate the influx of knowledge and you will *pass out*.

"The Earth is actually slowing in its rotation. Eventually, Earth will seek to return to its original and natural rotation—counter-clockwise. This fact is evidenced in many of the ancient temples. During the time of what is called the Age of the Pharaohs in Egypt, your Earth was still rotating in this counter-clockwise manner. The reason for the altered rotation is due both to manipulation by extraterrestrial forces and cataclysmic occurrences resulting from experiments by the then ruling civilization, the one we call Atlantis.

"It is not certain exactly when this rotation reversal will occur; we know only that it is eminent. When this event happens, for a brief period of time, your Earth will actually stop rotating. This could happen as

Jupiter is being birthed, which would result in intense light, much brighter than the present sun is capable of emitting.

"While it is hard to determine from where we are, it appears that you will emerge fully into the Photon Belt near the year 2009. The reactions within your emotional field will be extreme. The human drama will intensify and you will find that gaining control over your emotions will be of the utmost importance while you will play out the effects in your personal psychodrama. There is no longer a leisurely road to enlightenment.

"Your dreams and thoughts are more real than the cold steel of a sword. There is a reality beyond your present logic and your pictures of reason. You cannot reason the occurrences of this time with the intellect. In the higher understanding, thoughts of the Divine and thoughts of a lesser nature are *felt*. Feeling will become your new-found wisdom.

"The true language of the God I AM within you is experienced through your emotions, for emotions are the language through which you feel and Source expresses. This is the language of the Angels. You have neglected these regions for a very long time. The use of intellect alone is as archaic as the steam engine.

"Linear thought does not exist in the higher octaves.

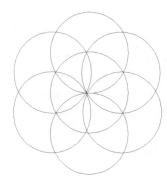

THE PURGING OF THE DARK FORCES: THE EMERGENCE OF EARTH INTO THE FIFTH DIMENSION

"The Dark Forces are losing ground. They are running out of time -- the window closes without discernment and they are aware of that fact. It is imperative to their objective that limited perception continue, for their kingdom resides in third-dimensional reality and they know they will descend, so to speak, when the shift occurs.

"These Dark Forces feed upon your negativity. They need your fears, your anger, your passions and obsessions for sensuality and self-destruction. They need these emotional reactions. Your negative emotional reactions are the grist in their mills. They use those emotions to perpetuate the spell of mortality in which you are all enmeshed. This concept of mortality has been twisted by organized religions like a vise which crushes you.

"These Dark Forces are not real in the higher sense; however they are a real manifestation of humankind's altered-ego, and a manifestation of their altered reality. Therefore, those souls experiencing existence within the confines of the human reality, can experience their effects. These are thought forms that have been given life, so to speak, by your great attention put upon them, your focus of energy that fuels their reality in your plane.

"Their nature is that of a collective consciousness creating an illusion. They possess no form, nor individual life essence. They are an aspect of humankind's unbalanced consciousness. As you approach the Photon Belt, these thought forms will dissipate. However, there are many who hold onto this form of negativity as a source of justifying their limited reality. Let us use the example of a person suffering severe hallucinations. These visions are very real to them, though those around them can see nothing and consider them the ravings of madness.

"The choice is yours whether to hold pure mind or altered-ego. An important distinction must be made here. Pure Ego is the God Force, altered Ego is the *"man-u-factured"* force. You must qualify and quantify your thoughts, now more than ever before in your experiences upon your plane of reality. In some ways, the energy of the dark forces is more real, more infinite, than your physical bodies -- because you have given them your power through your belief in them.

"Remember the principle of the Universal Law, like draws like, the Laws of Attraction. What you express through your thoughts, what you declare through the emotional experience, what you judge, so shall you become. The universe is simply affirming your declarations. For even though in your present state you are not in full awareness, you are still powerful Gods. The essence that is within you, the one having the experience, is pure GOD I AM.

"There is a new Earth being formed at this moment. Presently it is existing within the confines of the fifth dimension. In this time, a separation of the wheat and the tares will occur. Those who choose not to move forward with their natural evolution, clinging, instead, to the old forms of limited thought of tyranny and oppression, will stay behind. Those who will not move beyond the imprisonment of their own creation, by their own choice, will stay behind and begin anew. Perhaps they will join the rest of you once they have completed the cycle again, growing in their awareness, into full ownership of their Godhead after the next cycle.

"The new energies coming into the Earth plane will allow for many to be able to read each other's thoughts. This is already beginning to occur. Clairvoyance and prophetic thoughts are beginning to become a common reality. You, like your brothers from beyond the sun, will have little need for spoken language. Language will become something you experienced in the limited world of your past. What you think, so you are. You will no longer be able to hide behind the many guises you have created in this past experience, nor will there be a need to do so.

"You will soon become more aware of the fact that time is an illusion. The artificial time/space matrix created during the time of Atlantis, was created to enable humankind to hold onto some semblance of their consciousness. The final days of the destruction of Atlantis were of such magnitude that there was little hope that anything would survive on the surface world.

"After the sinking of Atlantis, there were many years of nuclear devastation. It was during this time that you remember the Inner Earth and your sojourn there. That period lasted some 580 years. After that time, you emerged into this world, the Fourth World.

"What you express through your thoughts, what you declare through the emotional experience, what you judge, so shall you become. The universe is simply affirming your declarations."

"Confusion will reign during the remainder of this Century. All over the globe, people will rise up against tyranny. Souls even within the most primitive of cultures are realizing that no matter what their color or degree of technical knowledge, they are GOD I AM.

"The rise in frequency level among people will cause the final downfall of the tyrants as they struggle to hold onto the control they have exerted over the world. This is a contest of consciousness. One force pushing to control what is occurring naturally. There will be a brief period where, in your urban areas, a monastic political force will try to dominate. They are also waiting for the merging of time space continuum to occur, and they will call themselves, brazenly, the "New World Order".

"But this One World Government will be short-lived, for the control will slip away from the tyrants quickly. Great polarities will become more and more apparent, as the world observes, through the eyes of the media, the crumbling of social structures, religious groups, and sciences.

"The forces of the universe can not be reversed. As the Shift of dimensions continues, only natural states of reality will prevail. ALL manifested forms of illusion created by the *altered-Ego* will crumble within the next decade following the millennium. All synthesized items that are a part of this altered consciousness will actually vanish from this plane. Therefore, those who might not have your best interest at heart are themselves governed by the window.

"The Hopi have told their children, "Close the doors and windows, and under no circumstances look upon the outside world until the shift passes." The collapsing of the artificially created time/space matrix will truly be a sci-fi experience.

The Breakdown of the Existing Social Structure

"As fear spreads throughout social consciousness, most will also be drawn to their addictions, as polarities intensify. Those needing intense involvement with people and conveniences will be drawn to the cities. Those in the spell of the fear of total collapse of the global society will seek refuge in the rural areas, where adjustments are hard to make. Coming to terms with your obsessions can be very uncomfortable, but it is necessary at this time. Vast numbers of humanity have become strangers in their own world, let alone their own *being-ness*.

"As the current world religions continue to breed separatism, there will be a great fracturing of spiritual beliefs, not only from others who hold a different view of God, but from those separated from God. The belief that *He* is out there someplace, hiding in a piece of real estate called Heaven, designed for a very special elite group is quite a preposterous point of view. Nevertheless, this belief has spilled over into your perceptions, leaving you feeling separate from one another -- the chosen and the not chosen.

"Many racial conflicts will arise in America, and your media will feed this drama. This mistrust and separation will turn into religious madness, reminiscent of the Salem witch hunts and the insanity of the Medieval Inquisition. Again, most of the truly awakened spiritual people are already aware of this. They are getting prepared to go underground, and they will be hard to find. They will find a safe place in the mountains and just *be* allowing the drama to unfold.

"Inner city social structure will return to the gang and War Lord system comprised of social outcasts and marauders. This aspect of Orwell's book, 1984, will become a reality. The cities will become virtual confinement areas for these less desirables. Very shortly, cities will be quarantined. You will be told that this is in the interest of national health and to protect good people from the undesirables. The people will buy into it.

"Those in positions of power are already creating communities in rural areas where they plan to retreat. This will become apparent in about 1997. They will attempt to control your sources of water and woodland game-filled areas. You are already being monitored by those little devices that enable you to communicate through your cellular phones, facilitated by the little orange orbs a/k/a repeaters for cellular phones. The farm lands will offer little shelter as they are already heavily monitored and under corporate domination.

"International borders will break up and the American military will create situations that will support their need for unobstructed power. Soon it will become impossible to travel from state to state without the National ID card, which will soon replace the existing debit system.

"A National ID Card, called "The MARC" is already in use by your military. This is to evolve into an international card prescribed by the New World Order, all of which is manipulated by world bankers. This MARC will also become the means of exchange. America will be a cashless society before the end of 1998.

"As the dimensions merge and the time/space matrix collapses, many will question their sanity. Many who think they have had an abduction experience have actually simply experienced this collapsing and merging and don't know what it is. As these experiences multiply, it will be impossible to suppress public knowledge of them.

"The artificial reality created for purposes of control, left behind by the extra-terrestrials from the Wormwood Planet, is breaking down. It was their intrusion into our natural evolution that genetically altered our path so gravely. The beings from the Wormwood Planet regard you as they would cattle (which, by the way, is a genetically created breed of being). Your government leaders are preparing you for the release of information concerning the Wormwood Planet now approaching your solar system.

"The breakdown of this artificial reality will leave you feeling weak and vulnerable. The sanctioned religions will not have the answers for you. This is where the indigenous people will help. In their genetic memory they hold the knowledge of the original teachings. The

Cogi in South America, the Hopi of the Southwest, and other nations that were here before the tragic intrusion of Columbus, still remember and can teach you.

"The corrupted order of the Jesuits of the Catholic Church in Rome, above all other sects, have access to the thousands of artifacts and writings that were the booty from their pillaging of the indigenous people of this land. In America, over a five hundred year period, over fifty million people vanished from the face of the Earth in one of the most senseless displays of barbarity in the history of humankind. Some genetic strains were forever erased from the physical plane during this invasion.

"The responsibility for these violations will eventually wreak havoc for those offenders, and it will inevitably become apparent that many of you played a role in that time. Humankind has been fumbling with the natural order and has thrown their consciousness out of balance. As the Hopi say, *KYANASQUATSI*, a world out of balance. Mother Nature herself has created an alternative plan. She would not allow the total demise of indigenous people from the genetic pool of the Earth.

"The breakdown of social structure will be complete, total. No leaf will be left unturned. But the indigenous people who carry the genes of mixed blood will be charged with the influx of energies of the Christ and they will awaken to the ancient truths that are buried deep within their genetic memory.

"In America, these mixed-bloods are called Metis. In this particular blend of genetic consciousness, you have Cro-Magnon (the original species before the genetic tampering) and Homo-Sapiens. The gene of the Metis will be in alignment with the natural vibratory rate of the Earth, and many of the ancient wisdoms will be awakened within people with this blood. The weed is always stronger than the hybrid. It has not lost its natural ability to adapt to new environments or harsh conditions.

"It is through the mixture of the cultures and races in America that doors will open for a blending of consciousness. Through the gradual assimilation of blood, a new race of man will inhabit your planet after the transition.

"The puppet governments of South America will cease with the collapse of the world banking system. This will allow for a change in social conditions and many will return to the natural ways of their ancestors. This will not be a hardship since more than 95% of the people currently living in the areas impacted by this change now live far below the poverty level.

"Events will assist the Seventh Manu, or the new strain of human, to come into full development. Already you are transmuting into this new species. The ancient Earth energies are fairly intact in these South American areas, although there is a potential danger in the cutting down of the old growth forests that have kept the consciousness of nature in balance. The climate and the consciousness in the mountain regions there have been held intact since the existence of the ancient civilizations.

The Manipulation of the Magnetic Poles— Full Consciousness Self Destruction

"The magnetic poles will shift. Many beings from the planet Sirius are already working on this problem, trying to slow down the effects. In the past, the pole shifts have been manipulated by renegade tyrants from the Wormwood Planet. The Wormwood Planet has also been called Murdoc, or Marduke, and Phaeton. This manipulation of the shifts has not allowed Earth to return to its natural rotation, which has contributed to the state of unconsciousness that exists today. The result is that you have been purposefully kept in a state of amnesia.

"At best, humanity has reached the stage comparable to adolescence in consciousness, not quite over the final hurdle which would enable full consciousness to bloom and full memory to return. Previously, when a civilization reaches this point, a self-destructive mechanism automatically kicks in, so to speak, and the pattern of growth halts. Previous civilizations decayed from within at this point and destroyed themselves. Since the time of Atlantis, it has been the fate of each civilization to bloom but for a brief moment, and then decline after only a few years of great achievement.

"Perhaps you are already aware that the level of consciousness of previous civilizations far exceeds the current level on this plane today. We have not achieved the level of technology of past civilizations. We have not surpassed the art of the ancient Greeks, nor are we capable of the architectural feats created in ancient Egypt. We cannot travel on laser ships like the ancient Mayans did. These comparisons illustrate our relatively limited achievements.

"In the past, those of the Wormwood Planet have kept your planet under control through force. This has been accomplished by switching the natural direction of your planet's rotation. The natural direction of your planet is counter-sunwise (counter-clockwise), rather than sunwise, or clockwise.

"The current sunwise rotation of Earth is unique in your universe, as your scientists are now finding out. Earth develops a natural tendency to correct itself every 3500 to 3600 years in your counting. This is, essentially, how long it takes for your solar system to totally reproduce itself through physical matter, much the same way your body does through the process of cellular regeneration. This total regeneration correlates with the reappearance of the Wormwood Planet, whose inhabitants are quite like farmers coming to check their crops. But guess what the crops are -- the human race!

"In the past, the manipulation of the magnetic poles often caused severe geophysical changes. Frequently, humanity was totally annihilated as a result of the extreme changes in frequency. If there were survivors, there was also much chaos, and consciousness suffered radical shifts as a result. This is the reason why some civilizations appeared mysteriously out of nowhere, and why others disappeared without a trace.

"Consider the new information from the Sumerian Records and you will see documentation of such occurrences. Search the petroglyphs of early America, and you will find evidence of some of the early people and even drawings depicting the great wars between the brave ones who stood in defiance of the Lord God Jehovah and his reigns of terror and exploitation here upon your planet. Even the severely edited and altered Bible still speaks of the Nephilim, who were in league with Jehovah's tyranny upon your plane. They are, indeed, much taller than your present manifested form.

"Did you know that your Dead Sea was once a beautiful region? Its shores were inhabited by a great people who remembered their origins and stood in defiance of the Lord God Jehovah. There were many, in those times, who still possessed the memory of their Divine origins and knew well the nature of the grand experiment that was being conducted upon the Earth plane, the Cradle of Christhood.

"When the initial wars with Jehovah were over, renegade parties returned with the Ark of the Covenant. It was the most terrible weapon ever devised, possessing inexplicable capabilities of destruction. It was buried on the Plain of Sharon and will be discovered again, but not before the consciousness of the planet is fully awakened. At this time the weapon will be dismantled once and for all, forever.

"Those who had the courage to stand against the God Jehovah were destroyed in a flash of laser-like rays that could, and did, melt entire cities into living stone. The destruction was so complete that, even to this day, many of these places are, for all intents and purposes, devoid of life-supporting energy. This happened over three million years ago!

"There was a second destruction upon your plane during the Atlantean experience. This concluded in a nuclear explosion that left the surface of your Earth devoid of life for a period of almost six hundred years. Only those life forms which could seek shelter within the confines of the Inner Earth were spared total annihilation.

"This was when the Pleiadians had guardianship over your planet. They had, however, become decadent and tyrannical in their rule. The beings of the Inner Earth manipulated volcanic eruptions in an attempt to transmute the damage from the nuclear explosions, but there was too much damage.

"First, the animals ventured into the newly restructured world. You were warned about the possible dangers from radiation to your bodies and your consciousness. With the help of your forefathers from the system Sirius, a layer of protection was developed against these rays. You call it the ozone layer.

"The ozone layer has been damaged recently by the abuse of fossil fuels and chemicals, threatening the life forms of the entire planet. As a result of this damage, the Sirians, and other like-minded beings, were allowed to intervene, and this intervention continues to this day. This was done to allow your continued development, so that you might be able to fulfill your destiny to attain Christhood.

"Over the past five hundred years there has been a noticeable decline in your electromagnetic field Your electromagnetic field could be likened to the screen which holds the frequencies by which the holographic image is projected by consciousness. Another of the effects of this condition is causing erratic fluctuations of your magnetic poles.

"This is actually quite a normal occurrence, and the poles do fluctuate from time to time on all planetary bodies, including your own physical body, throughout the universe. The fluctuation of Earth's magnetic poles, however, is due to the breakdown of the artificial electromagnetic grids that were established by your forefathers -- those which were established through the placement of pyramids and the Atlantean crystals.

"This, combined with the incoming effects of the Photon Belt, which activates Scalar Energy waves, will cause a severe disruption of energies over the next five to seven years. This is becoming more and more evident and will continue to affect you more and more. (Have you had computer problems lately? What about the instruments in your plane?)

"As you approach the Photon Belt and align with the natural Earth energies, this is causing an increasing of the metabolic rate of the Earth. As She readies Herself for emergence into fifth-dimensional reality, these occurrences will escalate. In the end, the archaic technology currently being used by the industrial powers of Earth will be neutralized entirely. Your scientists are even now attempting to utilize HAARP in attempts to control weather, but it can not stop the Shift.

The Truth About Gods, Governments, and Little Green Men

"Many ancient truths will be revealed within the next five years of your counting, upsetting what your world societies would have you believe are the stories of your origins. An ancient pyramid will be discovered in Turkey. It will appear near the surface as a result of Earth activity (earthquakes) there. It will be discovered nearly intact and will reveal the technology used to build the pyramids. We will learn of their magnificent nature, their intricate design, and their precise architecture, which has yet to be achieved in your contemporary world.

"Information will be discovered beneath the Great Pyramid in Giza that will reveal your Galactic origins. These truths will shatter the misconceptions that have manipulated you throughout this civilization. Through their discovery, it will become evident that you have been here for a very long time and that you have interacted with beings from other galaxies from the beginning. This evidence will shake the scientific world.

"Your concept of extra-terrestrials will be altered far beyond your present comprehension. Evidence will be discovered that they have lived amongst you in many civilizations before this one -- civilizations whose grandeur and beauty shadow anything you can imagine in this present world. A discovery in Alaska will reveal an ancient advanced civilization there that existed there before the last shifting of the poles.

"The truth about Jehovah's reckless, irresponsible, adolescent, and warring nature will be inarguable. The true relationship between the Gods will be unveiled, and you will come to understand the true intentions of Lord God Yahweh, ID, Ishmael, and many, many others. You will remember much and through consciousness, as you begin the process of reconnecting with your Star Brotherhood. All in all, it will be a splendid show.

"There will be many more landings of inter-dimensional craft beginning in 1997 and 1998. The frequency and visibility of these landings will make it virtually impossible for the world governments to continue with their present policy of *official denial*. You are being prepared through a manipulation of the media for the visitations, and you are being readied for the government's admission of their cover-up. That is why you are seeing so many programs and movies about UFOs and aliens.

"The contracts your governments made with the aliens during the Roosevelt, Truman and Eisenhower years are running out. Under contract, your governments "sold you out," so to speak. Your governments were given technology in exchange for non-interference and easy abduction of the population.

"These contracts run out in 1997. This is why the Hubbell Telescope was placed when it was. It is actually an early warning device to warn you about the return of the Wormwood People. Remember the Hopi Prophecy. It refers to the final days and says, "one of the signs of the End Times is when they build a house in the sky." Well, it's there. It's the space station, and there are people living aboard it right now.

"Soon the truth behind the dissolution of the Soviet Union will be known. The Soviet Union has spent billions of dollars on research on the subject of extraterrestrial life and other paranormal phenomena. The truth is, they were ready to announce their discoveries to the world. Secret meetings were held in South America and Switzerland, and the decision was made by the leaders of the New World Order that this was premature and the results might disrupt the plan for the New World Order. The simplest solution was to dissolve the USSR, and this was accomplished within 90 days. An entire nation was dismantled for the purpose of withholding information until a more convenient time.

"We will not dwell upon the acts of inhumanity to man, nor the oppression that will be attempted by the World Government. According to the terms of contracts written fifty years ago, the government is to deliver control of the mass population to alien interests. Your world will be run essentially by alien beings, while a privileged few who consented to the agreement are permitted to enjoy the wonders of the new technology.

"Certain things have not gone as planned. At the time of the agreements, neither your consciousness nor your technology was capable of discerning or understanding the information about the shifting of the poles, the existence of the Photon Belt or the Wormwood Planet, and the underlying intentions for Earth's inhabitants, much like what happened to the native Americans of North America in the nineteenth century.

"All attempts by the World Government to show defiance against these alien beings have met defeat. However, there is now help coming from Sirius A, the Andromedans, and other inter-dimensional task forces. They have surrounded the planet and have successfully prevented full-scale retaliation against you on several occasions. The Nephilim and others who are aligned with Jehovah are determined to harvest all they can by their own free will. They intend to continue manipulating the consciousness of those who they regard as their personal property.

"The Sirians have enjoyed a long and sometimes painful co-existence with human beings, the Children of the Sun. They were among the first beings to help with the development of physical embodiments that could survive the conditions of the planet.

"Earth was not the first home of human beings. You had origins in the Pleiades and on the planet Mars. Each one of these cultures grew self-destructive, due to their competitive natures. When you inhabited planet Earth, you needed an improved model, so to speak, one that could exist in harmony here. This was after the destruction of the stratosphere which caused the waters to fall to Earth, causing the creation of the great oceans that you have to this day.

"The Sirians that were here were from a water world and so they had the necessary experience to undertake the task. Consider, if you will, how it is that your bodies are basically designed to run on an electrical network that functions in water. Human blood is, after all, basically the same composition as sea water. Essentially, you are fish that can survive on land. You are far more closely related to the dolphin and the whale then you are to the ape. Once again, this will be realized as soon as the pyramid of Turkey and the underground chambers and anti-chambers of the Great Sphinx are explored.

The Rise of the Anti-Christ

"The Anti-Christ will possess the knowledge and abilities of an avatar, and he will seem to perform miracles. His emergence into world prominence will be a signal to those who work in the light that this is the time for them to step forward.."

"Within the next seven years, the impending effects of the Manasic Radiation Belt will be announced. This belt is presently merging with the Earth's atmosphere. The Manasic Radiation Belt is interacting with the Earth's own radioactive waste that has been released into the atmosphere after multiple nuclear explosions over the last fifty years. The effects of this contamination are now evident within the Earth's inner atmosphere, affecting everything from trees to oceans and rivers.

"Earth and your solar system are rapidly moving into the Manasic Radiation Belt, and as a result, the planet is experiencing global warming. This radiation is also creating increased deformities within the human consciousness. Ironically, as the planet is warming and the ice caps are receding, there is a scarcity of water and drought in many areas.

"Although some Humans who are feeling the effect of the Manasic Belt are definitely moving in the direction of Christ Consciousness, there are many more reverting to Neanderthal Consciousness. This is especially obvious in the cities where there is pollution, as well as manipulation of the population through constant inundation of electromagnetic frequencies. The expansion and contraction of human consciousness will intensify the geophysical changes as dimensional realities merge.

"Your religious institutions will have no answers, and their failure to assist people during this time will act as the catapult for the emergence of a being who the desperate and gullible general masses will decree as the "Savior of the World." This false "Messiah" is already amongst you. Remember, YOU manifest your fears.

"This "Messiah" is approximately 35 to 40 years of age and, although he is aware of certain abilities he possesses, he has not yet been thrown into the role of Messiah. It is the mass consciousness and the constant creation of the events, over and over, that will occur in the drama of the Armageddon, that will cause much grief to those who cannot let go of this thought pattern. It will be the their own patterns of thought, through the laws of manifestation, which will bring forth this false Messiah.

"The emergence of the Anti-Christ will coincide with the renewed outbreak of war in the Middle East. At this time, the world societies will become paralyzed by fear. It is the very patterns of their beliefs in the Armageddon that will call forth his being. He will be viewed as a last hope by the crumbling religious organizations that will fall around you. Although his reign will be short-lived, he will be regarded as a spiritual wonder by millions, and he will emerge as the crowning glory of the New World Order. He will be a charismatic politician, spiritually advanced in his grasp of ancient knowledge. He is being trained by the negative side of the surviving mystery schools, what you might call the Dark Brotherhood. Through these teachings, he is being given a very powerful understanding of the forces of nature. This is the Dark Brotherhood's last attempt to control billions of vulnerable people, as the final days of third-dimensional reality come to a close.

"It is the increasing intervention of extraterrestrial forces in the next three years that upset the plans of these dark forces, however. Eventually, this entity will be confronted by these ambassadors of the galactic legions. The years between 1997 and 1999 will be years of great revelation, as the awareness of the masses expands to comprehend the presence of this extraterrestrial involvement in your world.

"Ultimately, the true nature and essence of this Anti-Christ, who is no more than a master manipulator of human consciousness, will be revealed. This Anti-Christ will possess the knowledge and abilities of an avatar, and he will seem to perform miracles. His emergence into world prominence will be a signal to those who work in the light that this is the time for them to step forward.

"As those who work in the light use their abilities to access a level of consciousness that aligns with the Christ Consciousness, they will expose his weaknesses and cause him to return to his true natural state, as he is confronted with an energy of a non-destructive nature. This effort will be unified and accomplished with the assistance of those from the higher octaves, in an attempt to preserve the hologram of human consciousness.

"It is necessary, as you bridge the dimensions and enter fifth-dimensional existence, not to cause the destruction of the alternative Earth. The alternative Earth must be saved as a landing pad for those who do not choose to embrace the fullness of Christ Consciousness. These light workers, in cooperation with the Grand Council, are slated to dismantle the Manasic Radiation Belt. Through the understanding of the higher octaves of human consciousness (the Christ), they will create a natural group Merkabah around the planet Earth to allow the final stages of the transformation to take place.

"It should be noted here that your planet, as a living entity, has already evolved into the fifth-dimensional vibratory field. In her nurturing way she has never given up on her children. She is allowing humanity to move ahead by their own free choice at this time. All of the galactic bodies in the heavens, even the stars, possess consciousness. All is connected to the Divine Source.

The Re-Emergence of Beings from the Inner Earth

"As we draw closer to the year 2000, the people of Earth will witness the re-emergence of those beings who dwell from within the Inner Earth and the Hollow Earth. These are the beings who helped you in your transition after the destruction of Atlantis. Some of them are human, the ones who chose not to return to the surface world after the destruction of Atlantis. These beings have evolved far beyond your present ability to understand science and technology. For the most part, they rely on the abilities of the mind, rather than external technology and devices, as you have chosen in your reality. They have chosen a parallel path, but they are connected to you in consciousness.

"Many of the ships you will witness in the heavens are not the ones created in Nevada and New Mexico with the assistance of the Grays, nor are they, for the most part, inter-dimensional craft. The majority are the ships of those who inhabit the Inner Earth.

"The Inner-Earth beings have monitored our development here for eons, and they have their own agreements with the Nephilim. Although they also possess superior technology, like the Grays and the Nephilim, they are a peaceful people whose origins have well-established links to human beings through genetic lines. These beings are also preparing themselves for the emergence into Christ Consciousness.

"The beings of the Inner Earth have often been sighted on Earth. They are known as Yeti or Sasquatch. These are the beings who appear at Mount Shasta, who come and go through the "windows" in some of the vortex areas of the southwestern and the northwestern United States. They interact and communicate with the Trans-Himalayan Brotherhood, the Ascended Masters, and with beings from beyond the stars. Unlike those of you on the surface, they have not fallen prey to the artificial reality in the biosphere. By your current definitions, they would be considered immortals.

"There have been countless experiences with these beings reported throughout England, Ireland, Siberia, and South America.

While their existence is accepted with only mild interest in these countries, they are at least not the subject of sensational tabloid attention as seen in the U.S. Much evidence is purposefully being withheld from the American public by the American media.

"For example, in 1994 over a million people witnessed a UFO over Mexico City. Also during that year, many government officials and tourists visiting ancient sites in South America simply vanished. There were two major volcanic eruptions that year, so large they threw pumice stones the size of small boats into the waters off Mexico. Almost no news regarding these occurrences reached the American public. Why?

"The people of the Inner Earth have remained an enigma throughout most of our history. The reality is, they simply chose not to participate in the destructive consciousness of the surface people. On the other hand, the people of the Hollow Earth, a land also known as the "Land of the Smoky Sun," are a very ancient race of beings who have inhabited this Earth from its inception. Inter-dimensional by nature, they possess tremendous powers of the mind. Their form is not like yours at all. These are fifth level beings who have no desire to experience the limited reality of those who chose to emerge onto the surface world.

"Your government in America is aware of their existence. It was the government that sponsored Admiral Byrd's exploration of the North Pole, where he was taken into their world. His private journals speak of his encounters and that material is available from several sources. Why, you ask, have we not heard about these beings through the media? Why have they not made contact with our race as a whole if they are truly so advanced?

"Consider this. With all the prejudices between the peoples of your world, based on different cultural and spiritual views, why would advanced beings, who do not choose to control you, expose themselves to such a savage race of destructive beings? We are not yet ready to hear them, let alone accept or appreciate their existence here. Remember that it has been less than one hundred years since the chief mode of transportation for humanity was the horse.

"If you cannot overcome your own self-hatred, why would you be expected to act differently to others from another planet, or from within your own Earth? You must understand, these are beings whose physical appearances are quite different from your own. Be assured, however, that you will witness their existence before the end of this century. As the activities of the Pacific Rim intensify, great ships will emerge from the openings located at the poles of your planet. Also a great ship will emerge off the Western Coast of Central America.

"Another phenomenon will occur. A great funnel of water will rise up from the ocean. At first it will be a total mystery to your scientists. They will identify this phenomenon in the ocean as the "G Force." From within it a great ship will emerge, a mother ship. It will host thousands of beings from the Inner Earth. They will make a statement to your surface world as they, themselves, prepare to leave this plane on their inter-dimensional craft.

"Their ship will virtually block out your sun. It will be witnessed by millions, and their message will be projected to the entire population of the surface world. Accompanying its presence, there will be heard throughout your world a great hum, an Om. The frequency and the methods by which their ships are powered are beyond your present understanding. These are the great light ships remembered only in your mythology. There will be many other ships that emerge by the same method. The region in which this will occur was once your homeland, the land of Mu, or Lemuria.

"With all the prejudices between the peoples of your world, based on different cultural and spiritual views, why would advanced beings, who do not choose to control you, expose themselves to such a savage race of destructive beings? ... If you cannot overcome your own self-hatred, why would you be expected to act differently to others from another planet, or from within you own Earth?"

"Within the next few years racial tensions in the United States will escalate. Initially, this will be a war resulting in great strife in the streets of America. Ultimately, the revolution will swell and include people who are not in agreement with the philosophies of the New World Order. You must use your inner strength to avoid involvement in these situations. Conflicts will be agitated by those who would establish a One World Government. The inner cities will be unapproachable. The degree of human degeneration will produce a state of complete collapse in urban areas, just as the Elders of the Hopi foretold 12,000 years ago.

Excerpts From the Hopi Prophecies

"In these times (end times), many of the people will be as hollow vessels. They will not remember their Mother, nor will they be connected to their own spirits. Man will be living as in two worlds, a dream state -- one dream ending, another not yet formed.

"They (modern humankind) will find themselves lost within great caverns that are made of strange stone and mica; they appear as mountains that touch the sky itself. There will be no connection to the Earth there at all, for everything is stone, even the dark rivers they walk upon. No plants or trees will exist there, and the sun will always be behind a dark cloud. Even the sky will have no color. From inside one of these caverns, you will not even be able to see the mountains or the stars.

"There will not be Human beings there. The people will be as monsters that exist by killing themselves. They will have become worse than wild animals that are sick with the frothing sickness. Still others will be as spirits, not knowing their bodies, having no tie to the Earth -- or its people.

"There will come a day when a Great Star appears, so bright that it will outshine the sun. When this happens, the people of this time will stare into the sky, for there has been no day and night there for so long. And upon seeing the Great Star, they will become filled with fear. Then in a moment they will disappear, as smoke rising into the sky. It will be as if they never were.

"Then the Earth will bury what these monsters have created. She will make herself clean. There will be the purification of fire, of water, and of the winds, winds that will blow down the mountains of mica. Even the air will be on fire in those times. Only those who sought refuge in the mountains, kept away from the sickness, and held the memory of our ancient teachings will have survived. Their numbers will be few.

"As you approach the year 2000, many regions of the United States will expel noxious and highly explosive gases. This will result from the movement of the tectonic plates. This will be so intense that your government will have to severely restrict the use of combustible engines.

"Your weather experts will create a new term -- *Fire Storms*. The air will literally catch fire. This will be caused by natural elements and the tempering of the Earth's atmosphere by the raiders from above.

"There will come a time during this next decade when a different kind of fire will be seen in your skies. It will appear as if the whole of the sky is engulfed in flames. This, however, will be the reaction to the massive shifting of the dimensional fields which will happen when you come fully into contact with the Photon Belt. This fire will be cold in nature, and is what is meant by those who have seen visions of the Red Dawn. This phenomenon will be similar to what some have experienced as St. Elmo's fire. It is the field of illusion that you have created around yourselves, literally burning itself up and dematerializing.

"There will be many such displays in your skies in the coming times. These will be hard times of adjustment for many. However, humanity will survive. As a whole, humanity is creating its own experience. What is not understood by enough of you in this time is that each individual's thoughts *will* and *must* manifest. They always have; they always will.

"You have known about this event and been in preparation for this time for eons of human development. You knew about it when you were Angels. The human reality is only one of your dreams in the Unified Field of Eternity.

"The key to making it through these times is your ability to get out of your own way, allowing the God Force, the I AM, to do its thing. There is too much belief in the notion that you must be in control of your human destiny, when in fact, humanity has never really been in control of anything -- especially itself.

"There is nothing to achieve and no place to go. It is more important to *allow* reality to occur, to be in the world, but not of it. There will be many people losing it all around you, but that does not mean you have to. If the energies of a particular place or relationship do not harmonize with creating your happiness, then acknowledge that, and break your patterns of creating the limitation and allow the change.

"If all you did was follow your joy, you would find that things would work out in your lives with much less resistance and friction. Part of being out of balance is the resistance itself. If something isn't working out, or if your relationship is failing, it might be your God desperately trying to communicate with you, to change your situation. The situation might just be your attitude.

"If you want to love God, then you must first love yourself. For it is within yourself that you and God meet. It happens every day. It has been happening all your life, but you've excused it as madness and run away to linear reality.

"If you want to change the world, then change your attitude. Become unlimited. Think about it. Even with everything occurring within the human drama, humankind has never been so free. Now, it is only a thought that can bind you -- only a thought!

"Desire and thought are one and the same. What you embrace with your thoughts is what will manifest in your future. Your bodies are, after all, simply recycled minerals, water, air, and fire. What gives these elements life is what we call *the great mystery*. The key to harmony is in understanding and dealing with your emotions.

"All fear is simply the fear of the loss of immortality, and mortality is only a thought -- a concept. You are eternal Spirit; you can go beyond trivial experience and the spell of mortality. You can go on to I AM. All thought returns to the creator of the thought. We are all, no matter the nature of the being, aspects of the Creator.

"The outcome of tomorrow will be determined by what you decide this moment and the actions that follow. The whole of every prediction of this coming time/space event, every prophecy that has ever been foreseen, is all predicated by your decisions and your thoughts. As you enter the Photon Belt, it is your own chosen truth that will prevail. The emphasis must be upon each individual *becoming* and *allowing* sovereignty.

"Interaction with the lesser vibration is also a matter of choice. The fish that does not swim will not experience the ocean. Life was meant for living. You created this reality for experience. Go out into the world; go within yourself. Work at it, and the nature of your reality will change.

"This can be a time of great magic, or it can be a time of great sorrow. What is your choice? Follow your joy, but not at the expense of everything around you -- that is not true alignment with Divine Harmony. Watch your thoughts, qualify them and re-quantify them as you realize their error. Remember, the action always follows the thought. When you truly learn to love yourself and enjoy yourself, then the universe will respond accordingly. It is Divine Law.

"There will be decisions that you make in these times that will be unlike other experiences. Relationships are changing, and the effects are multitudinous. Many times you will find yourselves in abstract situations, with no reference for comparison. Trust in your hearts. You are entering strange waters.

"You live in a 3-D world: Discernment, Discretion and Detachment. You exist in a field of infinite possibilities. You are the one having the thought; you are not the thought. Follow your desire. Use discrimination and discernment, and the results will be in harmony with your thought. You are not responsible for the thought patterns of others, nor are you responsible for anyone else's choices in their time/space event. You have the right to pick and choose your experiences; that is discernment, not judgment.

"Everything around you responds to vibration. If you raise your vibration, then reality will respond accordingly. That which is of a lesser vibration will fall away as you come closer to standing within your truth. Your truth is not in your past experience, nor in your future experience -- it is in *the Now*. If you alter your reality by raising consciousness and exist fully in *the Now*, you will alter the outcome of your future events.

"The old, archaic consciousness that is locked in its own prison will fade with the passing of planet Earth through the Photon Belt. Consciousness will be renewed like a clean slate. What you put into your dreams will become your new reality. Everything in your reality is the result of thought.

"Matter itself is not solid. Matter is particums of light, responding to willful thought. You see a tree and you identify it as a tree, therefore, the energy that makes up that experience responds to your perception as a tree. The shaman who sees it as the God Force, sees a totally different reality.

"How you construct reality is mainly based upon your attitudes. Disease, for instance, is a total manifestation of your attitude. Your attitude determines the degree of clarity in the perception of thought. Divine thought can only be experienced by having no attitudes. The natural state of human experience is joy. When you enter the House of Joy, *dis-ease-ment* ceases to be.

"To heal the mind is to open the heart. The pain you will or will not experience is equal to the love you withhold from yourself. You are the crucial element that causes the whole of your perception of reality to have the results you are experiencing. Tomorrow is going to be determined by the next step you take today.

"We bid you farewell. Go forth with love; know that you are the Children of the Sun.

Aho Mitakyue Oyasin

The Wisdom of Tawa

T he Hopi have shared much of their prophecies about these times, times when we walk in two worlds. There are stories that they tell of our interaction with those from the stars. The event that begins this time translates close to these contemporary Hopi words..............

"When they build the House in the Sky (space station,) this is the signal to us that several other events are about to take place in our heavens, as well as events on Earth that you talk about called the Earth Changes. In those days we will witness the return of the Kachinas. Much will be out of our control, for many of us will have lost our ways. It will seem as though the Earth will be for the taking – everyone will be claiming a piece of Her, even the Kachinas will want to take a piece of Her. But we must remember that all prophecy includes the prophecy of choice. And the prophecy of choice has everything to do with consciousness. Knowing this is what makes us human beings, and not like the animals. "When we see a vision, we cannot say this is how it will be, or it must be this way. We simply say, "Let us see," and we may or may not be given the vision to see what is coming. When we tell the vision to the people, it is their choice what to do. We are only seers, not creators."

Grandfather Martin

The New Sun

Although the creation of a new sun is not yet fully recognized by conventional science, a new sun is most certainly being birthed. It hasn't been publicly announced yet, mainly because science and the consciousness that allows science its dance upon this plane, does not understand it. True knowledge and wisdom of the highest order are first delivered through the human spirit and then *dreamed* into the experience of reality.

During the summer of 1994, a swarm of comets was discovered by our telescopes. These comets were headed on a possible collision course with planet Earth. Ultimately, we were told the course of the comets was altered by Jupiter's gravitational pull. Some people were actually disappointed that at least one comet didn't make its way into Earth's atmosphere, fulfilling an ancient prophecy that a comet would hit the Earth and usher in the full brunt of the Earth Changes.

I was with the Hopi a lot that summer and we watched the heavens. This was not the time, but it was seen as the coming of the Red comet . Hopi don't look at comets necessarily as flying rocks. To the Hopi, and myself I will add, these occurrences are most often seen as ships, not as shooting stars.

However, our scientists are now aware of yet another comet making its way towards the Earth, and this is the one you can expect to enter the Earth's atmosphere. Earth will cross the pathway of this comet in the spring of 1998. The certainty of our running into some of it's debris is very clear. We are in trouble, and the Hopi would agree, only they see the comet as a ship that gets blown up in an encounter with those benevolent to we little Earth beings. They see it as a ship – not as a chunk of space rock.

To the Hopi, the significance of this kind of activity, which occurred to Jupiter, is that it was in direct response to Mother Earth calling for assistance from her own family in the heavens. These comets were, in a manner of speaking, cosmic eggs. They were absorbed into the atmosphere of Jupiter, much like the human womb accepts an egg.

Jupiter is scheduled to become the new sun. These eggs will replace our present planetary solar system when the existing planets go through their transformational process, as a result of our solar system passing through the Photon Belt.

This has been foretold as the reappearance of two suns in our heavens. This will not be the first time this occurrence has been experienced by the evolving Earth species. This was the situation when our current Sun, the Yellow Sun, gave birth to our present solar system. As each planet was birthed, it gave substance to various forms of consciousness. The prophet, Edgar Cayce, gave much information relative to this understanding.

To the Hopi, we already have two Suns. One is hidden behind the present Sun we see everyday. Because of where the Earth is in its orbit, it is hidden from our view. This is why we have Man and Woman in our solar relationship, the nucleus of the family unit. When the change comes, these two Suns will travel with us to the new heaven. Jupiter will become the new parent Sun here. Only Jupiter will not be as our Sun, it will be like the other Suns -- blue. Our Yellow Sun is very rare.

The planet Venus is quite like Earth was before the early lasers of the Atlantean's broke through the cloud cover and stratosphere which incubated the Earth. Before Atlantis, the Earth was a greenhouse under the protective clouds, the fabled Garden of Eden. In those days, the Earth was illuminated constantly by light refracting through the clouds of water that surrounded our globe. When these clouds were ripped apart by the use of laser beams by our Atlantean ancestors (who, by and large, were us) the rains came. These were called the Great Floods and have been written about in all Indigenous cultures.

This cataclysm was partially due to a natural purification process undertaken by Mother Earth Herself. The Earth required purging because the Atlantians had experimented heavily with nuclear power and corrupted genetic experimentation. They partook in slavery and debauchery over the Lemurians. Consciousness had become corrupted;

it was the first war of valued life. The elements of the Earth were in rebellion.

The only natural catharsis was, and is, a long bath in saline solution, or salt water. The devastation that existed in that period of time was far greater than our present nuclear pollution. It was so bad, in fact, that there were many mutations of the life forms upon this plane.

It was during this period of our experience that the Hopi, who were the Fire Keepers within the Temples of Atlantis, took many of us into the safety of the Inner Earth. Here we stayed with them, and the many other beings of the Inner Earth, for a period of approximately 580 years, waiting for the devastation that was occurring on the surface above to balance and for harmony to return to the life forms.

During our time within the Inner Earth, we dreamed the reality that we would later experience as the Fourth World. The manifestation of that, the Fourth World, is the world in which we are currently living. After that purification through water, some of us desired to return to the surface world to experience the new reality which we were partially responsible for creating. Others of us did not desire to return and, to this day, some of our relatives remain within the realms of the Inner Earth. The Inner Earth has sometimes been referred to as the Middle Earth. This should not be confused with the Hollow Earth, or what has sometimes been referred to as the Land of the Smoky Sun.

To this day, many of the openings to this Inner Earth remain accessible. It is here that the Hopi and others meet with the Kachinas. There is some very interesting information that can be obtained from the diary of Admiral Byrd and his encounters with these beings in contemporary times.

The Photon Belt:
Days of Light and Days of Darkness

Many religions of the world speak of a time when we will experience several days of light and/or several days of darkness. It is now estimated, based upon certain recent events, that this time is very near. Perhaps it will even occur before the year 2000, or at least by the year 2005, and by another calculation, 2012. It is hard to tell when this will happen in *linear time* sequence, because the effects of the Photon Belt will neutralize the effect of our perception of time as we now understand it. One thing is seen in a commonality throughout all the seers in the world, this event is an inevitable experience, whenever it actually begins.

There is a great field of light (the Photon Belt) that exists in our universe. Earth has passed through this field of light many times before. Each time has brought about a new world. This is when the Kachinas will return and interact with us again upon this Earth. We now know that this field of light is identified as the Photon Belt. A photon is an element of pure white light having no structure and no weight. It has no polarities because it does not exist within the electromagnetic plane. It is not physical matter, but pure energy.

One of the effects of the Photon Belt, which we are already entering, is the speeding up of time as the metabolic rate of the planet is infused with this energy. This will cause physical matter to become less dense in molecular structure. The spaces in-between the molecules will actually expand.

This expansion is accelerating and this acceleration will continue. The vibrational rate will increase very rapidly. This expansion will allow for more and more light to reach each molecule. The intensification of the light field and the metabolic increase within all life forms will allow our consciousness, and the consciousness of the Earth, to enter new dimensions of reality. This will affect all life forms, even the stones, even the Inner Earth planes.

As our planet Earth continues in its cycle around the central sun within the constellation of the Pleiades, it is moving in a counter-clockwise rotation. The *natural* rotation of the Earth is counter-clockwise. This is why many ceremonies are performed to honor this turning. This shifting of energy should, once again, connect us with the natural rotation of the stars and our solar system. This energy will help us to tap into the memory of our natural beginnings.

So as the Earth moves through its natural cycle, we will once again enter the Photon Belt. Ten thousand five hundred years ago, Earth was on the other side of the Photon Belt. This was at the time of Atlantis, and the pole shifting during that civilization was cataclysmic.

The Earth will again change completely when we enter the Photon Belt. This time we will enter the fourth dimension, the bridge between the worlds. Some of us will go with Mother Earth and become pure light; others will not be able to align with these higher energies, or octaves, and will find themselves on a *New Earth*. On this new Earth, those who did not align themselves with the higher octaves will begin the process of evolution again -- from the beginning.

Those who can raise their vibratory levels will be able to go with Mother Earth, and will experience what is now recognized the world over as Christ Energy, or Christ Consciousness. This is when we enter the Fifth World, which is also the fifth dimension, the fifth octave of the light spectrum. This is where the Masters exist. This is where the Kachinas come from, and go to. This is from where the great light ships come. This is from where the Dolphins come and go.

Our solar system will also move from its present dimensional location to a new higher octave of existence, much like the etheric cities described by the Masters. A new solar system will be born to replace the third dimensional reality that we are presently experiencing. It is during this merging of the dimensions that, for a time, two suns will appear in our heavens. There is even a possibility of three suns for a brief moment in time.

The factor determining whether we have days of darkness or days of light is which body enters the Photon Belt first -- our sun or the Earth. If the sun enters ahead of the Earth, we will have days of darkness. If the Earth enters first, we will have days of light. And for the briefest moment in time, all people, the whole of the Earth, all Her creatures and even the stones, will exist in a state of pure consciousness. This period will last for approximately 110 to 160 hours, as it is now understood in our current calculation of time. So the darkness or light will last from 3.5 to 7 days, but there is no way of knowing exactly, because in that experience, time will no longer exist.

Thε Fiεlds of Enεrgy

One of the differences between this world and the Inner Earth is energy. The reason some of us are able to see the doorways into the Inner Earth, and some of us cannot, is all a matter of energy. Why some can see devas and the great light ships and others not, is a matter of energy.

If you were to take two magnets, one with a hole in the center like a donut, and one that was shaped like a straight bar, and attempt to pass the bar-shaped one through the hole in the donut-shaped one, it will move easily through one way. Turn the bar-shaped magnet around the other way, and again try to pass it through the donut-shaped magnet. It will resist furiously.

Our own energy is quite similar. When certain people enter a room, we can often actually *feel* their energy. Try holding your hand out towards someone and notice that when you reach a certain distance from their physical body, before you actually touch, you can feel the energy of their body.

We perceive this world as solid, but even the great God of science has now proven that it's not. Most of us have yet to catch up to this simple realization. It's all energy. But from the understanding of Don Juan, let us forgive the scientists. They are always coming from behind, looking at what happened, and trying to explain it from the pieces. They actually never had the experience themselves.

The people from the *Inner Earth*, or the *Kachinas*, or the *Ascended Masters*, for example, vibrate at a much higher frequency than do ordinary people. Also, they do not exist within the same magnetic polarity that we do. Their energy utilizes scalar waves more than electromagnetic energies. That is how they appear to walk through walls or the side of a mountain. That is how they travel through dimensions and can travel from another star system in the twinkling of an eye.

There are openings to this inner world. There are places where the Earth's crust is very thin. Although you may perceive it as a rock wall, only your sensitivity to the energies in that place will give you a clue to the fact that something is actually very different there. Objects placed at these sights will sometimes vanish in the brief moment that you look up, distracted by a passing bird. Or a whirlwind may suddenly blow through the site and take your attention. If you make yourself very pure in vibration, attuning to the natural energy of the Earth and harmonizing with it, you may experience the appearance of these beings; you might even be taken on a journey with them into their world.

When this occurs your physical body would be left behind. If someone is nearby, they might think you're unconscious, or even dead, because the physical body is only a shell. Without our *essence*, the body has no life force of its own. That is why when one passes over, and the spirit of that person leaves, the body returns to the elements of the Earth. This allows your old robe to be recycled, so to speak. Another spirit can choose to take up these elements and wear a new robe in their chosen experience upon this plane.

As we enter the field of light, the Photon Belt, we will experience similar energies. We will not be able to enter the field of energy unless we are able to raise the rate of our vibratory field to match that of the Light. Only our light bodies will be able to merge with the new energy. Our old bodies will then be left behind, like shells, at the entrance to the opening.

There are some in this contemporary world who would call this ability Ascension. It is a very old process. The difference this time around is that the whole Earth will be experiencing this energy shift, the bird, the butterfly, the human, the snail.

Everything and everyone around us is like a dream. When you experience these energy shifts, it is almost like waking up from a deep sleep. At first it can be hard to move, or perhaps you will not be able to move at all. That is because you are moving energy, not the body. It will be quite like our current awareness of dreaming. At first you are aware of everything around you, like being a huge eye! With practice, you will slowly become aware of your new body and master its new energy field.

The Pathways

As we enter the final days, the prophecies speak of four pathways. Humankind will have choices. There are several locations where the story of the prophecy is written in ancient stone.

I have elected to share these drawings of petroglyphs which are located in the four corners area of Arizona. It is said by my Hopi elders and I have experienced that these locations are actual portals, or windows to another dimension. The photographs and location of these sites remain undisclosed to protect the sites, from vandals and souvenir hunters. These petroglyphs are older than the Hopi.

They simply refer to the people who left them as the old ones.

There is land in Arizona upon which are the remains of an ancient temple which was also built by these old ones that are well over 20,000 years old.

It was an exciting find when I was shown this particular petroglyph (left) as it was very similar to the now famous petroglyphs near Hotevilla telling of the Emergence into the Fifth World and the possibility of World War III. What is intriguing about this one is that it shows that mankind will have choices as to the actual outcome of our fate as we merge with the Fifth World.

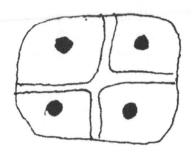

We are shown *Sotuknang* (who was the Son of Tawa, sort of what Apollo was to Zeus) emerging from the Third World. He is leading mankind to the surface of the Fourth World (left.)

Sotuknang showed them of the future and promised them that if they kept to the ways of the original teachings they would have choices at the end of time (the Experiment.) For the world would have been destroyed those from the red land in the south (Atlantis) and was now beneath the great waters. I have heard two versions of the story of the petroglyphs. In one version the balls or globes represent the three shakings or warnings to change our ways . In the other it is said that they represent the first, second and third world, and the ending of the fourth world is represented by the half globes. This also represents the possibility of four chosen outcomes.

One path shows that mankind would lose it's mind by forgetting their original teachings. They would wander in a meaningless world and disappear into the blackness of the void when this world ended.

Those however who held the original teachings close to their hearts would know abundance, would prosper.

But there would be those who would hold on 'to the ways of war,' as a result their transition would be one of suffering.

Still others would find themselves alone, without dreams and the ability to create. So they would become trapped between worlds for an unknown time period.

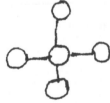

Upon the emergence from the third world each brother had to take their knowledge and go to the four corners of the Earth (left.) They were to go and bring back what they had learned through experience to the circle (medicine wheel) so that the wisdom would all be shared amongst the family of humanity the children of *Tawa* and the Spider Women.

We here on Turtle Island are known as the grain eaters (right.*) This same symbol can also be found on ancient Japanese writings thousands

of years old. They translate to the same meaning 'the grain eaters', or 'the rice eaters'. It could be noted that most of the Pacific coast a few hundred years ago was marshland and wild rice was a main staple of life. It has to do with *Sotuknang* and *Masah* gave to us four sacred grains *[1] Rice, Millet, Wheat, and Corn. These the four brothers took the grain upon their journey to the four corners of the Earth. For from a small handful one could grow enough food for a whole village.

*[1] Detailed information on the sacred grains and their correlation to "the Teachings on the Blood" can be found in the Authors' book, *The Nagual Returns with Kryahgenetics the Alchemy of Self-transformation, Through the Eye of the Shaman* co-authored with Laura Lee Mistycah through Mistyc House Publishing.

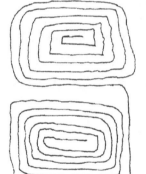

Their path would not be easy, but they were eager to see the new world (left.)   The reality experienced as the Third World was no more, except within the inner Earth. It (*Atlantis*) had been destroyed by greed and competition.

There were many beings (right) that fought in the heavens and tried to dominate mankind in the end times prior to the end of the Third World.

Their path would not be easy, but they were eager to see the new world (left.)   The reality experienced as the Third World was no more, except within the inner Earth. It (*Atlantis*) had been destroyed by greed and competition.

There were many beings that fought in the heavens and tried to dominate mankind in the end times prior to the end of the Third World.

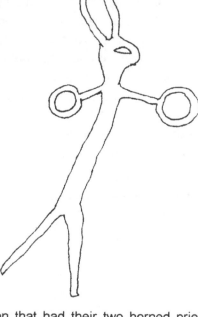

There were those who came from the constellation of Orion that had their two horned priest (above right) that ruled the people in their name.

We had the help of the winged beings (above left) that taught us the original teachings.

These beings are eternal and enter this world through portals (left). They come from the seven universes in light ships (right.)

If the above left petroglyph was reversed, or inside-out, it would be a representation of how we are existing in this dimension. That is why everything is 'turned upside-down." The person shown has reversed their polarity. By reversing their polarity, they are capable of moving in and out of dimensional portals. This indicates that the ability to egress and ingress between dimensional portals is possible.

For they possess a knowledge of energy that we have forgotten (left.)

Soon they will return as we enter the Fifth World. We will be given signs and know of its coming (below.) There will be a great bow in

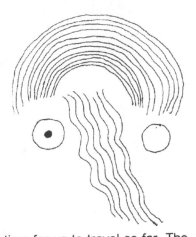

the sky that will have twelve rays, these will be the lords of all the universes. The lords of the seven rays shall surrender this universe to the new age. There will appear in the heavens two suns. And *Saquasohuh* will change the Sun to blue. There will be many changes in this time as we travel through the labyrinth to the new world. We will enter a period of darkness, and

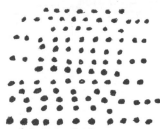

it will take time for us to travel so far. The transmutation will not be easy. The time it will take from when the Twins arrive is Seven years of changes, leading to the purification. Then it will take seven years to become fully awake (left.)

The secrets to the universe could be known to anyone who understands the meaning of the numbers 3, 6 and 9, and how they apply to physics and all the sacred writings. This was also the understanding and belief of Nikola Tesla who used this knowledge to create technology that would give us free energy, and the ability to move things through time and space as well as time travel. There is information that I will disclose in later works concerning the numbers 3, 6 and 9, and how in fact they can be used to decode certain works of history, as well as recreate the music of the spheres.

One of the possible interpretations of the petroglyph below would be the following: The purification of Earth will be by various degrees and achieved by the elements. First Water, then Wind, then Fire. Then the powers that are pure consciousness will change the nature of everything and the Earth herself will move from her belly. Many

new mountains will be born during this time (left.) Some will choose to leave this Earth and go with *Saquasohuh* to the new world in the stars. Others will remain here and start over again. For we will remember the knowledge of the Energy (below) again, which will enable us to move between worlds again, as it was in the beginning when we could communicate with the animals.

An interesting note is that I have found almost identical symbols in China, India, South America, and North Eastern Oregon, and Tennessee. The story seems to be as universal as the symbolism upon the living stone.

The Elders tell us that at the close of the third world and at the emergence of the fourth world, in the occurrence of the great 'star wars' that ensued that those who were given the original teachings were instructed to carve them in the living stone so they would not be forgotten as we would eventually lose the memory of them. From my observations, there is much that indicates many of these petroglyphs were burned into the stone with some sort of laser device.

THE WISDOM OF *TAWA*

The Hopi way of life -- the natural way of life -- Return to the simple ways

Here is where the wisdom of the ancient Hopi people can begin to give us viable solutions. The ways of Creator are simple. Let's start with your personal world, your body.

All the elements of Heaven and Earth are represented in our bodies. The Wind is in our breath, the Trees in our lungs, the Water in our blood, and the Earth in our digestive system. Thunder is in our words, and Spirit is in our minds, and should be in our hearts. Sound is heard with our ears; light (the stars) shines through our eyes.

As light comes from the Central Sun toward Earth, it is known that it passes through twelve constellations. We have twelve main organs in our bodies that are influenced by these constellations. Also, we have twelve energy centers that impact the human body. We identify them in our contemporary world as the twelve chakra centers, or great seals, seven of which are located within the confines of the physical body; the remaining five are presently perceived to be outside the physical body, or located in our Light Body.

To all living things there are cycles or seasons. To each form of plant there is also seasons. Those of us who work with herbs understand their seasons. We understand when it is the right time to harvest them, how the energy moves through them and at what time of day, or in what season they are aligned with the natural ebb and flow of the Earth energies. In the summer there is an abundance of male energy. In the spring there is an abundance of female energy, and so on and so forth.

We used to live in the natural way. Once we were in flow with the Earth and Sky energies, but today we have created a world of artificial environments and it is easy to fall out of sync with nature. Living, as most people do, within buildings and automobiles for the better part of our 24-hour day, we have moved away from our natural instincts. The industrial age brought great mechanical technology, and this has now moved into the age of computers, the technology of the mind. However, in the process of moving away from nature in our relentless charge into technological progress, we have become weak and sick in our bodies. We now lack energy and creativity.

There were cycles in the consumption of food, in order to keep the body, the animal part of us, alive and functioning within the Divine order that Creator meant for us to thrive and evolve within. Our artificial environments leave us diseased. We *are* the Earth. Our bodies are made from the same elements; we share our consciousness with our Mother. So, like our Mother, our physical bodies are also contaminated and diseased, and many are dying from incurable diseases, the plagues.

There are natural energy patterns observable in our universe which surround us, like how a star is born and how it dies. Similar cycles and patterns reflect the universe within our bodies. In falling away from the natural way of eating and breathing, we have thrown ourselves into physical chaos, so it is only natural that the energy moving through our minds, which affects the thoughts that create the cause and effect of our reality, have become distorted.

> *"We are the Earth. Our bodies are made from the same elements; we share our consciousness with our Mother."*

The very source of all life on Earth is the water. It is the birthing place of all life forms. Like our Mother Earth, we also need the waters to be able to function in balance within our bodies. Our oceans and our rivers are the pathways of the blood of the Mother. Our blood is where we transform food into the life source. Human blood shares the same composition as the water in the oceans. It has the same mineral composition and salinity. Like our oceans, our blood has become polluted.

Within our bodies, the ebbing of the tide is synchronized with the pulsations of the heart. Our lungs are the inner forests. By breathing properly we maintain our relationship with the Earth and all life forms. The rivers are our blood vessels, the lakes are our liver. Springs equate to our salivary glands, and the rain is our sweat.

The functioning of our internal universe is maintained and powered by the blood. Through the purification of our blood we can, once again, regain the true state of good health. Through proper eating we can regain our vibratory connections to the stars as well as the Earth. Through the thoughts which pass through the mind, we can regain our natural vibrations and our relationship to the Creator. We can, once again, enjoy a full sense of being.

By bringing our bodies into harmony, we can transmute our food into the higher frequency of the heavens, allowing us to experience the joy of freedom. Only then can we truly experience the great miracle of Creation -- being human, living the awareness that the Creator has taken the very same elements of the field and the ocean and combined them into the living expression of Divine Thought, what we are -- Humanity.

When we are out of balance within our physical bodies, we lack the sense of synchronicity between the Creation without and the Creation within. This insensitivity is the seed of disease itself, and the obvious manifested results are witnessed in the mental instability of the human society and our self-destructive patterns of behavior. There can be no peace without while we are experiencing an environment of inner conflict and violence and perpetuating a diseased universe within. This lack of harmony distorts everything we perceive.

The natural order in the universe is the way of TAWA. TAWA means Sun in the Hopi language, and it also means Moon in the Tibetan language. The unifying force that unites the two is Mother Earth. The Moon reflects the Sun within us, manifested as feelings. Within our bodies, the moon is represented by the sack that encompasses the heart (in physiological terms, the pericardium.) The Sun is represented by our heart. Thus, the sun and moon within the physical body function within a union of Heaven and Earth.

Our Sun is a star connected with all the other Suns throughout the Universe. Every physical manifestation upon the Earth is transmuted energy. This energy, once again, comes from the heavens, passing through the twelve constellations, the cosmic clock, on the way to Earth. This energy is then transmuted into all life forms that grow upon the Earth.

Like the Sun, our heart also seeks the interaction of all our inner Suns. This is achieved through the movement of liquefied sunlight, our blood. From this universal source, everything that grows within our inner world grows and receives life, as the plants in the field receive the life source from the Sun.

The secrets to solving the problems of the world lies within each one of us. Unfortunately, as a human race, we have elected to sublimate our problems with an attitude of acquiescence -- learning to adapt to disharmony and disease, instead of choosing to clean it up and change it. This has become our preferred syndrome because we have chosen the *feel good* approach to healing.

Our present methods of treating disease enable us to *think* we *feel* good, but seldom heal the cause of *dis-ease*. Allopathic (modern) medicine almost always treats the symptoms, not the cause, parceling out pills that mask the pain, while the real culprit goes undetected. Because we have developed an insensitivity to the Laws of *TAWA* (Sun/Moon) within, we have created *Kyanosquatsi,* a world out of balance.

> *"Our present methods of treating disease enable us to think we feel good, but seldom heal the cause of dis-ease. Allopathic (modern) medicine almost always treats the symptoms, not the cause, parceling out pills that mask the pain, while the real culprit goes undetected."*

We have entered the Final Days. We are in a transition. In this transition we are going through the Light. How can we make conscious choices that contribute to the evolution of human consciousness if we cannot utilize our will fully? How can we make conscious choices that contribute to the evolution of human consciousness if we cannot utilize our minds fully? The poor quality of our blood and its impact on our mental ability makes it difficult for many people to determine what is correct. It is hard to know the Laws of Creator in our present state of moral and spiritual corruption.

Our world within reflects human consciousness on a global level. The minds of the world's societies are represented by their governments, and they have all become corrupt. Now it is even proposed that all governments be formed into one central government, A NEW WORLD ORDER. If they succeed, they will seek to control our very thoughts, perhaps even our dreams.

The central governments, as history will confirm, continue upon a pathway that supports a material world which only serves to separate us further with each passing generation from the Natural Laws of Creator. This regression is symptomatic of our addiction to self-destruction. In denying Creator's Laws, we are left only with the Laws of Man, which differ from village to village, culture to culture, belief to belief. All too often our diversity breeds judgment; it is the disease of separatism.

Our *WILL* represents the inner *WILL* of Creator that flows eternally within us, the *WILL* to live. We can, like the plants and stones and animals, continue to exist beyond this transition. We can transmute and connect with the Light from which we all come. This integration of the Light and the Earth is the greatest transmutation that has ever occurred in the universe. Bringing our bodies back into harmony with the Natural Laws of Creator by eating properly, we will be able to regain our connection with the higher vibrations of consciousness and *willfully* integrate the physical and the Light. It is the wisdom of *TAWA*. It is the original teaching.

We can enter this time of emergence with our whole mind, and make the conscious choice to *live*. This is achieved through the simple understanding that we are part of Creation. The fundamental law is to become, once again, One with Creator.

These are the Final Days. The world as we know it is coming to a close. We cannot change the course of events now set into motion. The experiment with the temporal dream is finished. We now face the final test of human consciousness -- to restore our Oneness with Creation. We are going home. It is a process; it is like the seed becoming the green shoot and then the flower.

There was once a wise man who, upon struggling to reach a certain village, asked the Sun to remain in the sky until he reached his destination. His words stopped the Sun and it remained fixed in the sky until he reached the village. The wise man was impressed by his own power, and he thanked the God Of All That Is for his blessing.

That night he dreamed, and came out from his tent and cried to the heavens his lament. When questioned by his brethren as to why, he replied, "Alas I am a fool with my wisdom." Had he truly learned to overcome his fear of traveling through the dark, he would have left the heavens in their natural order, as would the God of all things. Then he would not only be a Wise Man, but a Master as well.

Do not blindly accept these descriptions of possible future occurrences as an immutable reality. Feel them! Come to your own understanding of them. Watch the world around you, for while these things are occurring, only our awakened consciousness can alter the final outcome. If you do not know the most extreme outcome, how can you make an intelligent, willful choice?

IT IS ALL CHOICE. THIS IS THE WISDOM OF *TAWA*.

The Final Days

Creator sends his messengers to us every day of our lives. Very often I hear people say to me after one of my lectures about matters that concern the Earth's well being, or about the latest development in genetic research that has gone awry, causing new viruses to break out, or about galactic exchange between extra-terrestrials and our world governments, they respond to me with:

"Why weren't we being warned?"

"Why were we not told of this? How could this have happened? "How did we lose so many of our rights as citizens?"

"How could the government just give away 18 million acres of our national forest?"

"What will happen when we reach point zero and there is no electromagnetic field?"

Well, when you can no longer hear the sound of your own heart, how can you expect to hear the sound of the heavens? Why haven't you listened to the messengers?

While sitting on the red rocks which grow and rest upon my sacred ground in northern Arizona, I am awed feeling energies from the ruins of an ancient temple they once formed, a temple that is well over twenty thousand years old. I ponder at what these ancient people must have been like. There were once children playing here, laughing and crying. Aqueducts that once carried water to a labyrinth of gardens are still there carved in the living stone, but those people and their civilization have long vanished from human experience.

Sometimes I can hear the laughter of those children, the murmuring of women working within their living quarters, the sound of ceremony rising into the sky from their ancient kivas. These people are so old no one knows by what name they were called. You're pretty old when you are older than legends, older than memory. They are just called the Old Ones by the Apache, and by the Hopi who are older than everybody. The Old Ones -- I can still feel your presence, Grandfathers. It is as if somehow you are still very much here, alive now seeing through my eyes.

I raise my pipe to Grandfather, and we sit in council together and ponder the dream called Life while we watch the setting Sun. We talk of some of the warnings that have come to me, to the world. What is going on? Everywhere I can see the madness within the hearts of the people of this time, the time of the emergence. My Hopi Grandfather, Martin, once told me people in these times, known as the Final Days, will be living in two worlds. It will get very confusing as the Spirit World and the world we walk in come together. But it will only last a little while, just a moment in forever. Laughter will be a good medicine to have in those days.

In 1993 a verbal warning to the Peoples of Earth was given by the Cogi people of Colombian Mountains. The Cogi are perhaps the oldest surviving society of people, still maintaining a presence here in either North or South America. They call themselves the Elder Brothers. They refer to the *Ameripeon* (European-American) societies that presently dominate the global environment as the younger brothers, the brothers who were sent away so that their defiance and irreverent attitude towards the Earth and the guardians would not interfere with the harmony of life. Of course, that was when the Earth was still a lush and cared for garden.

In a recent video released throughout the media's global communication systems and PBS Television here in the United States, the Cogi elected to give their younger brothers a warning before they blindly stumble into a cavern of inescapable self-destruction, causing not only their end, but the end of every life form upon our Mother Earth. You can expect another warning from the Cogi people very soon. They have a new message. You could hear it around 1997 on national media.

This most recent message was born from the very mountain tops of the Earth, the places where the life-giving rains are born. The places where the mountains give birth to the Cloud People are being reduced to lifeless desert landscapes. The process by which the clouds have sustained life upon our planet for eons is now breaking down. The Cogi tell us that if we do not quickly change the way we deal with our Mother, the rains may end altogether. The Cogi Elders say that it does not have to be the end of the world. It is still our choice.

In March of 1994, the Hopi Traditional Elders went to the United Nations for the fourth and final time. They were refused recognition by the members, and no voice has yet been established in the United Nations for the Indigenous People of this land. A letter was sent out through various avenues of media communication by the Spiritual Council of the Hopi Traditional Elders, the Hopi Sinom. In the letter, the people of the World were notified that events had transpired conforming to the warnings of their ancient prophesies. The Hopi Sinom know that we are now entering the Final Days, that all the prophesies had been fulfilled except those that pertained to the final days themselves. What will occur during these times is once again a matter of choice

In March of 1995 thousands of people were sent yet another message. This time the message was given by the Mayan People of Central and South America. At the spring equinox there was to be a grand occurrence. An entirely new light grid was about to be formed if enough like-hearted and like-minded people could be pulled together. The ancient Mayans understood and mapped the cycles of our planet and the orbit of our solar system around the central sun, Alcione, which can be seen in the night skies near the constellation of the Pleiades. This orbit causes patterns or cycles to occur within our immediate solar system that could be referred to as solar seasons.

These seasons have been described through the language of Sacred Geometry by various civilizations ever since our first emergence upon this plane. Here in the Western Hemisphere we have enough of the pieces of this ancient knowledge written upon the living stone that we can assemble the story of our origins and our future pathway through this time of total transition.

We have been told -- "as above so below" -- that our bodies are a microcosm of the universe itself. Indeed, this is a grand truth. The appearance of numerous crop circles are not a coincidence, nor are they manufactured by some radical sensationalist or advanced mystic cult, riding bicycles in the middle of the night. Oh, there are the few of these cases, but most crop circles defy the feasibility of human construction by their very complexity of structure and form. They are indeed messages from our Elder Brothers, of the Inner Earth, those you refer to as the Ascended Masters, and as well there are those that are from our brothers who come from the stars.

Through the crop circles, we are being given the codes to our genetics, as well as information about the changing nature of physics affecting life forms on this plane as we near the great shift already occurring upon this plane of third-dimensional reality. You are being given the doorways to forever. Some of these circles are actually codes given to help the Earth Herself transmute the dense consciousness with which we have bound Her during our long experience in limited thought. Through some of our oldest forms of written communication we are being given specific dates and locations of events and occurrences that affect our future as a people upon this Earthly domain.

Our global climate has already been thrown into cycles that will only intensify in their chaotic nature. The projections for plate tectonic movement and the methods by which the Earth must heal Herself are very linear and quite predictable. Any child can guess the ramifications of global economics upon our present lifestyles. We tend to focus entirely too much upon the negative aspects of these changes that are upon us. We have, for the most part, developed a tabloid, subjective consciousness. Since there is a multitude of sources concerning geophysical changes (some of which are inevitable,) the emphasis here will be on the changes within the individual.

The changes that will have the most dramatic impact on the days to come are those that effect our attitudes and social order, those that allow us our belief systems as a species. Civilization can not exist without a belief system. The embracing of a belief system gives the human being a sense of order, and that is what distances us from the beast -- social order. The emotional storms that humankind is about to experience will require our greatest focus to get through. Structure must and will break up; it will begin within our inner universe. What occurs in the exterior reality is a direct result of the balance or lack of balance within.

This is a time to strengthen your love of self and your connection to the God Force within your own being. The polarization of energies which is occurring at this time is causing the human dream upon Earth to split into two distinctive groups. The result of the culmination of our consciousness to this point of evolution is the emphasis on duality. The two groups are those who are fear-based and stuck in limited mind, and those who are God-realizing and who allow a state of limitlessness to occur.

I suppose Grandfather would say to me, "Perhaps you are confused about the future. Perhaps things you once thought were truths upon which you could rely are now shifting. Perhaps there is war in the hearts of men. This is what has always been the condition. You must decide now if you will choose the warrior way or the Hopi way. We know how things go with warriors, but the Hopi way will always be, as it always has been, the way of peace. Is this not the way of all the great masters - - to follow the Hopi way?"

Realists and Earth Dreamers

The limited thinker is the realist, very often not Earth conscious. These are not the Athenians, these are the Spartans. Instead of the theatre, they go to Wal-Mart. Spirit is something that is okay for Disney and children but, "*I have a corporation to run.*" Thinking that their technology will get them through, they have bought the dream of the artificial reality. To these people, a hike in nature and getting out is walking through the mall, the white man's forest. "*Well that is an interesting concept, but here in the real world.....*" You know the type. You will never change them so give up. Just get out to where there is a little more space to feel and allow.

These people have limited vision. They will not hear you if you are of the other polarity -- the Earth Dreamers. Earth Dreamers see the fantasy, they are basically visual, and very sensitive. This sensitivity can and is often misconstrued for being shy, or even backwards. They are very Earth conscious, and the proximity of the spirit world is their second attention. They are inseparable. These people are usually in constant pain, because the world at this time is not being controlled by the Earth Dreamers, it is being controlled by the realists.

The realist says, "The scientists say it is a comet, they should know, so it is a comet. I have given them my authority to dictate the nature of reality." They have used remote vision, it is now law.

The Earth Dreamer says, "A comet, well maybe....let me feel this a little deeper. Let's use our own remote vision....I know what I see now....by God, it's a ship....How do I know? I have Nature's law within me and the nerve to trust myself. Remote vision—well, I have dream vision." You know this type also. I am one of these types.

"This is a time to strengthen your love of self and your connection to the God Force within your own being."

The polarization of human consciousness cannot be easily seen by most who are caught within the confines of the human drama. It is not often that the fish realizes that it is swimming in the ocean. Most people are like children while they are evolving. They do not see the whole picture yet. We have grown accustomed to existing within the consciousness of subjective reality. Because of this condition, we often find it hard to see the forest for the trees.

Simply by distancing ourselves from any occurrence and not taking on the energy of what we are witnessing, we cease to become a participant in the drama. Then we do not charge the drama, and it goes away most of the time. We continue and succeed when we keep focus upon what we are doing -- fulfilling the dream.

When we take the willful action of not charging the drama, we awaken within us the natural ability to *see* the true substance of what is occurring. We achieve understanding without the filters of mind affecting what is going on in a given moment. Clairvoyance is but an exercise of this ability that has been worked with effort and achieved. The problem with this art today is that a lot of people take advantage of the other guy who does not have the ability. But the charlatan is short-lived and soon discovered. In the end there are no lies.

True sorcerers are not evil by any means; they do not have time for this foolish attitude. Nor is it by parlor tricks that they derive their power. They derive their power from their efforts toward application of consciousness, and maintaining clarity while exploring pure mind. They care little about outside opinion, or whether what they see is going to be acceptable by the masses. They are simply independent thinkers, adept at accessing higher thought frequencies, free from the chains of dogma.

They are *alchemists*. They are aware that thought creates. They are aware that the hologram is sustained by frequency, and everything is impersonal movement of energy. Above all they are mastering their emotion which directs the flow of energy. Thus, they can alter the perception of reality and dimensional doorways, because they are beyond judgement.

Everything is energy. Everything is vibration. The external manifestation we experience in our day to day walk is only the result of the Divine Source expressing Itself. We are realizing this through the higher consciousness and the merging with the higher octave of vibration, the emotional language. *All experiences on this plane are the result of our thoughts, feelings and actions*, which manifest in the external drama according to the intensity with which they are conceived and embraced within us. Consciousness, quite simply, creates the nature of reality.

The Great Shift is already in motion. We are realizing the effects of this Great Shift within our lives as personal shifts. These shifts are being influenced by factors that are presently occurring in our universe. There is a measurable breakdown in the electromagnetic field of Earth and in our entire solar system, including our sun. In the breakdown of the electromagnetic fields which hold matter together, the very nature of reality is changing. The foundations of cause and effect are themselves shifting. We are in the process of becoming Light. We are realizing through experience that all reality, and its forms visible and invisible around us, is the result of thought. We are realizing that thought, like the Photon, has no weight, as well as no structure.

This new realization is causing us to change our present understanding and patterns of thinking. There is a new energy in the plane of third density and the old archaic form of thought process no longer applies. Thought carries a vibration. We can even feel it. We can feel if someone has benevolent or negative thoughts towards us. We feel it in our energy field, radiating from their energy field. So we can deduct, then, that thought most certainly is alive, can we not? Sometimes we feel it even if the sender is physically far removed from

us. So from this realization we know that thought can even travel of its own will. Thought travels via vibration. If we can feel this from another human being, imagine what we feel from a planet, or a Sun, or from a solar system that is going through the throws of change.

"All experiences on this plane are the result of our thoughts, feelings, and actions, which manifest in the external drama according to the intensity with which they are conceived and embraced within us."

Now realize that at this very moment the entire universe is in the throws of change, changing into something it has never been. The implications of this kind of vibrational shifting are limitless. Vibrations strongly effect our consciousness and our ability or inability to access the higher vibratory fields of *Hu-man* awareness. We ourselves are changing into something we have never been.

Many of you have had the sensation that time was either speeding up or slowing down. Time is a product of human conception, a method of measuring the passing of experience. It is not a real thing born of its own energy. It is not alive and has no consciousness of its own. It is merely a manufactured concept, in other words, *an illusion.*

This breaking apart of time, so to speak, at first can be alarming, strange and abstract. It can cause much emotional stress if resisted. In fact, it is simply the language of nature, a way of reminding us that this structure, too, must fall. Nature, like the God Force, works through our higher emotional octaves causing us to feel. Feelings are an expression of vibrations, emotional vibrations of the inner spirit.

We are presently rapidly experiencing a phenomenon referred to by our scientists as the Photon Belt. They have been aware of this coming event since about 1961. The governments currently in power have made extensive monetary investments in preparation for the eventual shifting in energies that will occur as a result of our entering the Photon Belt. Even the Vatican, the very church in Rome, is taking quite expensive measures to investigate this occurrence. They are building a huge observatory on Grants mountain in Arizona. Why would the Vatican want to do this? Maybe they realize something they do not know how to tell us about yet.

The essential nature of a Photon is within the reality of light. It is born of light, possessing no form, no physical structure whatsoever, and therefore has no weight or density. It is not affected by either the force of gravity or the effects of electromagnetic polarities.

It has been understood for some time now by our physicists, that time and space are nothing more than a state of illusion. What still remains beyond their understanding, however, is how an illusion of such magnitude could have been created in the first place. If the public understood that time and space are an illusion, then they would ask the obvious questions: "Time and space were created by whom? By what means were they created?"

Our entering the Photon Belt has to do with the rapid increasing of the metabolic rate. The planet is made up of matter. Matter is comprised of molecules. Molecules are comprised of atoms, which are comprised of particums of light.

We are part of the planet, we are not separate from it, even though separation seems to be the ruling attitude of the masses at this point in our evolution. The very elements that comprise the physical structure of the human body are identical to the elements that comprise the physical body of the Earth. So it is, we are one with the Earth. Likewise, as the metabolic rate of the Earth increases, so does the metabolic rate of our own physical body.

We are not keeping up with the vibratory rate to which our consciousness resonates. Our body, with which we have become out of sync, is already moving in sync with the Earth's new velocity. For centuries the Native Americans have spoken of the heart beat of the Mother. Resonating to the rhythm of this heart beat is what keeps us in balance with the rhythm of the Earth. She has quite literally picked up speed. There has been a quickening of the resonance to enable her to align to the new rhythm. We have, in separating ourselves from her, lost our natural ability to stay in alignment with that new beat. We are existing in a world out of balance.

The results we experience from being out of balance are quite easily realized. Time seems to speed up, or slow down. Life too often seems to be running away from us. There is never enough time to accomplish things that need to be done. How did Grandma and Grandpa do it all without the convenience of our modern technology?

The very structure of our lives seems to be coming unglued. Family structures are taking on new forms or collapsing altogether. We are losing whatever fragments of human heritage we have left. More than fifty percent of the children in America today come from divorced households, single parents, or dysfunctional homes. Unfortunately, we have come to accept this condition as normal. We can clearly see the de-structuring of our consciousness. It is being played out through the human drama.

With the speeding up of our metabolic rate, we also experience the expansion of our molecular structure. People today are experiencing out of the body occurrences at ever-increasing rates. Books about near-death experiences are the rage. Stories of encounters with inter-dimensional beings are becoming a daily occurrence. Our lives are moving so fast that, in certain instances, many of us are developing Chronic Fatigue Syndrome. We feel that it takes many times more energy to accomplish simple tasks, and we are suffering in epidemic proportions a lethargy that makes physical action actually painful at times.

We can see in many of our children being born over the last ten years or so, an attitude that questions our concepts of parenting. Every action or position that the adult assumes is questioned and put to the test. They are maturing mentally faster than their years would seem to support. Likewise, many adults are experiencing major life changes or career changes at a later and later age. This is another example we are experiencing of the *de-structuring* of time.

Personal relationships are another story. We are growing out of relationships at a faster rate than we seem to be growing into them. People no longer accept the pre-determined roles that the antiquated rules of society have established for us. This has evolved, in many instances, into a war between the sexes. Not only are we in conflict with our inner emotions, we are at odds with our partners. The very foundation of the male/female relationship is being questioned, because we no longer hold in balance the male/female energies within our own being.

We are, for the most part, drowning in the flash flocds of an information highway. We are reacting without realizing. The media, coupled with the accessibility of computers, has had tremendous ramifications upon our attitudes towards life and the images we hold of what we are supposed to be. It would appear as though many of us desire to live our lives as fast as a computer can generate images upon a screen. Don't forget to hit *SAVE*.

Our bodies, as well as the physical manifestations of our mental pictures into third dimensional forms, are in conflict with each other. One can talk about changing our global society within a matter of hours through the use of modern technology, yet it still takes us four to five days to drive an automobile from New York to California. We listen to speakers talk about what is occurring. But are they asking to hear our thoughts or our solutions? Does the every day person, living reality, have a voice in whether the world is going to end or not? And if aliens come to take over my ranch, well I think they're in for a little surprise.

We as a people, as a global society, appear to be riding a runaway train, speeding ahead on tracks laid down by those whose patterns of perception no longer apply to our contemporary situations. We are headed towards an unknown destination and very often seem to be traveling in circles. Due to changing magnetics and shifting polarities, the compasses we once relied upon and the perceptions handed down through the generations have altered, resulting in new perceptions of our manifested reality. We are in conflict with the external world, and at most times in complete denial of this conflict. We are caught in a labyrinth whereby we keep recreating the patterns over and over, watching ending after ending. Illusion always has an ending. It is built into the dream.

"It would appear as though many of us desire to live out lives as fast as a computer can generate images upon a screen. Don't forget to hit Save."

For those who rely upon the existing structure for their source of inner strength, these are very hard times indeed. For those who cannot flow through their changes of circumstance, these are times where the struggle and the friction of change will bring about great pain. The Buddhists have a saying that applies to all times: "It is the tendency of the limited mind to cling to that which brings about pain and suffering." We have been repeating our actions for so long, we have become enmeshed in the patterns. It is time to break our addictions to outmoded perceptions and patterns of existence before we become *lost in the flood.*

It is a time where we must break with traditions that limit our realities. The concepts of the world religions were not created by the God I AM. They were created by men. They were then, for the most part, custom tailored by the reigning lords of power of the day, to accommodate a specific social doctrine or political order.

But it isn't working -- it never did. It's just recycled old movies. Their dogmas and archaic doctrines can only be enforced through force. So we solve each situation that ends up in failure by resorting to war -- religious wars, my concepts against your concepts.

It may be helpful to consult the existing definitions. This is the current definition of the word religion in WEBSTER'S DICTIONARY:

> re-li-gion: coming from the Latin Root religio-supernatural, constraint, sanctioned religious practice, *perh. Fr. religare.* to restrain or tie back. Archaic: Scrupulous conformity: A cause, principle or belief system held to an order and faith.

So it appears that in Webster's definition the term religion means: "politically sanctioned beliefs in the supernatural".

> be-lief: a state or habit of mind in which trust or confidence is placed in some person or thing.

In order to create something new, you must access an energy greater than that which created the reality in the first place. There is a new awareness that is being birthed in spite of the negative intentions that is being hurled against it. It will continue to swell and grow because it is life itself, seeking itself. Conditions are no longer conducive to healthy, joyful realization of self. We are no longer learning; evolution has been stilted. We have come to almost a complete stop, and unfortunately, in many areas we are regressing.

Life as we have known it is fast reaching a precipice whereby it must change in order to continue. Science calls this event taking a jump. Life must take a leap and become something beyond what it presently is to adapt to its changing environment. It is how the whole game works. How it changes, how each one of us changes, is a matter of choice.

There is a body of knowledge which has survived the onslaught of the conquistadors and the Inquisition of the Holy Mother Church. This knowledge stood through the desecration of contemporary society. It is a knowledge which the descendants of the Mayan People are trying to freely share with the people of the world. It tells us that in accordance with the cycles of civilizations, we are at the end of a season. The ending of this season brings with it the end of the structures that have been established by this present civilization based upon Judeo-Christian belief patterns, established and tailored, for the most part, by a select order of Roman Emperors and sanctioned to become part of the social order of their day.

So altered are the original teachings of the Master Yeshua Ben Joseph, the Nazarene, that as they exist in available text today, they contain less than one-fourth of their original content. The mention of the existence of this great teacher to peoples of other lands, has all but been eradicated from the writings accessible to the common individual. The position of women in the established hierarchy of Holy Beings has also been manipulated by organized religions. Women have been kept to their allocated roles as inferior beings, for the sake of preserving the established patriarchies of the sanctioned religions.

To separate woman from spiritual expression of ceremony is to deny the very nature of the Creator. To forbid women entry to sites or temples is a display of the preposterous ignorance of our times. And it is man who declares such a separation—man, not God.

God, Creator, is the foundation of the creative force, neither male nor female, but the balance of both, and thus neither. I have even heard from the lips of some of the contemporary leaders of some organized religions here in America, while they claim to be of the Melchizedek order, that women cannot prophesize. God, they say, does not speak through women.

This archaic practice of embracing a dogmatic philosophy of separatism has resulted in humanity's present situation. We have created a belief system based upon a limited perception achieved through habit, and not conscious realization, from one generation to the next, under threat of genocide and torture. We have twisted the Divine Principles of a limitless and loving Supreme Being who holds no one separate, above or below another, regardless of even their galactic heritage.

We are rapidly approaching a time where these ancient forms of dogmatic enslavement will perish and be exposed for the illusions they are. If the chains of tradition hold one back from embracing the Divine Truths of Creation, then we are better off seeking our wisdom and understanding of spiritual truths from Nature and from within ourselves. The wilderness has been long known as the great teacher to poet and sage alike. We can turn to Nature at any time. We can choose to live in Her nurturing, balancing setting. We can mirror Her truths in ourselves.

It is inevitable that Women will again take their rightful place along side their brothers, and the structure that has supported philosophies of separation shall fall by the wayside, shattered by the winds of change. The Age of Patriarchies is past. Their principles no longer apply. They have outgrown their usefulness in the grand experience.

> *"It is inevitable that Women will again take their rightful place along side their brothers, and the structure that has supported philosophies of separation shall fall by the wayside, shattered by the winds of change. The Age of Patriarchies is past."*

In the Great Shifting that is upon us, *the Christ* has already risen. It is *the Christ* that is within all of us. Call it the God I AM, call it by what ever expression you choose. It has risen even within the stones. It is part of the raising of the vibratory field of the Earth Herself. The Mother must be acknowledged as the great being She is, for those who refuse to appreciate Her will fall behind in the wave of conscious awareness that is sweeping throughout our universe. In acknowledging her greatness, we shall know ourselves and own our true nature.

Be aware that our scientists are very aware of her consciousness. They are trying, as you read this book, to alter her genetic codes by duplicating crop circles through a technique called Synetics. They are broadcasting frequencies into the Earth's Body and implementing codes which they hope will effect the molecular structure of the Earth, by which they are telling those who have found out about this research the process will enable them to control violent reactions within the Earth's crust during the time of Earth changes.

They are creating man-made crop circles within the Earth's crust. We must grasp the reality of the technology that overtook Atlantis. This was technology with a total disregard for the Earth, which was partially responsible for the cleansing of Atlantean consciousness from *the Holographic expression*, or what you could call *Life* in conscious projection by the species as thought form.

At this time it is nearly impossible to predict with accuracy the events that shall occur in our immediate future, meaning the next ten to one hundred years. Time, as we have known it, is evaporating like old memories that escape the mind's ability to grasp, and the old paradigms which have governed the outcome of occurrences are shifting with each moment. In addition we have entered a gateway, or window. The outcome will be determined totally by our thoughts and actions day by day. What seems in one moment to be inevitable can be altered in the next by one individual who chooses to embrace Christ Consciousness.

There will be many opportunities for us to utilize smaller, more intense dimensional portals that will open as we enter the period of 1997 to 2003 -- portals by which we will actually be able to walk between the dimensions by will, if not by circumstance. These portals will be created by the stars themselves as they answer the Mother's call for assistance. Many souls will elect to take advantage of the energies afforded by these portals to leave this limited plane of reality, and wait, in a manner of speaking, on the other side.

The Gateway is about choice. In the next decade, we will all have to make the choice whether to walk into the light or to remain holding on to our limited realities. This will cause a splitting within our species, both genetically and consciously. There will be those who consciously choose to accept moving into a higher vibratory plane of being. They will allow the archaic restraints of a dying belief pattern to fall away. They will embrace merging with unlimited reality, the oneness with Creation. This will cause many of them to withdraw from the accepted social order of the day. They will seek the renewal of the inner spirit that Nature can provide. In nature, they will be able to release the pain that results from clinging on to belief patterns and not allowing for change.

There will be a second group who will refuse to accept the actual oneness of our relationship with the universe. They will insist upon holding to old beliefs, to worshipping dogmatic systems that have kept them and their kind enslaved lifetime after lifetime. They will cling to material idolatry, which will only continue to create it's own chaos, and eventually end in complete collapse. Perhaps, in a strange way, this event of the actual collapse of the entire world economic system will bring about the realization, and the probability, of us creating a new system. It must be if we are to continue along with the rate of expansion of our consciousness in which we are presently evolving.

They who hold on to the current structure of human enslavement through economic chains, will experience the magnification of that very structure which keeps them enslaved in their own web of ignorance. It is this group, in particular, who will have a very rough go of it over the next twenty years or so. It is this group that will experience the Earth Changes as a cataclysm, for they have dreamed it so.

These are the ones who will choose not to break their addictions to suffering. They need to perpetuate their pain in their everyday life so that they can identify with the specific form of reality they are comfortable with. Think about the number of people who do not seem to know how to thrive in an environment of peace and harmony, the ones who seem to have to blow everything up around them, the ones who have to create an environment of agitation and conflict in order to *feel*. Many people will not adjust to the shifting of vibratory levels that we will experience as we move from third-dimensional existence, through the fourth-, and into fifth-dimensional reality. The fourth-dimensional impact will bring with it much confusion, for again it is only a bridge. It is not yet home, for home is in the fifth-dimensional level. It is the return home, full circle back to where we began this journey long, long ago.

There will be yet another group, a third group. These souls will be like the children. They will be unexplainably impervious to the diseases and madness that will be rampant during these times. They are the ones who will be *the watchers,* experiencing the changes and holding the creative thought for the next world. They will be incapable of holding judgments, judgments that might become the seeds of disharmony in future generations. *The watchers* will only hold objective memory of pain within their molecular structure, therefore, they will not need to experience it in another incarnation.

Many in this group will in fact be true star children. Their origins will come from far away, for in actuality they will be seed from different universes -- hybrids of another kind. We must realize that portals and star convergences allow for passage both ways through the dimensional highways. The Holographic universe does not necessarily follow the rules of creation as they are seen from this limited reality. Change in paradigm means complete change.

This two way highway will bring about also the manifestation of Neanderthal-like beings. As the time space matrix flexes, both past and future consciousness will manifest upon this plane. They will project through a variety of levels of our earthbound social consciousness. They represent the manifestation of rage and judgment held within our beings for eons. On the whole, the archaic structures of a militant and tyrannical social order will decay into a cycle of self-destruction. Through this *de-structuring,* the new world will enable itself to emerge free of the karma of the old and passing age.

It's been suggested that you take any measures necessary to change your physical locations from urban to rural. Those of you who have not yet developed your skills of living off the land will fare much better on your five-acre lots beneath the trees, than you will in the sea of a soulless humanity in the throws of madness that will exist in the inner cities.

It will also be of the utmost importance that we develop stronger connections with the spiritual essence of our inner being. It will become next to impossible to rely on outside protection. The very nature of reality will alter around you in ways you cannot yet perceive, for you have no experience of what will come.

It is through these shifting perceptions, as the old consciousness implodes, that people all around you will become dangerously disoriented. Even with Her constant flux and change, Nature, the hologram of the Mother, will be a source of comfort and renewal as we progress through each level of a shifting consciousness -- perhaps our only source.

As it has been said, reality, as we know it, is the result of the group consciousness. Thought will be recognized as the power behind creation. It will eventually be apparent to the laggards who hold onto dying perceptions that the weird occurrences of a seemingly science fiction nature are the result of improper thought patterns. But the struggle of the individual under the avalanche of imploding minds and the consciousness they weave, will be too much for even the strongest of them to stand up against.

Ironically, they will suffer from the very vibration of separation they have created in their attempts through the vibration of fear to maintain control. Only as community, exercising free will, and understanding the individuality within the whole, can humankind hope to survive the frequency of change that is already upon us and intensifying with each moment.

The re-birthing of consciousness, creating a humanity in balance, will generate basically from the rural areas where those brave souls who chose to realign with the natural order of life will be rejuvenated by the very elements from which the dream was created. At the moment of the completion of this fourth world dream, we will experience the phenomenon of perfect balance. At that precise moment, the dream as we have experienced it will cease to be. Life will alter and change in that single moment, in *"the twinkling of an eye."*

Our scientists will be increasingly intrigued by the phenomenon of lights they will see in the heavens. At times, the entire stratosphere will resemble the *aurora borealis.* These lights will be caused by consciousness imploding and by the attempts of our galactic brothers to help hold together the consciousness of humanity, the Dream of Earth, during these shifting times. Keep your eyes upon the lightning; the *Wakinyan* will bring with them an array of colors and occurrences that will prove to be very exciting.

Pure water, clean air, real food, and wild herbs necessary to maintain health will become increasingly precious commodities over the next few years. The levels of disease in our cities will reach uncontrollable proportions, which is the underlying reason the government will insist upon the issuance of the National Identity Card to control movement across state borders.

The military is already being trained in elaborate programs for civilian containment. Regional areas have been established since the days of the Nixon administration for such containment and they will be openly declared as installations designed for the purpose of public well-being and national security. Be aware of all immunization programs! Accept nothing blindly!

The Photon Belt

Let us speak now of our interaction with the Photon Belt. This is not a singular occurrence; we have been through it many times in our journeys around the central sun. Due to our passing through this Photon Belt, life upon this plane has altered dramatically many times. In previous experiences, whole life forms have vanished, never to be seen again. Great civilizations, far advanced of our present one, have left this plane with little or no trace of their existence. Entire genetic strains have vanished forever from this reality. Earth has been the home to many expressions of the Creator before the introduction of the present human species as we perceive it.

We have brothers and sisters in the star systems that had their origins here, which is why some of us feel kindred spirits in the night stars. They are truly our relations. Each culture and each race has had its moment of grandeur, and this is part of the legacy of our Emerald Planet. Records of these peoples shall be unearthed as a result of the impending Earth Changes. Some are presently being discovered as the seas and ice caps are moving and shifting due to global warming, polar shifting, and tectonic flux.

There are openings at various locations on the planet that are again making themselves known as the vibratory rate of the planet continues to increase. Presently, the planet is moving along its orbital path at approximately 18,000 miles per hour. Within the time of the present generation, we will accelerate to greater than 234,000 miles per hour. So time is definitely speeding up. This acceleration of speed will cause many changes to our current understanding of physics and to the paradigm of cause and effect.

Within the next generation, our ability for inter-dimensional travel and the interaction with beings on other planes will become commonplace as it once was in our time upon this plane. First we experience a time of expansion. Due to the increased rate of vibration we will experience quantum leaps -- "hollow leaping" -- in our evolutionary realizations and development. It is because of this speeding up that we will experience both the intense *de-structuring* and the potential for intense growth in our world.

The phenomenon of UFOs will begin to occur with more regularity after the fall of 1996. Between 1997 and 1998, the degree of interaction will make it more than impossible for our governments to deny their existence. Many of the Indigenous Peoples of the planet will elect to stop reproducing young as we approach the time of the Great Shift, which will occur as we fully enter the Photon Belt and enter fifth-dimensional reality.

The photon belt has layers to its consistency. The outer layer of the Photon Belt is referred to as the Null Zone. As we pass through this zone we experience the intense *de-structuring* occurring upon this plane. Reality and all its structure fractures, to allow for greater expansion and intensified metabolic rate. When we enter into the Photon Belt, passing through the Null Zone, our speed of travel through space will increase to such an extent that life as we know it could cease to exist. Furthermore, it should be understood that pure photon energy is pure light, very similar to the white light that we hear people tell of as they go through near-death experiences.

In the Bible and in other ancient writings, the coming Photon Belt experience is referred to as a time when the planet will experience from three to seven days, and possibly as many as twelve days, of light. We hear also of a period of time we will spend in darkness. This phenomenon is about to happen to us. If the Sun enters the Photon Belt first, we can expect to experience a Great Light many times brighter than our Sun. It will be as if the whole of the universe were lit up. If the Earth enters the Photon Belt first, we can expect to experience the darkness. At the time of emergence, the Earth will actually stop. Consciousness alone will hold the nature of reality; there will be no physicality.

Regarding the concept of time, during this period it can be safely assumed that the artificially created time/space matrix that exists upon this planet will cease to function entirely, therefore rendering our present perception of time completely non-existent. This phenomenon will most likely occur, as it is seen now, before the year 2020 in our counting.

Our travel through the Photon Belt could prove very disastrous to humankind and their perceived reality. You see, we only have access to levels of consciousness that we perceive we can attain. Basically, we are prisoners of our own thoughts. However, there have been measures taken by those who love us and who are working continuously to assist us through this time of transition. There are those amongst the Star Nations who are working endless wonders to assure our safe passage through the Photon Belt.

One primary change that will occur upon entering the Photon Belt is the expansion of molecules. Simply put, as our frequency increases, all molecular structure expands. We will enter again the physics of light. This expansion is what will enable us to access fifth-dimensional reality. This expansion, on the one hand, enables us to merge into our light bodies, but, on the other hand, also causes an extreme polarity, almost a solidification, of those molecules that resist the dimensional shift and refuse to resonate with the higher frequency.

Therefore, the outcome could, for a lot of beings, be similar to the dinosaurs' fate when they simply moved into another dimensional existence, a dimension holding a frequency they could resonate with. Their purpose here no longer contributed or added to the evolution of valued life form. Simply put, they were in the way of evolutionary process.

"We only have access to levels of consciousness that we perceive we can attain. Basically, we are prisoners of our own thoughts."

The Jump

On its present path, humankind offers very little to the continuation of the Dream. We have polluted our environment to the point that it is, in many instances, irreparable. We have gone over the line, so to speak, and life as we know it, given present conditions, will self-destruct within the time period allotted to the next generation. There simply will not be enough food, oxygen, or life-sustaining materials to support twelve billion or more people. Life must make a jump to adjust to the new environment we have created.

Are you aware that our oceans are dying at an alarming rate, and it will be considered a miracle if, within the next twenty years, even ten percent of the sea life common in our grandparents' time is still upon this plane? We are, even here in the great waters, the Mother of all life, rapidly approaching critical mass. This again affirms the inevitable fact that we are about to take *the jump*. Life is mutating itself to adjust to the inevitable change that must occur for the Life Force to continue. However, as it is in the case of any jump, the life forms will mutate and adapt.

This *jump* must occur when life in its present form has exhausted its source of sustenance. Sounds very much like cancer, does it not? Well, it is. We have almost exhausted the life forms with which we co-exist upon the Earth. If we continue at our present rate, by the year 2010, with a population of twelve billion people -- even the scientists are saying that it is entirely feasible we will consume eighty percent of the known life forms that exist upon this planet -- animal, vegetable, mineral, as well as the oxygen -- within one year. So where will the next year's sustenance come from? A grim picture, isn't it?

In order for us to survive as a species we must make a quantum leap; we must make *the jump*. That is why there is so much going on these days in relation to the Breath of Life, accessing our light bodies, and so forth. We were created from Spirit. It is Spirit that will lead the way to our next destination, the fifth dimension. Those who hold the desire, those who remove the layers of illusion, those who comprise the image of what we are, will be able to stand in their truth, merge with the light and continue. Those who do not will inevitably experience, in their frequency, the full, spectacular force of the Earth Changes.

This is why it is so important for us to strive for balance of the spirit and the flesh. The flesh can only transmute in accordance with the spiritual fortitude we can hold within our consciousness. The season of the flesh is past. We cannot go backwards. We cannot return to Creation that way, nor can we slow its forward thrust. Life is on-going and forever. Light moves much faster than matter.

"... become one with your spirit. Learn to be one with the Creator. Learn to be one with the Earth. Learn to be one with yourself. To know God, know thyself! Rise from the pain of limitation and enter your forever dream. You shall become that which you judge – this is universal law."

It has been said in many of the prophesies of the Indigenous People that we have reached the final days. There can no longer be written the linear, predictable course that our future will take. It is a matter of choice. Each one of us must choose individually. Then, collectively, we will experience. Everything is frequency, it is a matter of harmonics. It is up to each one of us to accept and embrace the God within, the God I AM. No one will come to lift us from our own chosen dilemma. This is what we have created; only we can change the outcome. That is why it is so important to realize that humanity, collectively acting as individuals, each working with what is before us each day, can affect the outcome of our destiny as a whole.

So we enter the age of truth, where "the wheat is separated from the chaff." We are at the gateway of tomorrow. What will your future be? Life here will continue. Third-dimensional existence will follow its pathway. For many it will mean starting over at the beginning of the dream. For others it will mean continuing to realize we will no longer be what we were before *the jump*. Be assured that we who choose to make *the jump* will in no way be less -- in fact, we will be more, much more than we ever could have imagined. We will lose nothing; we will simply be more of what we are.

In these next few years, make the commitment to become one with your spirit. Learn to be one with the Creator. Learn to be one with the Earth. Learn to be one with yourself. To know God, know thyself! Rise from the pain of limitation and enter your forever dream. You shall become that which you judge -- this is universal law.

On the road to forever, remember your fears must be released, for fear closes down the heart center, it literally stops the creation process. You are the first born of creation. All of creation shall know what you, the radical few of God, have chosen to experience, so we could become all we can be.

Welcome to *the Quickening!*...

May you learn quickly that your heart is your only true shield.

The Lucifer Rebellion

The following is a transcription from a taped session at a gathering on Orcas Island, in the spring of 1996 off the coast of Washington State, where I maintained a home from 1992 until 1997. At that gathering I was asked the following question:

"I've heard that there really is no such thing as the Devil or Hell, but I see so much evil in this world. There must be a source to this evil. Is there, then, a Lucifer?"

"Oh yes, Lucifer. Well, that is really an interesting subject. Do you really want to know about him?"

"Yes."

"Let us take a moment and do the breath. It can be very difficult to access this information, you know. The events occurred so far back in time, so to speak, that connecting to this place in the time/space continuum could leave one stranded in space. However, the request is sincere, and perhaps the answer can help fit in a piece which will allow for completeness in your original memory."

The group went into a state of deep meditation and collectively pulled in information from the Akashic records.

"Before we begin, it must be understood that we are truly powerful creators. What we decree, so it will be. Understand that if in your reality you choose polarity and the illusion of good and evil, then someone or something must play the role of that thought declaration. No matter what the situation, someone will fulfill the role of the bad, and someone will fulfill the role of the good. Dark and light -- it is all the same game. Life really is a drama, you see. Your thought absolutely dictates the nature of reality; there is no exception.

"Let us begin our story with a point in the time/space continuum after Source created all known reality. All of us are part of the continuum of the Father/Mother when Source contemplated its own existence.   In that moment all things potentially, and yet no thing materially, were created in the great void.   Therefore, when the great Light burst forth from the void, it created an on-going energy force, in a manner of speaking, which continues to this moment.   It is known throughout your galaxies as the *SKA*.   It is what you are actually referring to when you say *Great Mystery*. You, me, and all who are present and all that is, are part of a forever process. It is called Life. For in that moment, all things potentially, yet no thing materially, were conceived, all within a single moment.

"All that is within our reality is purely potential experience. What makes it our personal experience is the choice to connect with a specific energy, a time/space event. Time is, of itself, a no thing; it is a potential that exists only for our experience. Where we come from and where we go after we choose to no longer experience the physical plane could be referred to as the Great Void, the unlimited, unified field of potential events.   These possible events are as numerous as our capacity to have thoughts.

"Light in motion creates energy. Energy becomes the sense of motion. This, in turn, becomes tone (sound), which then produces color. Color becomes emotion, and it is through emotion that we have the ability to realize reality.   It is the movement of light that causes frequencies to occur, and it is upon these wave lengths that thought travels.   In this manner, thought can fulfill itself and realize itself in a moment. All that we realize, all that manifests, comes from the Light.

"As light lowers its rate of motion, it slows or coagulates. When it has slowed down enough, the result is physical matter. Therefore, as Einstein reported, all matter is the result of thought, thought travels via light. As we think, so it is. $E=mc^2$ -- energy equals mass times the speed of light squared.

"When we were first created in the Light, we felt our existence through the light spectrum.   Presently on this plane there are seven rays. Soon there will be twelve rays, but that is another story we will discuss at another time in detail if you wish. These seven rays make up the entire composite of light that creates our known manifested reality through frequency.   In alignment with the light spectrum, fourth-dimensional reality is the Violet Ray. It is a bridge between that which is physical and that which is of the Spirit, or of the Light.

"Fifth-dimensional reality is x-ray. The vibratory rate of the light is very intense here, thousands of vibrations per second higher than in the third-dimensional plane. There are also many more colors in fifth-dimensional reality than exist in the lower third-dimensional reality. Can you imagine having twelve primary colors in your color spectrum, which now consists of three? That should give you some idea of what it is like. There is no need for structure in order to survive in fifth-dimensional reality.   In this higher vibratory state, we are thought concept -- emanations of the source. You know this concept as light bodies.

"Hence, those we call the Ascended Masters who reside in this dimensional reality have no need for structure, and can appear to walk through walls. They exist in these light bodies. Time has no influence upon light bodies. At this level of existence, one becomes immortal. This is man's natural state. It is where your God is, your I AM.

"There is then the matter of sixth- and seventh-dimensional reality. Here the light exists at such an intensity that there is, utilizing human capabilities of perception, no way to relate. The light in the sixth dimension is the Gamma Ray, and the seventh defies description in language entirely; they are both beyond words.

"In that life is ongoing and never-ending, in that all that ever was still is, you are still connected to the part of your being that exists beyond the seventh level of reality. In fact, you are actually twelfth-density beings. You are still GOD I AM. Existence upon the Earth plane is experienced by the lowering of your thought vibrations to such a degree that you can experience this third-dimensional reality. You really are not your bodies.

"That part of you which is still existing in foreverness, enjoys the totality of the Unified Field. It is the Lord God of your being. Hence, "...the Father and I are One. The Kingdom of Heaven is within." In actuality, there are twelve levels of density. Those of you who are Christed have actually created a twelfth density. You have opened up the heavens, so to speak, and have created the beginnings of a new universe. You have created a thirteenth, which is why you have created so much confusion in this time -- for you are the ones who created it. It is so new that there is very little known about it on any level at this time.

"It is the movement of light that causes frequencies to occur, and it is upon these wave lengths that thought travels. In this manner, thought can fulfill itself and realize itself in a moment. All that we realize, all that manifests, comes from the Light."

"In the lowering of our vibrations and in experiencing all that could be in the universe, there came the question, "How would we enter the vibratory field of third-dimensional reality?" The answer comes in our potential to master the fifth level. Physical form could only exist to this point in the third level. It does not exist in the fourth, nor in the higher levels of vibration. The fourth dimension is still the Light, yet a variation of physical form can exist in the manner of light projection or holographic reality.

"Out of this we created the thought of *Epigenetics*. It is the knowledge of *Epigenetics* which Sacred Geometry reveals to us. *Epigenetics* is, virtually, the blueprint of all manner of expression through the physical plane. *Kryahgenetics* is the knowledge of the flow or movement of life form related to thought, and is also explained through sacred geometry. Without these, life could not express in form.

"When one sees an entity in a vision, the entity is materializing from the fifth dimension through the fourth dimension, which can then be perceived by us in the third dimension, yet it cannot be felt as substance. If it is projected fully into third-dimensional reality, it has to take on physical form. The entity can alter time, and what you experience through time may only be a moment, yet it can be actually years in experience. So either the entity must take on physical form, or in many instances, you are raised in awareness momentarily, lifted via your light body into the higher octave to perceive its emanations.

"Returning again to our experiment with the denser third-dimensional experience, while we were contemplating this entrance into third-dimensional reality, there were those who could not understand why one would deliberately place themselves in such a place of confined reality. It was risky. One could get stuck there, because one of the side effects, so to speak, was amnesia -- a literal breaking of the thought continuum from the Divine Source.

"Due to this risk, many rejected this experience, this possible reality. However, there were those few very courageous angels, and we are the angels, who took on the project. We are the first born of God. The name of the game here in third-dimensional reality is to raise the nature of physical matter, to maintain its integrity, to remember simultaneously the Divine Essence of what we truly are, and to accomplish all this without breaking the thought continuum of the Divine Source. *Aho Mitakyue Oyasin* means in Lakota "*We are all one*" -- not just all one with a part, but one with the whole.

"The successful outcome of this experiment is what we now call Christ Consciousness, the Christos, and for the most part, we have completed this experiment. We are all going home. Some of us are here to help the slower ones of our family to move along. Some of us are here to maintain this reality as its cycles begin again in a new expression from zero point.

> *"The name of the game here in third-dimensional reality is to raise the nature of physical matter, to maintain its integrity, to remember simultaneously the Divine Essence of what we truly are, and to accomplish all this without breaking the thought continuum of the Divine Source."*

"But let us return again to when we were beings from the fifth-dimensional reality. We had never before experienced the taking on of physical form. It was new to us. While experiencing this new third-dimensional reality, there occurred within the framework of consciousness a group of these angels who got stuck on the other side, so to speak, in the third-dimensional side of physical expression. They continued to possess Super Consciousness, yet they were unable to access the avenue to successfully return to the Light. There was, as they had expected, a break with the continuum of the source. Our energy had stepped down; the frequency was too slow.

"Using our mental abilities we created many forms of technology, pyramid technology being one and the great light ships used in inter-dimensional travel another. This technology extended the capacity of the physical body to amazing proportions, all in an attempt to return home. Remember that time as we know it was not yet created; we were still forever beings.

"Like any machine that has parts which wear out, the physical structure has its drawbacks. It needs to be constantly renovated. The technology was developed to the degree that in a pyramid the physical form could totally renew, allowing it to exist virtually forever upon this plane. This was accomplished by accessing the inner temples of the great halls of Almenti in the inner Earth. Keep in mind that we are still speaking of the Gods/Angels.

"Jehovah was not, and is not, one of these beings who dwelt upon the Earth plane. He never lowered his vibratory field to the level of the body physical. Jehovah was never a human, but he did dwell within the higher electromagnetic planes of reality.

"We are *Hu-man* -- God-man. Actually, we went further than Jehovah into the evolutionary process. We actually lowered ourselves so deeply into the third-dimensional reality that we have all but lost our abilities to utilize the Light. We even believe that our temporal expression is all there is at times. The spell here is very powerful -- it is called the spell of Mortality.

"The Gods who lowered themselves into third density suffered uncalculated alterations to their energy fields. This phenomenon made it impossible, after repeated re-entry into the third density, to again return to the higher octave. After a time they literally became stuck in the third density, yet still possessed, what we would call today, Super

Consciousness. While on this side of the density, these Gods elected to utilize their super technology to create an artificial Merkabah as a vehicle to return them to the higher octaves from which they came.

"There were certain potential dangers, however, in using an artificial Merkabah to accomplish this feat. The desired effect was produced by manipulating the electromagnetic fields which make up the stuff that holds all matter together. It created a Merkabah which existed within a polarity, the polarity which is necessary to perpetuate the electromagnetic field. Souls traveling through this artificial Merkabah would then take on this duality in their own light configuration. Therefore, they could take on a distortion of the One Consciousness. It was a very risky endeavor, to say the least.

"Most every one was against it; it had too many flaws. There was one entity, however, who decided, "The heck with public opinion. I'm giving it a try. If it works, we could all get back. If there are accidents, we can get those souls back later, after we complete the experiment. I mean, this way we're stuck here. What real danger could there be? We're Gods, after all. We're immortal, aren't we?"

"This particular very bright Star Child, being very charismatic in nature, elected to go ahead with the experiment. There were many who elected to join in the game and create the artificial Merkabah. So, despite the warnings of billions of other souls, these few radicals went ahead. Oh, by the way, the entity's name was Lucifer. He was such a bright star he was even called Luciferous, meaning the Light.

"Lucifer is a sixth-level being of incredible consciousness, who once existed within the realms of all the octaves from the fifth and sixth realities. He elected to use the artificial Merkabah to lift those who became stuck in the image back to their Fifth Dimensional Reality. The experiment, as we now know, did not work as anticipated.

"In fact, what occurred was even worse than anticipated. This distortion of consciousness created a warped perception of themselves, in that they could easily conceive themselves to be the holographic image of their own thought projection, rather than the source of the image itself. It would not be a true emanation of the source, rather it would be a reflection of the emanation of the actual light. It was an image and not the real thing -- it was a distortion.

"So Lucifer is forever labeled the bad guy. Lucifer is a light being possessing neither a male or female body, and has never elected to take on this limited physical form. Only the Christ Beings did that, only those Angels who elected to go all the way and trust that Divine Consciousness would correct itself. These became the Children of *Yahweh*, the Indigenous People of Earth. Then there are the children of *ID* (Fairies, Elves, and the like), who were very gentle and loving by nature. Later in our history the genetic tampering occurred and really messed things up for a while. However, that occurrence is correcting itself even now.

"There are many stories that can be told of what happened as a result of the genetic tampering. Being where you are at this moment, asking this question, you, too, are one of them. It happened seven and one half million years ago in our counting. That's a lot of life times.

"The short of it is that *all physical beings*, including the Nephlium spoken of in the Bible, including the human species, including the Grays and so on, comprise those souls who elected to partake in the *Luciferian Rebellion*. We are all the Children of Lucifer, in a manner of speaking. You who are human, however, are the most blessed of all, for you are known in the heavens as the *Patal*. You are considered royalty. You are the Christs. You are the Archangels of God returning home.

"This has been called the ending of an age by some. Well, those are the defeatists. This, Masters, is the beginning of a new heaven, a new reality -- the Christos! What a grand time to be participating in the drama, is it not? You get to go home! You are experiencing a changing of cosmic seasons, a fulfillment of destiny. You have corrected yourselves and completed the grand experiment. You are coming home to God.

"So who is the devil? And who is Lucifer? What is man? And what is God? Is it not all born of the same source? Is not everything Divine? Is not all the *IS*?

"If you call forth a reality that has the necessity of someone playing the Bad guy, well then, you shall have your cake and eat it to. If it is necessary for Lucifer to play the roll of the bad guy to move you to your inevitable destiny of returning to God, well, he doesn't mind playing the role. Whatever it takes. For in the higher realization there can be no good or evil -- there is only God.

"The duality, like *Satan,* only exists in the minds of man. And it can only exist when we live the artificial reality that we are separate from the source. Lucifer is part of the source. Reason it out from most pure mind. That there is evil of any kind is a trick of the light. It is the image, the altered ego, tricking you into believing that you are less than God I AM.

"Man has long forgotten the Christ within him, becoming merely a surviving creature. Addicted to a mundane existence, they evolved themselves deeper and deeper into matter to such degrees that they lost all memory of their divinity. Lost because they forgot the priority of self and they separated that self from the creator. Through this separation, they became frightful creatures that fear the dark, rather than being the Lord of it."

"Blessings, and eternal awakenings. Have fun creating your own story, for you are Grand Gods indeed."

Understanding Events
Between 1996-2013

These can be very confusing times. There is so much information coming into our plane. We are experiencing an accelerated expansion of our consciousness. This is being manifested in the form of conflict, both internally and externally. There is confusion occurring to the very core of *Hu-man* consciousness, literally, to the very core. Our core belief patterns are being questioned to the point that at times we can find ourselves almost non-functional in this third-dimensional reality.

When this happens we are very susceptible to the multitude of entities that are offering quick fix cures and escape meditations. Or perhaps we ask ourselves if it is better to just "get real." Well, getting real has its costs too; we lose our *Hu-man* ability to dream. We find that "getting real" can translate into everything getting very unreal. The conflict of emotional swings and altered perceptions of self and the external world can cause such turbulence that we too often find ourselves lost upon the seas of confusion.

What we will discuss tonight is a simple explanation of some very ancient teachings. Teachings that were once an accepted understanding amongst the peoples of the Western Hemisphere, those who you would refer to as Indians. The ancient teachings are about the circles of life. This day we discuss the Sacred Circles, the cycles of our universe.

We are entering a new phase of evolutionary development, and what we share tonight will someday, once again, become accessible knowledge. At this time we are experiencing, amongst other things, the breaking down of structure. This process begins with the inner structure or the limited consciousness that, for eons, has kept us within our very limited perception of reality. *Hu-man* consciousness, as a whole, has reached its limits and is seeking to access its own Divine Source, its true nature, its beginning, when consciousness was limitless. As we experimented with the effects of limited thought, you might say we fell under the spell of limitation.

Presently, we are feeling our way around in a reality that no longer serves a useful purpose. Given our true nature, the end result is that we will, or at least some of us will, create an environment wherein we can once again access our true consciousness. Humanity must learn to maintain an environment of creativity, for without creativity we only experience death. We have grown beyond the point where death is necessary. We are fast becoming a species which no longer has a need for this limited existence. *Hu-mankind's* destiny is to move beyond the limitations of mortality to touch its "foreverness". This limited existence no longer serves a valuable purpose.

Creation is like a Sacred Circle; we are returning to our beginning point. *Hu-manity* is learning that deep within the recesses of its inner knowing, it understands how to recreate itself. We have created our reality over and over again. We have become so bored that we no longer feel the wonder of it all. We can no longer see the miracle of it, or the grandest miracle of it all -- ourselves. So we must move on and get with the true purpose of our existence as a *Hu-man* species. We are experiencing the pressure of life seeking only itself.

The advanced stages of boredom manifests in severe depression. Under the effects of extreme depression, one lets everything go. Humanity has let it all go, even the Earth, the very source of our existence. Science determines that at our increased rate of pollution, population growth, and consumption of the Earth's resources, within less than twenty years we will reach an irreversible condition of self-annihilation as a species.

Then again, modern science has always been the last to acknowledge new avenues of expansive consciousness. Science is now discovering, for the most part, that the accepted concepts of our "known reality" are not as absolute as it thought. You see, science is still unable to disprove the Divine Nature of humankind, the existence of Creator, or the Ascended Masters.

Science is only now starting to discover a language that allows it to substantiate that the metaphysical world is, indeed, real. In many instances, metaphysics is more real than what we have thought to be for hundreds, perhaps thousands of years. It is hard to be a realist when you enter an Inipi Lodge and experience the Buffalo Calf Woman. It is hard to maintain logic and linear thought when you sit inside a Hopi Kiva and see, within the confines of the darkness of the stone and mud room, in pure blackness, the rising and setting of the Sun.

We have been referred to by our Star Brothers as "the laggards of the universe." This is even referenced in the Bible (they have not yet removed it from the text). We have wavered for a very long time, and we have fallen asleep at the wheel. We are suddenly being awakened to what we have come to call the occurrences of supernatural phenomenon, when in reality they are simply the occurrence of natural events. They are seasons, if you will, that have governed the human species since its beginnings upon this plane of reality.

What has remained somewhat constant for some 7.5 million years is about to change. The change will be radical. Keep in mind that this change is not limited to just the Earth. No, it is occurring throughout the entire universe, the full implication of which the *Hu-man* species cannot yet possibly comprehend given its present level of awareness. What is occurring is something beyond known reality. We are, in essence, moving into another possibility, the possibility that we are more than we have previously allowed ourselves to believe, that we might even be related to this invisible anomaly known as Creator.

All records upon this plane that deal with what you would call prophesy, have to do with known reality and its potential outcome. But what we are about to experience has to do with something much bigger than that, which is why one will find that all the prophecies of the Ancients lead us to this time and go no further. We are at a precipice. We are about to leap into the unknown as far as the human experience is concerned. There is no precedence for what is about to occur, for we have never come this far before in the entire human experience.

There are some very simple understandings that can at least help make us aware of what we are about to experience in this next unfolding of the human drama. Let us first explore the possibilities of the knowledge relating to the Mayan calendar, and later enter into the experience of the Photon belt.

Let this be heard in the light of creation, may it serve to expand your horizons, allow you freedom from judgment, and assist you in remembering your ancient future. For you have fallen under the spell of the dream and think, for the most part, that this is all there is for you. You are so much more, if only you let your true inner being emerge. This is the time of the Great Emergence, the Emergence into the Fifth World.

The Mayan Calendar

Our Mayan Ancestors held the understanding of seventeen different calendars. These calendars go back to our beginnings some ten million years ago. For our understanding tonight, we will deal with three of them, the three that most critically effect present events. These calendars are called the *Haab*, the *Tun-uc* and the *Tzolk'in*.

The Haab is based upon the cycles of the Earth. It has 360+ 5 days totaling, like our present calendar, 365 days in one year. It consists of 18 months containing 20 days each and a 19th month called Vayeb which uses the extra 5 days. Each month has its own name symbol, and each day uses its own Sun symbol.

The Tun-uc is the Mayan calendar based in the understanding of the Moon. It utilizes 28 days that mirrors the female moon cycle. This cycle is then broken down into four smaller cycles consisting of seven days each. These smaller cycles are representative of the four phases of the Moon. They are referred to as Portal Days.

The Tzolk'in is commonly referred to as the Sacred Calendar of the Mayan people and is based upon the cycles of the Pleiades and the 25,480 orbital years of our solar system. For simplicity's sake, round this off to 26,000 years. This 26,000 year cycle is only a fraction of a greater 206 million-year cycle. We can relate to our present calendar by counting in units of 260 days. It utilizes the sacred numbers 9,13, and 20. The number 13 represents the numbers and dates, and the number 20 represents the Sun signs. Also in the Tzolk'in, there are four smaller cycles or seasons comprised of 65 days each. These seasons are guarded by the four Sun Gods, *Chicchan, Oc, Men* and *Ahau*.

Portal Days also exist within the cycles of the Tzolk'in Calendar, which create a double helix pattern utilizing 52 days. Accessed by the mathematics of the number 28, they indicate a balance of male and female energies.

To date, the Mayan calendar has never erred. It is the most accurate method of divining the time sequence of prophesied events that exists in all the records of humankind. However, this teaching is not about numbers and mathematics. Therefore, only the most general reference to the numbers and the mathematics will be used. That information is easily accessible; we are more concerned in this work with the deeper meaning. It is essential to our continuation as a thinking species that we move beyond the linear, binary mind set. To date, our scientists have endeavored to decipher the Mayan calendar through the intellectual process, solely through the use of limited mind. Therefore, it has remained a mystery, an elusive riddle. These ancient mysteries cannot be approached by the limited mind, nor by the mental body alone. This was not the intention behind the hieroglyphics or the petroglyphs found around the world. They were intended to spark within us feelings that would trigger memory.

The Mayans feel that during their ancestors' stay upon the Earth plane, much knowledge was exchanged between them and the beings from the Stars. Their ancestors' karma here on Earth concerned carrying the burden of the purposely created time/space continuum and its illusional effects on this plane and upon our perception of reality. Like us, they too experienced social consciousness by entering human bodies, bound to walk through the illusion of time in a linear fashion.

They were aware of the beginnings of our Earth, and the development of the *Hu-man* species. They were aware that over time the species might become caught up in its own drama and perhaps suffer the gradual loss of its ability to "ride" the cycles of time. This is accomplished by becoming the Light itself which creates the matter, rather than physical matter which is the product of Light. As they see it, our consciousness has, in fact, gradually become denser and denser.

Presently in our "advanced society", we have all but lost our once natural ability to *ride the Light*. In fact we are just now reaching the point of being able to conceive of this concept as reality. Just recently, we have created the language of quantum physics which enables us to conceptualize and work in a world where Light exists beyond time. Trust that our present understanding of time and consciousness is to change again -- radically!

We are being reborn into a new reality. In this new reality we will become less and less binary and increasingly more analogous in our thinking processes. What was once thought of as abstract will become reality, and present reality will become, once again, the abstract concept originally conceived.

Our Mayan ancestors understood this process and left, as part of our heritage, a picture language that through the simple means of emotional communication, bridges all cultures, all language, and all levels of limited consciousness, even through the passing of time. It is a heritage of the living word written upon living stone. The key to deciphering this picture language lies in our willingness to open our heart to the possibility that we are much greater than our limited self-perception has allowed.

The decoding of the ancient calendars and glyphs is a matter of intuition. The knowledge of the universe is available to all who dare to venture beyond judgment and limited archaic thinking processes. The information can only be accessed at light speed. Even in our present day use of computers we are finding ourselves relying more and more upon the use of symbols, are we not? The amount of information and the speed with which we must process information require a much more efficient system than that which is based on our present linear language and thinking processes.

To decode the messages held in the ancient calendars and glyphs, we must use the fullness of what we are. This knowledge cannot be accessed through limited consciousness. It is going to take full power, in alignment with ourselves. We must relearn to harmonize with our physical, mental, spiritual, and emotional bodies. If we do not, the doorways, the portals will remain closed. We must rekindle our dreaming abilities, for without dreams, we soon loose the desire and passion to live. Life becomes beige and we eventually close down; Divine Spark of Consciousness implodes. Presently, our entire species is nearing a situation of critical mass where our consciousness and life, as we know it, will implode. We must turn the tide.

If our intention is to be able to communicate with the Sun as the ancient Mayans did, we must relearn to travel through the Heart. Through the *Hu-man* heart and by mastering our emotional body we can learn to access Universal Consciousness at its own speed, the speed of light. Emotions can change in a second. We must understand our emotions so we can become masters of our own fate. The mental pathway is linear. The emotional pathway has built into it many turns, valleys, and mountain tops, and it is abstract by nature.

It has often been said by the sages that on the Pathway, the shortest distance between two places is frequently not a straight line. We cannot understand with our mind, yet we attempt to explain our experience through the mind. True understanding is accomplished with our feelings. Emotion is the language of GOD. Through emotion and feelings the Divine Source speaks to all life, to all It has created. Emotion is the essence of telepathic capability.

Communicating and understanding in this way can be very difficult for us. We have been taught not to trust in our own emotions. We have been taught to question our individual feelings. We have, in essence, been tricked into creating our own prisons. The bars are invisible to linear perception, so we continue to delude ourselves into thinking that we are free. It is the *Hu-man* desire that will lead us home. Our desire, when mixed with the passion of the *Hu-man* soul, will kick in, so to speak, of its own accord once we relearn to trust our own inner feelings. This is part of the riddle that the Mayans left us, their *Children of the Sun*.

The Mayan Sacred Calendar with its 20 Sun signs is a tool that works on the cellular memory. Through our intuitive and emotional abilities we can reactivate knowledge that has been implanted within the human consciousness since its beginnings. Each of us will remember our own unique relationship to the cycles of the calendar. Each of us has a precise connection to the Cycles of Life. Each of us will access our own specific awareness of our relationship to the cosmos, based entirely upon our position in the calendar system. We simply have to allow ourselves to remember. This is the true astrology.

Another aspect of the Tzolk'in Calendar is the understanding of these cycles in relation to a galactic cycle, the Tun. This is a cycle consisting of 5,125 to 5,200 years corresponding to our orbit around the Central Sun, Alcione, which is the brightest star within the constellation of the Pleiades.

Our evolution through these cycles is spun through thirteen cycles called by the ancient Maya, the Baktun. Through natural unfolding, this cycle has caused us to enter into a cosmic leap, often referred to as a Hollow Leap. The result is that the *Hu-man* species, as a result of our original DNA programming, initiated by none other than ourselves, created a *Quickening* of our own evolution. This *Quickening* enables us to transform our physical matter as we evolve without sudden shifts, disappearance of species, or cataclysmic occurrences. It is simply a *Quickening* of our evolution.

This *Quickening* effects the entire embodiment of the Earth -- the stones, the animals, the plankton. No-thing shall remain unaffected. We are nearing the ending of the thirteenth Cycle of Baktun, a period of time from12 AD through the year 2013 AD.

As a result of the *Quickening* there is presently occurring a wide spectrum of events. There is a dissonance of Earth's resonant field resulting in increased seismographic activities due to shifting tectonic plates as the Earth twists and moves through Her own evolutionary journey to align Herself with the Divine Order.

*"The Mastery of our emotions is our destiny —
Mastery, not denial ... Emotion is the essence of
telepathic capability."*

Once again this is reflected in the upheavals in our society, the overthrow of governments and institutions which have held us in captivity by exploiting our perception of limitation. Perhaps the Anti-Christ would be better referred to as the Anti-Creativity. The Earth is not angry with us; She is only expressing Her own creativity through acts of passion. In times past these things we call Earth Changes were seen as indicators, but we were closer to our true nature then, as well as to nature Herself. Now, for the most part, we live in envelopes, isolated and insulated from nature and Mother Earth.

As we are connected to Her, when the Earth twists and moves, we twist and move with Her. Her violence in creating should perhaps be looked upon simply as the reawakening to Her own passionate nature. It is translated into the human reaction as turmoil and chaos. It is the re-birthing of creativity, Divine creativity. We feel Her process within us, even unto our smallest atomic component, and we are reacting to it through our DNA. It is the web of life.

Most of the changes we are experiencing within ourselves are beyond our comprehension. They are the reaction of the DNA to the bombardment of radiation from Earth's collective radiation belt. The size of this radiation belt and its proximity to our atmosphere has been decreasing steadily for the last fifty years. The ecosystem's natural process that filters radiation has been corrupted by the overload of nuclear particles which our atomic explosions have dumped into the atmosphere. This is a major reason for global warming, the high incidence of cancer, and the degradation of the fundamental building blocks that make up cellular structure.

This mutated form of cellular reproduction is being mirrored by the insanity of our present day society. Like cancer destroying the body, society is determined to self-destruct. It has taken less than one hundred years to reach our current unbalanced ecological state.

We are also reacting to the shifting of electromagnetic polarities as Earth shifts into harmonic alignment with the galactic order. We are, after all, Her body. We are made of the very same stuff. The entire paradigm of the physics of the Earth is altering at an increased rate. It is picking up such momentum that our scientists are left stunned and amazed. At every turn of the road the old and archaic is no longer applicable. So it is we are passing this plane of reality, and we must. Humanity will no longer need this plane to proceed into our mutual future.

We find uncontrollable cancer and plagues ravaging our societies seemingly immune to contemporary medicine. Viruses and bacteria are mutating at such an astonishing rate that they defy our present methods of treatment. One could say that the Earth body is, within the infrastructure of her cellular being, experiencing a condition of "*divine fever.*" She is throwing off that which is causing Her illness and *dis-ease.* Affected by the vibration of her illness, Her orbit is altering -- wobbling. At this point, if She alters her rotation of orbit by even six degrees, then, like a gyroscope, She will lose her spin and fall over. The ensuing results would be disastrous. Our experience will be similar to a massive nuclear explosion.

Does this sound discouraging? Well, it is not. It is only discouraging if your understanding is incomplete. Prophesies can be dangerous if they are based on partial information. Knowledge is power. Enlightenment is acquired, not stolen. It is a gift that is earned through the arduous process of learning to let go of our judgments, even the little ones. This is why many of us are experiencing the manifestation of our conflicting thoughts. What we think and what we fear is coming up in our faces, is it not, often times almost as quickly as we think them.

There is much talk these days about the Native American experience, but be aware that these people, these Earth Keepers, are feeling the effects of the *Quickening* much more intensely than the rest of us in the United States. This is also true for the entire indigenous population of the Earth at this time. Many of the Indigenous Peoples have even elected to stop having children as they realize that these

Truths are occurring and we are, indeed, at the end time of this present cycle.

The Indigenous Peoples are going through the shattering of limited thought with such an intensity that perhaps less than 15% of them will survive the intensity of this transformation before we reach the year 2013. Tribal existence in its present limited form is in the way of the Oneness of all that must be attained in order for us to successfully complete the Emergence of the Fifth World.

All structure must break down so that the new can emerge. We are experiencing the de-structuring of limitation. All archaic forms of consciousness shall be transformed. This de-structuring is, in essence, the Armageddon. It is a war of valued life; it is our inner conflict. We must take care that our internal struggles do not manifest in external violence. The Mastery of our emotions is our destiny -- Mastery, not denial. Our key is the awareness of our higher aspects, our Divine Spiritual Essence, which only knows love and compassion, the feminine side of our being.

Most of the Sacred Calendar deals with events that transpire through the year 1987. The Mayans have encoded within the understanding of their calendars and precise mathematical formulas used in their calculations, an understanding which is very important to our continuation as a species. It has a lot to do with our understanding of the light and the darkness, good and evil.

Within the understanding of the Mayan Calendar there are cycles of light and dark. These have to do with the thirteen Lords of Light and the nine Lords of Darkness. There is no difference between the Darkness and the Light. That judgment is only seen because of the polarity of consciousness that presently exists here. To the understanding of the ancient Mayan and in our own higher octaves of reality, there is no such thing as good or bad. There simply is.

In a manner of speaking, the Lords of Light were the giving Energies, and the Lords of Darkness were the testers of Energies. There is a story . . . First, the Master comes and bestows upon the student the gift of knowledge. When the student feels that he has learned enough, he begins to grow bored and dismisses the teacher by a show of attitude. Being of the Light, the Master graciously retreats from this interaction to continue upon his own journey. The student is then visited by the departing Master's brother, the Lord of Darkness. The Purpose of his energy under this influence is to test true comprehension of what was given so freely to the student in the first place. The moral of the story is that the Lord of Light and the Lord of Darkness are *not* enemies; they are both great and necessary teachers in this realm of duality.

The thirteen Lords of Light each reign for fifty-two years. Then we are under the influence of the nine Lords of Darkness, each of whom also reign for a period of fifty-two years. We are presently coming out of the reign of the last of the nine Lords of Darkness. That period lasted from 1935 until 1987. The manifested form of the Lord of Darkness upon this plane was Adolph Hitler. Hitler did not pass away in the bunker in 1943, but, in fact, died in Argentina in 1987. There is evidence of this, and although it is difficult to come by, the information does exist in certain news records on micro film.

Even after the expiration of the manifested form of the Lord of Darkness, reality and the consciousness have continued to re-create the experience through an overlay of energy. We experienced this overlay of energies between 1987 and August 12,1992. During this time, we went through a sort of tunnel of confusion and darkness. We have emerged out of that experience and now are potentially able to access the beginnings of the next great Age of Light. On August 12, 1992, there was a well-attended ceremony held at Palenque on the Yucatan Peninsula of Mexico. Here the people gathered to celebrate the opening up of a great portal. A portal that allowed us to access an expanded degree of the energies from the Central Sun, Alcione.

"There is no such thing as good or bad — there simply is... The Lords of Light were the giving Energies, and the Lords of Darkness were the testers of Energies."

One of the effects of these new energies was a shift in consciousness. Simply put, the metabolic rate of both the human and planetary body was intensified. We are vibrating much faster than we did twenty, or even ten years ago. This shift is allowing us to access more of the feminine side of our nature. The raising of the feminine energy has allowed for the emergence of many women into prominent positions in the world theater once allowed only to men.

Many women are finally enjoying new positions of authority which have been closed to them before this time. This occurrence within the social structure of reality is no small miracle. After enduring thousands of years of ignorance, we are emerging from Patriarchy. As predicted by the Mayan, all structures have begun the process of transmutation. There is a fracturing that is occurring within the mind set of social consciousness allowing all of us, as a global consciousness, to access more of the Light.

Keep in mind that, in having *free will,* we can also access more of the Dark, or shadow side of our essences as well. This is why we are seeing much opposition surface as we advance upon our pathway to the Light. It is always a choice. Unfortunately, there is much evidence of this degenerating energy present within our society. The old and the archaic will not be able to continue. The Battle of Armageddon is, indeed, taking place. It is a war of valued life, a silent war within the heart of each of us.

After that date there is simply no way of telling which way events will turn. This is because it is now up to us. We must choose between limitation, a way that we are very familiar with, or limitlessness, Christ Consciousness. This will allow us to emerge to the next level of our awareness and experience the reality of the Fifth World. This step cannot be achieved by force or power. It is a process of allowing, maintaining our Divine Nature, and following the Spiritual part of our being which is experienced through our intuitive sense of emotional desire. This is desire of the spirit, not of the body. We are spirits encased in a robe of flesh. It is a borrowed robe at best.

Change is unavoidable, but we have the ability to master change and our actions and reactions to it. There has never before been so much information accessible to human consciousness. We are the captains of our own ships. In this case, the ship is going to be created out of our consciousness. We, like the dolphin and the adepts, will need to create our own Merkabah, great light ships, vehicles of the Angels, the Sirians, the Pleiadians, and many of our inter-dimensional neighbors who interact with our race and have done so since the beginning of our experiences here.

Understanding the Earth's Passage Through the Photon Belt

The emergence into the Photon Belt will totally alter the energy patterns and physics of planet Earth. The Photon Reality is very different than the one we have been experiencing, but is by no means a new experience to this plane. It happens every 10,500 years. In reality, there is no time, but in the present understanding there needs to be time in order for most of us to relate. Photons are essentially particums of light, having no structure. Structure such as matter cannot exist within their field. We are constantly experiencing mini-photonic occurrences, but they are short-lived and dispersed by the influence of structured reality which dominates third dimensional reality.

There have been many conflicting attempts to explain this event. Scientists have been well aware of the existence of the Photon Belt, and the Manasic Radiation belt since 1961. The Photon Belt is not some expansive area that exists within the heavens, actually, it is a small area. Presently, the Pleiades are experiencing the effects of this Photon energy. Soon Earth and our solar system will experience the Pleiadian influence as we go through our synchronization of planetary movement (which is well explained in the Mayan Calendar.)

What we will experience as we continue to move into the Photon Belt is dimensional shifting, for we will experience the full effect of light. It is almost as if we are moving into a space of anti-matter. All that will remain while we are in its full effect is the thought that conceived matter.

Electromagnetic fields are, for all intents and purposes, nullified within the Photon energy field. In the Photon Belt we will come to know the true meaning of the White Light, for, in essence, that is what the Photon Belt is. Mother Earth has been around for a very long time. The *Hu-man* species has been here for 7.5 million years, developing our abilities to create the most adaptable form of embodiment. We have been influenced by our space brothers who genetically altered our physical structures, as well as our mental capabilities. The splitting of the *Hu-man* brain was one of the most detrimental of these occurrences. This has slowed us down, but it can no longer affect the final outcome.

Earth has experienced the Photon Belt many times in its evolution. Each time has resulted in radical changes in life forms as well as consciousness. Sometimes moving ahead and sometimes moving backwards, these experiences are either progressive or regressive. Reflecting these shifts, *Hu-man* beings have developed their own consciousness along the way, sometimes experiencing great periods of growth and spiritual awakening, other times experiencing the implosion of *Hu-man* consciousness. Reality is actually like dream time. It has no specific rules; it simply is of itself. *I AM that I AM.*

We are simply the dancers in the dream.

26,000 year Cycle of our Solar System passing through the Photon Belt

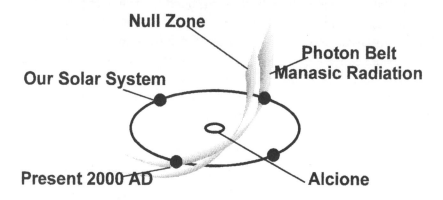

> 1. Our solar system moves in a counter clockwise orbit around the central Sun Alcione.
>
> 2. A complete revolution around Alcione takes approx. 25,860 years.
>
> 3. The Photon Belt is sometimes referred to by our scientists as the Manasic Radiation Belt. It is the white light of Christ Energy.
>
> 4. The Null Zone is the fragmenting particums on the fringe of the Photon Belt. We are presently in this Null Zone as we experience progressive intensity of light as we move closer to the central core.

If we were to look at the orbit of our solar system around the Central Sun, Alcione, on a two dimensional diagram, it would appear elliptical. The last time we experienced the Photon Belt was during the time of the de-structuring of Atlantis. That was approximately 10,500 years ago, and from that time we have been evolving to the present day experience. Many of our technologies today are simply primordial attempts at recreating forms housed in our cellular memory, those we once mastered during the Atlantean period. Once again, our cellular memories are being jarred into awakening by the activation of our DNA as we enter the influence of the Photon Belt and experiencing the *Quickening*.

Let us return to our two-dimensional diagram. We are presently opposite to our position in our galactic cycle, as we were during the final days of Atlantis and our last experience with Photon energy. Remnants can be found indicating the passing from one Photon experience to the next, where seemingly a civilization has mysteriously vanished. Examples of this include the pyramids of Giza in Egypt, the ruins of Machu Picchu in Peru, and the columns and roadways off the Virginia coastline and the Bermuda islands where Atlantis once stood.

Many of these sites show indications of methods used in the construction, that in our present limited consciousness, we have lost the memory of. We, therefore, create phantom explanations with no foundation as to how they were built, meaning, specifically, that it took 400,000 Hebrew slaves working 24-hours a day, three years to build one of the great pyramids at Giza. This concept is a total absurdity. We know now, in fact, that the building of the pyramids, whether in Egypt, South America, or the Mississippi Valley, occurred from the apex down. In other words, we worked hand in hand with the great light ships in the construction of the pyramids. Proof of this can easily be observed as we look at the Sarcophagus within the king's chamber of the great pyramid. One will notice that it is impossible to get the structure of the Sarcophagus in or out of the existing doorways. Reason deducts, therefore, *Hu-man*, that the Sarcophagus must have been constructed within the room, prior to the doorway being built. That means, further, in truth, the pyramids were built from the inside out. Can you see why this concept is hard for the linear, logical mind to grasp?

Remember that Photon energy will neutralize and totally alter the electromagnetic fields. These are only necessary in the lower coagulated realties, where light has slowed to such a degree that physical matter can take on actual form.

When the electromagnetic fields are neutralized, we will find ourselves working with a new form of energy, *Scalar energy*. Along with the altering of the electromagnetic field there will result an altering of our present laws of cause and effect. The laws of physics are changing at this moment and the old methodology of physics no longer applies. This situation has caused human consciousness to expand our scientific thinking to the new physics we now term quantum physics. Science is finally realizing that thought creates the nature of reality, not the other way around.

The methods used in building the Pyramids of Giza, the way in which the Egyptians lit the inner chambers of these Pyramids enabling them to see to create great works of art and construct the inner chambers, utilized *Scalar* energy. There are many physicists who are now publishing information about this topic, but the point that we wish to make is that *Scalar* energy is connected to our minds.

This form of energy cannot be accessed without the application of our consciousness. This is the way that Pleiadian technology works. Nikola Tesla knew it and tried desperately to release this information, but was stopped by a combination of government and corporate forces, who feared losing money with the advent of a technology that would essentially give the world free energy. Albert Einstein knew this as well, but he could no more change the mind set of the corporate world than could Tesla.

The present social order simply could not and cannot allow free energy. In the end, such decisions are made by the money changers, our bankers. So, as a result, access to unlimited energy has been denied to us for some 50 odd years. Tesla died penniless, bitter, and under strange circumstances in a lonely hotel room. The world lost a great genius.

But what about this Photon Belt? And what has this all to do with the Mayan Calendar or the Hopi predictions of the Day of Emergence. . . Everything! The Emergence has to do with the raising of the Earth's vibrational field as Earth, Herself, aligns to Her own energies already aligned with fifth dimensional reality.

Emergence of the 5th World

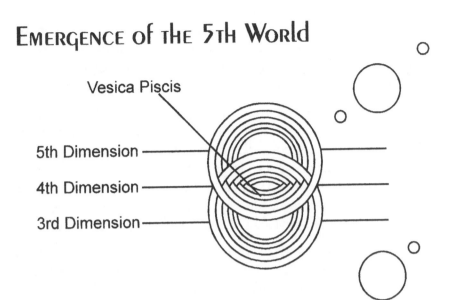

Vesica Piscis

5th Dimension

4th Dimension

3rd Dimension

As it is now seen, between 1998 and the year 2003, Earth will have physically passed through the outer layer of the Photon Belt, referred to as the Null Zone, and continue on it's path moving directly into the full effects of the Photon Energy Belt. At this time, we will enter 4th Dimensional existence. Here time as it is presently perceived will dissolve. Realities will merge as we experience the transformation to resonate to the frequency of 5th Dimensional frequency.

The full effects of the emergence will last an estimated 3.5 days. Presently, we are experiencing the fluctuation of time space continuum, or cross dimensional shifting. Simply put, it is like living in two worlds at the same time.

As this illusion indicates, with the merging of the dimensional realities, a Vesica Piscis is formed as the spiritual and physical consciousness of the planet are merged into one reality. It is within this Vexica Pisces that the new consciousness is birthed.

In a simplified explanation, once the merging is complete there will emerge two Earths. One third dimensional, where life will begin again at point zero, and the New Earth, which will vibrate to fifth dimensional frequency.

The New Earth will experience two Moons, as it did during the time of Atlantis. Physical reality of the 3rd dimensional earth which begins again at point zero will remain the same. Of course, this Earth will experience the full effects of the cataclysmic Earth Changes.

If you look at the above diagram, you will note that Earth is seen as two spheres. This represents the merging of the spiritual realm with the physical. The lower octaves that we have been experiencing for the past several thousand years are presently merging with the higher octaves. You will also notice that Earth Herself is surrounded by several bands. These represent different levels of consciousness, and therefore, relate to several levels of reality coexisting simultaneously.

We actually have been living a multi-dimensional existence since the first conception of Earth, the Fourth World. Our third dimensional reality contains the time/space continuum and our current perception of "past lives" as being separate from the present. This sense of separation is experienced without the clashing of these realities, much like fiber optics and the telephone wires which supply us with the Internet web of communication. Actually, as hard as it is to conceive, these past lives are really all one continued existence of the immortal soul.

Due to a catastrophic occurrence, a miscalculation, if you will, during the early times of experimentation in Atlantis, the one reality fractured into multi-dimensional realities. There was, for a time, so much confusion on this plane as a result of that miscalculation, that without the intervention of our Sirian and Andromedan relatives, the situation would have been irreparable. They assisted those who are often referred to as the Trans-Himalayan Brotherhood, or the Great White Brotherhood, in repairing this corrupted reality. Although repaired and made functional again, certain aspects of the original reality could not be replaced until this time. This catastrophe is responsible for our present perception of separated realities. Merging into the Photon Belt is a cycle that will re-initialize this plane of reality. Consciousness, once again, can continue on its evolutionary path to Christ Consciousness.

There are those who will not be able to merge at this time. It will be due to personal choice. There has finally been created, with the assistance of the Sirians, an alternative Earth (seen at the far right of the diagram). This will become the abode of those who choose to continue in third dimensional reality. It will experience the full effects of the Earth Changes, and this portion of humanity will start from the beginning, creating a new reality from Primordial Source.

You will also notice in the diagram that there is a larger circle, the outer ring. This represents the Astral Belt, which, because of the stratification of the atmosphere, is falling down upon the Earth's surface like rain falls from the clouds. This belt was created by the collapse or implosion of the Third World and contained within it the unbalanced thoughts of *Hu-manity* as it progressed through its altered reality. This was established by the Sirians to protect the rest of the universe from being infected with the *ids-ease* on this planet which resulted from the ripping of our stratosphere and the opening of the dimensional planes. This belt represents every unaligned thought that humanity has created in the last 26,000 years. Perhaps this helps explain the high degree of insanity and fear we are experiencing at this time.

We must pass through this astral belt in order to enter the higher octaves. Do you ask, why must we endure this? Why would the Earth allow this to happen to us? Why would She endure this Herself? The answer to these questions has to do with a story that goes far beyond our memory. It is a story about our creation. Earth has made an agreement, so to speak, to transform all negativity throughout the entire universe. This goes back to the first Earth, called Melina, which was in the Pleiades. Melina was destroyed by the consciousness of competition. Earth was her child.

As Earth's Children, we have taken on a shared responsibility to transmute all negativity that might possibly block the growth of Christ Consciousness through the physical form. Hence, the Astral Belt was not constructed against our will, but rather with our knowledge so as to enable us to continue with the Great Experiment -- *Hu-manity*.

Presently, we are moving through space and into the Photon Belt at a rate of speed which correlates with the Light that is emitted from the Photon Belt, the White light. The metabolic rate of the Earth, as well as the solar system, is intensifying to such a degree that within five years this group of heavenly bodies will have increased its speed by approximately twelve to fourteen times its present rate. So yes, time is speeding up. This is not an illusion.

Eventually, this increase in speed will cause us to begin to live beyond time. We will also feel the effects of those experiments, such as the Philadelphia Experiment, wherein they created an artificial time/space continuum that still exists to this day. Those experiments have not stopped. Many of them have to do with the past and future, so we can expect some very unusual things to be occurring in our very near future.

Prophetic News Update -- December 1996

There are those who would ask for information concerning geo-physical Earth Changes. Therefore, before we close, let us examine some of the experiences that will occur in the near future if the choice to raise consciousness is not made.

- It is essential that you find homesteads that have a natural source of "deep rock" water. Water will become more valuable than gold within the next three to four years.

- In North America, you can expect the volcanic activity on the western coast to become very active. This situation will reach a point over the next seven years where we will even experience several months of near-darkness, similar to an Alaskan winter.

- There will be rains of such abundance they will rival the Great Biblical Flood. Expect coastal areas world wide to rise between 200 and 300 feet accompanied by massive mud and rock slides.

- There will continue to be a shifting of the magnetic poles, which will be stabilized as we enter the Photon Belt around the year 2000.

- Weather around the world will become increasingly erratic. Europe will be hard hit by storms, as will the United States.

- Famine will reach cataclysmic proportions as we experience massive crop failure due to the weather changes. Earth will only know two seasons -- winter cold and severe summer heat. Expect the average temperature to rise 15 to 20 degrees globally. For example, in Arizona (U.S.) you may see temperatures reach as high as 140 degrees Fahrenheit.

- The movement of the tectonic plates will cause earthquake activity to intensify, some reaching as high as 9.7 to 12.0 on the Richter scale. The activity will begin on Pacific Rim. Japan will totally reform its land mass as new areas rise up from beneath the ocean.

- Scientists will be awed by the appearance of a large water funnel in the Pacific Ocean off the Central American coast. The cause of this water funnel will be referred to as the "G force."

- Through this funnel ships will rise up from the Inner Earth. Your brothers and sisters of the Inner Earth will make their presence known and give a global warning to us who live upon the surface.

- There will be an increasing number of children who live outside of family structures. Many will become homeless and live wherever they find shelter, as there becomes increasingly less room for them in an over-crowded and decaying society.

- Seventy-five percent of the world's population will not survive the intensity of the on-going Earth Changes after the year 2003.

- Many survival communities will be formed in the Pacific Northwest region of the U.S., and the majority of the population seeking refuge there will be youth under 20 years of age.

- Diseases, which present medical treatments will not be able to control, will result in the forced containment of large numbers of people within the cities of the U.S. and Europe.

- Europe will stand by watching the Earth Changes, as well as the social and economic collapse of the U.S. Government system during the period of 1998-1999.

- Concurrently, Europe will be devastated by tremendous storms and volcanic activation in the Mediterranean area.

- Between 1997 and 1998, thousands of canisters dropped by the Russians into the Bearing Sea, containing radioactive and chemical waste, will begin to break up due to seismographic activity below the ocean's surface. This will cause massive pollution of the Bearing Sea.

- This condition will cause the Northern regions of the polar ice caps to become over-burdened with toxicity. This toxicity will follow the ocean currents, creating "*red tide*" that will move along the Pacific Coast of North America, terminating many existing forms of life. By the year 2000, given present conditions, the Pacific ocean will be 90 percent devoid of life.

- Severe northern storms will cause massive flooding in the Northern regions.

- Planned bio-diversity programs, initiated by world power structures who have been manipulating the United Nations, will make a decision to infect millions with killer viruses.

- The U.S. will break up into five regions, as the Federal government is challenged by states' rights groups.

- Forced issuance of a National Identity Card will begin during the year 1997.

- Certain areas of the U.S., especially the South West, will experience fire storms. Therefore, use of combustible fuels will be prohibited.

- The severity of winters will increase. Expect winters that will last six months in what are now moderate, temperate areas.

- Desert regions will witness the appearance of strange insect and animal forms created in response to increased radioactive pollution of the atmosphere. This increased radioactive pollution results from the merging of radioactive fields in the outer atmosphere.

• Many will become insane as radiation causes mutations in the development of the human brain.

• When the world's population becomes aware of the bio-diversity plan for controlled population, unilateral uprisings will occur. This will lead to the emergence of the Anti-Christ personality, due to the dark consciousness created in this reality.

• The reign of this Anti-Christ individual will last from two to three years. During this period of time, those who understand the science behind his apparent miracles will join forces as the Christ Consciousness enters its final stages in the year 2000.

• One's abilities to reach higher octaves of consciousness will be the only defense against the madness that will infect the world populations as fear, mistrust and confusion of opposing forces intensifies.

• Many people will awaken to the memory of the beginnings of their creation, and through the chaos will see the re-birthing of many forms of the Ancient Schools of Wisdom, each drawing in the consciousness of those who were part of that belief system before the last age of cataclysmic activity. Much of this resurgence of consciousness is due to the collapsing of the artificial time/space continuum.

• Many individuals born between 1943 and 1947 will come into full memory of their consciousness during the Atlantean Age. These individuals are presently working their way through the maze of our artificially created reality to atone for their past actions.

• There will be many discoveries that will help the survival of the *Human* species through the times of change.

• By 1998 the world power structures will no longer be able to keep knowledge of their involvement with extra-terrestrials from the public.

• Presently, there is a major war going on in our heavens between those forces of the Wormwood planet and the Pleiadian people. This conflict has reached such intensity that the Andromedan and Sirian forces have now intervened in this struggle over control of the Earth's population and resources.

- Contracts made between the world power structures and the extra-terrestrials are coming due in 1997. Payment is expected in exchange for their advanced technology and services.

- Intervention of the chaos and struggles will occur only if the population of Earth can effectively raise their present levels of limited consciousness. Twenty-five percent is the required amount to lock in the grid of Christ consciousness and save those who cannot go on after the shift.

- Given the present method of counting, the shift will occur between the year 2000 and 2004.

- There will be a rekindling of religious war in the Middle East that will, as Nostradamus predicted, spark the release of many nuclear devices around the world. Yes, America will experience some of these as their defense systems malfunction due to deliberately placed computer bugs.

- Some of these devices are, what one would call, designer weapons, specifically designed to terminate certain "types" of life forms.

- New forms of alternative energy will be shared amongst those who have fled to hold out and rebirth in the high country regions.

- If the warfare does not stop of its own accord there will be an intervention. The Earth will not be allowed to be destroyed as *Humanity* experiences the final stages of a consciousness inflicted with unbalanced thought patterns.

- In order to stop the situation in the Middle East from escalating toward total annihilation of the Earth's life forms, there will be three warnings given:

    1. There will appear in the heavens the holographic image of one's perception of the Supreme Deity. This will be a message to humankind to stop its aggression.

    2. The fields of battle and those upon them will be frozen in time, so as to expose the nature of the holographic reality that exists upon this plane.

3. The entire region and accompanying holographic life forms will be dematerialized, and the Great Light Ships will appear by the thousands in the heavens.

• There will be racial violence in the U.S. and third world countries, so severe that Marshal Law will be established in many cities and in surrounding suburban areas and will last for quite some time.

• The cause of humanity's self-destructive tendencies will be recognized as a mutation of the very foundation of life itself. The Protet that all life utilizes to create physical vehicles, is the building block of all third dimensional matter.

• Forced encampment of those in opposition to the New World Order will be common place in many areas of the US. We are talking about entire regions and groups of people.

• Less than fifteen percent of the indigenous people of the U.S. will survive the Earth Changes. Those who do will lead many others to the new way of unification, as their remembrance of the higher octaves in their genetic inheritance is awakened. They are the Elder Brother.

• There will be the establishment of a new race which is already taking form on your planet. This new race will be composed of the children that survive the events of the change and the final shifting of dimensional reality.

• There has already been an alternative Earth established for those who do not choose to open to the higher octaves.

• After the fall of the Anti-Christ, those *Hu-mans* who make up the collective Christ Consciousness will come out of hiding. They will begin their teachings and will gather those who need assistance completing their journey through the final shifting of the dimensions.

• There will be an awakening of the true nature of our interrelationship with Mother Earth as co-creators of her life forms.

• In the final hours there will exist only consciousness.

• It will soon be impossible to advance on any level unless *Hu-manity* deals with its thought process. The stratification of the consciousness which holds together our reality is already fracturing. This is inevitable as we approach the Age of Light again.

- We will merge with the New Photon Experience within five years.

- Many surviving artifacts and surviving evidences of past civilizations will be discovered as a result of the shifting Earth.

- The discoveries soon to be released from the ancient Sphinx will shatter our perception of our origins and belief systems.

- There will be the tones, or sound waves, that will emerge from the Inner Earth. These will cause many to open to the various levels of reality that co-exist upon this plane.

- We will continue to experience many freak storms. Hail the size of golf balls, even the size of grapefruit, will fall during the summer. It will even snow in July in the desert areas of the U.S. Lightning storms will occur in mid-winter. Wind storms will sometimes reach speeds greater than 200 mph.

- In many places the Earth will open up and swallow whole buildings.

- Much of the land, the prairies and the forests will burn in wildfires.

- Much of the water in the Southwestern U.S. and New England areas, as well as Europe, will be contaminated by radioactivity.

- There will be much government intervention in spiritual freedoms and expression.

- There will be a violent tax revolt in the U.S. as the Federal Government begins to collapse.

- Electronic devices will experience strange malfunctions as we merge deeper into the Photon Belt, and eventually they will be rendered useless.

- Strange and freak accidents will occur in our everyday life experiences as we lift from the bonds of physical illusion and find the new mobility a strange experience.

- Urban society's increasing violence, combined with the Earth Changes, will result in a mass exodus from the cities crowding the rural areas in many regions.

- Expect massive interaction and sightings of UFOs. During 1997 and 1998, they will make their presence undeniably known to all the nations of the world.

- There will be a level of human awareness that would astonish even the masters of old.

- Everyone will be psychic.

- Healings of miraculous nature will increase.

- The Indian Nations will rise from the ashes, and along with the Metis, will bring into the consciousness of the world the true nature of our spiritual balance with all things, as well as a new race.

- During the next five years, great prophets and mystics will rise from a reborn Indian Nation, which will include the Metis, or mixed-bloods. Thus, the completion of the Sacred Hoop and Black Elk's rainbow vision will manifest upon this plane.

- Expect many phenomenon in the skies -- strange colors and inter-dimensional openings.

- Earth will be impacted by the Red Comet. This is the prophesy of the Hopi realized in the Red Kachina.

- There is a blue comet that will be talked about soon. This is actually a great Light Ship.

- Jupiter will become a sun, and the prophecy of the return of the two suns will be fulfilled.

- We will interact with many who exist within the Hollow Earth, the land of the Smoky Sun, as well as those of the Middle Earth.

- Many of you will have interaction with beings from different periods in time.

- The presence of new plant life as well as animal forms will soon be undeniable.

- Prehistoric animals will be discovered in South America and Canada.

- An armada consisting of over 180,000 ships is waiting just outside our solar system. At this time there are at least two Mother ships within our solar system. One of them is Andromedan and the other is Sirian. The Andromedan ship hovers just the other side of Jupiter, conveniently out of sight.

- By the year 2003 there will be much phenomenon occurring in the Earth's skies. All those who are of interstellar origin and who might interfere with the Earth's final emergence or inhibit humanity's final jump in consciousness have been ordered off the planet, be they inside the Earth's shell, or upon Her surface. This is the main reason for the close proximity of the Andromedan ship near the planet Jupiter.

• Within ten years, Earth will be orbiting within the influence of Sirius.

• Everything in the *Hu-man* experience of the 1996-1997 time/space will be about realizing the need for transformation and letting go of previously conceived belief patterns that were born of the altered ego. This time you are entering is not about time, space and distance; it is about light, and the oneness of all things.

• Within the individual, emotional storms will devastate relationships as well as destroy core belief patterns which do not hold true to the higher octave of God I AM.

• Many relationships will be devastated almost overnight, although when viewed on a more intimate level, the seeds of destruction have been dormant and lying long in the field.

• Expect violent and tumultuous emotional storms. It must be understood, that as we raise in vibration, old, heavy, emotional seeds which we have buried will come up to the surface. We are now giving ourselves the opportunity to learn how to navigate through these emotion with grace and poise, enabling us to become the Masters we truly are.

• In the year 2000 the Earth will be hit by major Solar shifts. There is a strong possibility that all electromagnetic fields could corrupt. If this occurs the ascension process will be instantaneous.

• You may find yourself removed from situations that are not complementary to your new path. If you insist upon holding on you will be, quite literally, ripped out of your dilemma and dropped off at some other location in the dreamscape.

• You will experience many periods of not being able to think. It will be almost as if there is no thought there. This is merely a process of the mind creating space in the only way it knows how -- to allow for new thoughts. These new thoughts are of a higher vibration than you're presently allowed. It is as if your mind were clearing its "hard drive" of all unnecessary data for the journey ahead.

- There will be much confusion within your physical bodies as your hormones race to balance the inequities of your male-female energy patterns. This is nature trying to balance its creations.

- Allow yourself and others to *be*. Forgiveness is the weight of the ages being lifted from your back in the moment of this experience.

- We are all "Christs in Training", creating reality as we go along, moment by moment, in *the Now*.

- Ice Storms will begin to rage around the year 2001. This will prove to be a phenomenon that will shock the world. Hardest hit areas will be the North Eastern US, Eastern Canada and Northern Europe.

- Meteor Storms will make contact with Earth in the spring of 1998.

- Intervention by Star Nations is eminent to protect Earth. Most likely we will see the benevolent beings that are already here make their presence known in 1998 on a global level. Essentially they are waiting for us to evolve.

- New technology will be found in the next four years which will be available to us to help many survive the weather that is ahead. Nature is about to become totally unpredictable as she interacts with the dimensional shifts. It is knowledge from the Stars.

"There were others who came before us who also resisted the coming of change. We can walk through worlds where once children laughed, women busied themselves in the market place and farmers  *tended their fields. We can dig up their bones and tell what diseases they had. But the bones do not tell us what they dreamed, what they thought, or what they new in consciousness. Our life is but a moment in time, the turning of a page ..."*

Update on the state of the Quickening

an open letter to those who asked.....

*D*uring my seeming disappearance from the public eye from August through November, I have gone on spiritual quest, and visited with many people. I also participated in several ceremonies with several tribal factions from Alaska to Canada to the Hopi and Denè people here in Arizona. Sometimes we just need time to live it. My entire life has altered as a result of my experiences over the past 5 months. I have some interesting information that comes from above as well as below our Surface reality. Here are some of the things we can look forward to as we enter 1997:

Let us speak for a moment about this new Star in the heavens, the comet that is being called the companion to the *Hall-Bopp*. Be assured that this "Star", which has made a sudden and dramatic appearance in our heavens, is the Blue Kachina spoken of in the ancient prophecies of the Hopi. I have heard the Hopi Sinom talk about this Blue Kachina since I was a very young. This is the herald of the completion of all prophecies. We are without a doubt in the Final Days. The message from the Hopi and Athabascan people from Alaska, from the Shooshwap in Canada to the World is "It is time."

I have been speaking about this "Arrival" since 1994 and for most of 1996. There will be many landings that will lead to one of the major significant events in our remembered history between November of 1996 and March of 1997. This event will be quite common. It could lead to a confrontation with our military forces if the world governments do not deliver their part of the bargain. This is when the contracts between World Governments and the Star Nations are up. The item of interest, the payment, is *US* -- each and every one of us!

For purposes of clarity, I have been taken as a quest upon these Light Ships several times. After my most recent ceremonial experience with the Hopi, we communicated with this Great Ship which is coming. You would call the method used remote vision and telepathic communication. We call it ceremony.

I returned from Hopi land and went to a certain location in Arizona where I know the veils between realities to be very thin. There is a location near my ranch in the Arizona Mountains, several actually, where these *Ships* move quite freely between the surface world and the inner world. They are seen by the local populous quite frequently.

Presently, there is a bit of commotion and a lot of vacillating stories about this huge "Star" that has suddenly appeared near the location of the erratic "Comet" *Halbopp*. In fact, this is not a star at all, but perhaps the largest LIGHT SHIP to appear in our heavens in over two hundred thousand years. This will clear up over the next two weeks when there the reality of the situation is announced to the world. The question in my mind is, do we the people announce it or does the world government. It will be interesting to watch.

This is, in fact, a living LIGHT SHIP of enormous size. It is almost a living planet in its own right, which carries within its living structure the Lords of Light including those who are referred to as the Galactic Tribunal, or the Great Council. This would include not only inter-dimensional beings, or Star beings from other Suns, but also those who are referred to as the Ascended Masters.

Within this ship are many souls who have, in a manner of speaking, disappeared from this plane, by either intentionally or accidentally stepping out of the time space continuum or stumbling through dimensional openings that exist at various locations upon the Earth. The Kachina is not the Ship. You could say that the Kachinas are the beings that come forth from the ship.

I say it is the Blue Kachina because it is foremost an Andromedan-headed expedition, or at least they have had the most contact with members of our race. And Andromedans have bluish skin. They are very tall, some reaching the height of probably nine feet. So if

I were a native of earth and I happened to be Hopi, I would call one of these beings a Blue Kachina, wouldn't you?

Many truths will be revealed about World Governments, including ours and their inter stellar relationships, beginning in the Spring of 1997, as the presence of many of these ships and the beings they host begin to interact with the peoples of our planet. We can expect many "landings" starting at about this time and continuing through the year with more frequency, as small emissary ships make their rounds throughout different locations and people upon and within the Earth. Know that there is a very direct and unbroken relationship with those who come from the stars and those who dwell in the inner Earth.

Let us consider that this *Hale-Bopp* was not the ship I see, and others also see. Rather, let us consider that it is, in fact, a flying piece of hot rock, called a comet. Consider this then. What creates the spectacular light show we see in the heavens known as the tail of the comet? -- debris, burning debris. This comet, then, will cross the path of Earth's exact orbit around the Sun. In the spring of 1998, the Earth itself will cross into that very pathway where the Comet crossed. That means the Earth may, in fact, be moving through the debris left behind by the Comet.

In 1908 a small asteroid (comet) about 50 yards across exploded some five miles or more above the forest of Siberia. This is documented everywhere. The results were that an area of almost two thousand square miles of that forest were totally leveled. The area was almost devoid of life form, the exact extent of which can only be estimated, for it was many years later that scientists from outside Russia were able to investigate the site.

Consider what could happen if we ran into a meteor shower where there were many of these particles of debris. What if only one piece of that debris hit the Earth as it progressed upon its orbit? What if it were larger than the one that exploded over Siberia in 1908? This is as much as I will give to those who do not see. I am a visionary, and a time traveler. But I am human like the rest of us. I am two-legged, and have my own perception of the universe.

What if that piece of debris had contained within it some form of life, which could destroy certain biological life forms upon the Earth plane? What if it were not a comet and, in fact, it were an Orion Ship? And what if that ship was destroyed by another force, and upon it was a cylinder containing something which could eliminate certain biological life forms here upon Earth?

There will be many prophecies fulfilled in the spring of 1998. We are entering the year of responsibility. We must be responsible for our actions, our thoughts, and our own lives. The power of Earth societies must return to *We the People*. All prophecy is a potential manifestation, it is consciousness that dictates the manifested outcome. In 1998 the map of the new Earth will begin to take form. For what you have not been told about is the map of rings, the map that includes the changes within the inner Earth. It is the map of the new grid, which shows new energy grids that are forming upon this plane as a result of the dodecahedron grid that now surrounds the planet.

If I am financially able to take and allow the space and physical time necessary, I will prepare this map in the course of this year. It is the map of Native American visions of the Earth changes.

Now let's talk a little about *the Quickening*. It must be realized at this time, that which could be referred to as the frequency waves which hold the present Earth consciousness intact, are being fractured by increased frequency waves currently focused upon the Earth and it many species. This phenomena is being caused by both natural occurrences as we enter the heightened effects of the Photon Belt, as well as by deliberate actions and manipulations of what could be called divine intervention by our Galactic brothers, who are benevolent to humankind and wish to assist them in the raising of the vibratory rate of the species upon the planet. This means not only the two-legged human variety, but the beasts, fowl, fishes, and plant life as well. All is consciousness, all is divine. There is no special group, species, or order. Planet Earth and all her children are heading towards graduation into our fulfillment of a divine plan.

Also at this time there is a phenomenon of the warping and fluctuation within the layers of the time space continuums, something that many people should be feeling the affects of. Our perceived reality is little more than the prolonged experience of a time space event. We are beginning to experience sensations of living in multiple time space events, because in fact they will be overlapping and merging. It will sort of feel like you are living in two worlds simultaneously. Or perhaps some might experience even more than two. You might be experiencing this when at times you feel like different people, as if different personalities are your expression.

Your sleep patterns will become erratic, and at times it seems like it doesn't matter if you have slept a full night or a few hours. People will change in front of your eyes, with the passing of each moment. You will see their true intent behind the masks. All of you are becoming clairvoyant. We all can see now if we choose. No one said it would make things easy.

Truth is the order of the day. Nothing which is not harmonious to the true nature of our spirit will be able to cling to us with the intensifying of frequencies that are presently occurring. That which is false will literally be ripped away. So expect radical changes to occur within relationships and life circumstances. Like the Earth, we will experience a lot of rumbling within, as we break out of our limitations that bind us from our fulfillment of being.

We are also beginning to experience the phenomena known as *Hollow Leaping* through time space experiences. Many of these experiences will seem abstract, perhaps even surreal in nature. There is much that has been and continues to be manipulated by science, such as the multitude of "rips" and artificial time space continuums that were created in and around the Philadelphia experiment, and the many others that the world governments have tried to keep under wraps.

There is a lot of negative energy flying around out there in the market place, due mainly to the inability of people as a whole to grasp the bigger picture of what is really going on here on Planet Hollywood. For instance, it has been said that the Earth's magnetic fields are degenerating. I even heard one teacher say that our Sun's magnetic poles have degenerated to the point that they appear to have vanished. This is entirely incorrect information. Rather, what is occurring is our own frequencies are rising to such heights that we are moving above what was once our norm.

There is a lot you have not been told. For instance, there have been many times that our own people have, through technology possessed by our military institutions that you are not yet aware of as a people, gone to other planets. There have been times where they have actually commandeered ships, weapons, and other things including beings with the hope of gaining technological information. We have been doing this since the thirties. It has all been accomplished with extra-terrestrial technology. We have had a long relationship with those from beyond the stars.

Time is collapsing. We are experiencing more space between our experiences, with less congestion of conflicting energies. So to some this is experienced as confusion, or even chaos. Perhaps it should be realized the degree to which we have had to exist within a polluted, over-loaded sea of contrary emotions and energies, that did not allow the space for something new to occur. We are creating a new paradigm, a new consciousness, as we prepare for unlimited thought and reality. We are feeling creation in process -- *the Quickening!*

"Truth is the order of the day. Nothing which is not harmonious to the true nature of our spirit will be able to cling to us with the intensifying of frequencies that are presently occurring. That which is false will literally be ripped away ... Like the Earth, we will experience a lot of tumbling within, as we break out of our limitations that bind us from our fulfillment of being."

I was at Lake Mead in Nevada about two weeks ago. I was asked to do some ceremony there. One of the things we became aware of there is that the land has had a number of bulldozings to camouflage the unusual nature of some of the rock formations there, formations which clearly indicate a massive explosion of indeterminable proportions, which were fused back together seemingly in a moment.

Okay, so something is hokey here. What really scared us was that the result of the USS Eldridge being zapped here on four separate occasions created a strange radiation that is emanating from the area. I believe without a doubt that the water is extremely toxic with radioactive residue that is a direct result of the experiment. When I was asked by an interviewer from a local television station what it all meant I replied, "Love each other more."

Love isn't corny. I cannot emphasize how important it is at this moment to place ourselves into the Love vibration. For what you are embracing in your hearts and consciousness this very moment, so shall your path be as we enter the final stages of the shifting. Control of our emotions and focus upon that which we desire to experience within our realities is the KEY! Our choices now will determine the manner in which our life experiences are realized in these final days. It takes just as much energy to create lack as it does to create abundance. It is all a matter of choice!

I was having lunch the other day when I was in Las Vegas, at a very electric table where Uri Geller, Zecharia Sitchen, and a few others were discussing the deliberate actions by our own Governments to manipulate weather conditions through their "HAARP" experiments. These experiments are causing the natural order of weather patterns to be totally thrown off kilter, meaning that we are almost out of control. The Freeze of `96-`97 will prove to be one of the worst winters ever experienced in the history of the US. The conversation went on to bring up the issue that not only was "HAARP" being used to manipulate weather, but it was also being developed to manipulate human emotions. Now is this starting to sound like a Stephen King story yet?

Also discussed was the intensity in which the United Nations is backing up programs all over the world, the US included, that are deliberately infecting populated areas with infectious viruses. Now I ask you, why would the Governments of the World deliberately spread infectious viruses to the world population, engineered to kill specific groups? Well the answer comes out of your asking yourself why would they initiate such a policy?

This goes right back to a program adopted by the UN back in 1993 in Brazil, which they called "Bio-Diversity". Henry Kissenger said, "Seventy-five percent of the world's population is no more than useless eaters." What the horror show is really about is that many of these viruses are now mutating. Science has no cures in sight. Population control is getting to be big business with the governments of the world.

I am a recognized Natural healer. Well, I have been working on ways of healing these new forms of viruses and cancers for several years. You see, I have a sister, Osage, and several years ago she came down with the Navajo Flue. I worked on her. She is well today. Many of us sat in deep ceremony to find out the cause of this strange virus that only seemed to effect people of Native American descent.

So ask me about Hanta Virus, common name "the Navajo Flue." We can talk about genetically engineered viruses here. Or would you like to discuss the Native women who, while going to Government clinics, were being sterilized while supposedly receiving immunization shots.

I strongly believe that people should not get immunization shots under the circumstances of these times. Tell your friends to refuse these public genocide policies. People can refuse based on religious beliefs; there are ways that you do not have to conform. They cannot force us to take the damn shots yet. These maniacs are literally killing our children. It is no joke! Do you want to talk about Dr. Jonas E Salk, Reese Monkeys, and the Polio shots in 1947, and the millions of people who today have Retro Virus?

My partner in life, Laura Lee and I are working with many people who are at the end of their ropes, and desperate from NO results.

Usually they have been diagnosed with terminal conditions to which it seems the Doctors have no answers to how to end their suffering. We are also working with an overwhelming amount of trauma patients, crimes of violence, rape, depression, cancer, CFS, PTS Syndrome, Aids, herpes, and, not to be overlooked, many, many people who have had UFO abduction experiences.

The results Laura Lee and I have had thus far have been great. Most of the people who have come to us thinking there was no hope for them are healed, and the results are permanent. Others we work with where the damage is extensive and has been ongoing for years, find immediate results and seem to heal within a very short period of time, from a few weeks to several months.

We are now working with naturopaths, bio-chemists, and herbologists across the country, because people seem to be coming down with new health crisis situations every week. Some of the more difficult situations are repairing what has been done by allopathic physicians in their attempts to "cure the disease", especially chemotherapy. It is like trying to rebuild Hiroshima after the blast.

We call our process of healing *Kryahgenetics*. The result of what we do is to literally reprogram the DNA within the cells of the body. Therefore, the conditions that cause the disease in the client are removed permanently. The result is that the condition is not only reversed, but usually within a few weeks or months the diseased part of the body is totally regenerated. And in response to some of your generous offers, *"Yes, we could use some help getting clinics off the ground and printing the book to get this information to the public."*

We are in the midst of a major health crisis in America. These viruses are not natural, and in more cases than is comfortable the outbreak happens after immunization programs are introduced into an area. Are we being murdered by our own Government? I say bring the question to the people before it's too late. Allopathic medicine is a dinosaur, and it is being perpetuated by corporate policies developed by thieves. It is like the organized crime. If they heal you they are out of business, reason it out.

Perhaps now it is time to consider a different course of emphasis. We might think about switching our focus from the phenomenon of what is occurring to what it is we could be doing to accommodate our inevitable destiny. How and what do we do to make this transition easy? What information is out there to help us prepare? UFOs, Ayurvedic healing, and holistic healing are all very real. If we come together and work as a force of one humanity, in the end we will move through this time of confusion, for we are the ultimate survivor race in the universe.

In the Light,

A Message from Andromeda
Atop Mother's Mountain in the Golden city of Gobean • Arizona

"Know we are aware that you have come with hope to bring back words of clarity to your arena of human drama. We will share this with you at this time. Tell your brethren be not concerned as much with what comes from out of the deep, for the deep is not as bazaar a reality as their own inner worlds. There will be contest in your heavens for sure. Within a decade from the turning of your millennium, there will be many engaged in conflicts of sorts in your heavens. And the light flares resulting from this conflict will be seen and felt throughout the nine universes. But this is not where the danger to humankind lies.

"Fear not your heavens; know, however, that in that confrontation there will also be many of your own seed. For your domain is vast indeed, oh man. And your seed now knows the grace of many universes. Look you within, for there is where the storm is rising, growing in the clouds of doubt. There is much which has been kept from you, but it was by man's own decree. There is a darkness upon the light of man at this time to be sure. Long ago, in your history, these formless shadows were driven far into the deep by the Masters of old. But some of these wild remnants of lifeless shadows managed find refuge in places where the consciousness of man was not aware to go. There they did lie, undetected, like the seeds of the Dragon's Coat, waiting for the right moment to take form from an unsuspecting host, greedy for power and material Godship.

"Now, once again they are able to manifest in the form of man and move they amongst man. They have taken the form of many of your leaders. It can be seen in the eyes, and felt in the Heart. Remember the eye of man is not the true sight, for the true sight is within. Adorn they themselves with much glamour, and the manner of their expression is smooth as silk.

"Those from the shadow world cannot take form unless it is given through the blood or consent of man, for they possess no light source of their own. Find within you the strength of heart to know thine own self, man. Engage not against those of your brethren that might be of reptilian descent. Know that you yourself have within you this same seed. Nigh, even though when uncloaked, these shadows from your deep past display around their crown the features of the serpent. Do not give into your own superstitions. Do not confuse the serpentine with the serpent.

"Dwell you always in the light. Keep your vision always upon the cosmos, and know always that all is divine. In the end, light will always reign supreme over shadow, for no thing can be if not for the light. These shadows that we speak of are the results of your own creations, and not of the higher realms.

"There is much that can be rendered in the folly of blind tampering with that which has been purposely closed. It would suit humankind best if they opened their minds to the pathways of their higher consciousness. But many of your kind are like children, seeking the pleasures of what is hidden behind veils, rather than to pay the price of devotion. Hence, you are now within the collective initiation. The light is returning to man. The darkness is stirred and in flight.

"Be it declared here, there is an intrusion that has already come to be upon your plane. Already those of the lower vibratory worlds have been called and walk amongst you, cloaked in lifeless ritual. Look into their eyes; there is no spirit within them. They seek the light that is within you. Be not a slave to your desires, for that which is truly formed of the light is formless. There is no war upon your race by those of other Suns. Wake up, Suns of Man. What is occurring is the playing out of your own drama. Great Gods you are truly, but you have forgotten your beginnings.

"The shadow is of your own creation. We are here to assist in clarity, not intervention. Now there will be great Ships that war within your heavens, and from beneath the depths of the Earth the Lion's roaring shall again make itself known. Its power shall be loosed to clear the shadows from your plane. On wings of light and in serpentine motion shall they drive the shadows from your plane, once and for all. It is these shadows, after all, that you are gathering. Awaken to knowledge. Awaken the Living Sun within your center, and the light that is already yours will be accessed.

"There is a contest occurring for sure, o' man. But know that you are the ones who have declared the terms and conditions of the game. For we are here to but serve the will of your desire. For you are the Patal, the supreme Lords of Light. Continue to sing your songs of light, drawing down the light, allowing it to enter your hearts. The light is responding in tones and hues of new magnificence, for the rays are now nine, and nine lords shall be there to stand by your side as the tenth is called in by your own voicing. Make thyself a vessel

for the light, and stand out of the way. It is a good day to shine !

Tamuksiwa